A SELF-REGULATED LEARNING APPROACH FOR CHILDREN WITH LEARNING/BEHAVIOR DISORDERS

ABOUT THE AUTHOR

Dr. Joan A. Benevento completed an undergraduate degree (Southern Connecticut State University), a master's degree (University of Connecticut), and doctoral degree (Catholic University of America) in special education, and taught special education youngsters in Connecticut, Alaska, California, and Maryland. She also holds a graduate degree in guidance and counseling (Boston College) and completed a postdoctoral program in Gestalt therapy in New York City. Recently retired from St. John's University, Queens, New York, Dr. Benevento has been involved in the training of special education teachers for thirty years.

Her ideas about constructivist education, which she has been developing for over twenty years, derive from a synthesis of Piagetian concepts of child development and Gestalt concepts of self-regulation. Dr. Benevento has given several presentations at national and international professional organizations describing this approach.

A SELF-REGULATED LEARNING APPROACH FOR CHILDREN WITH LEARNING/BEHAVIOR DISORDERS

By

JOAN A. BENEVENTO, Ph.D.

CHARLES C THOMAS • PUBLISHER, LTD.
Springfield • Illinois • U.S.A.

Published and Distributed Throughout the World by

CHARLES C THOMAS • PUBLISHER, LTD.
2600 South First Street
Springfield, Illinois 62704

© 2004 by CHARLES C THOMAS • PUBLISHER, LTD.

ISBN 0-398-07535-2 (hard)
ISBN 0-398-07536-0 (paper)

Library of Congress Catalog Card Number: 2004051663

Printed in the United States of America
GS-R-3

Library of Congress Cataloging-in-Publication Data

Benevento, Joan A. (Joan Ann), 1934-
   A self-regulated learning approach for children with learning/behavior disorders / by Joan A. Benevento
    p. cm.
   Includes bibliographical references and index.
   ISBN 0-398-07535-2 (hbk.) -- ISBN 0-398-07536-0 (pbk.)
   1. Learning disabled children--Education. 2. Problem children--Education. 3. Self-control. I. Title.

LC4704.B45 2004
371.9--dc22
                                             2004051663

PREFACE

. . . [the learner is one[1] who is more than just the theater on whose stage various plays independent of him and regulated in advance by physical laws of automatic equilibration are performed; [the learner] performs in, sometimes even composes, these plays; as they unfold, he adjusts them by acting as an equilibrating agent compensating for external disturbances; he is constantly involved in self-regulating processes.
(Piaget, 1970b, p. 59)

Research over the years indicates that standard intervention approaches for children with learning/behavior disorders* have not been sufficiently preparing them for the world they enter as adults. Unlike problems faced by adults that may be mitigated by their ability to manipulate and change a hazardous environment, the problems of these children may be centered on interactions with environments they cannot control or readily change.

Most children in need often do not receive the full range of necessary and appropriate services to treat their academic and affective problems effectively.

Adequate help may not be given until they clearly deteriorate and manifest significant academic failure or emotional disturbance. These children must be helped to generate more rewarding actions, thoughts, and feelings that will, in turn, result in more adaptive behavior (Combs, 1981; Elias & Maher, 1983; Dougherty, 1988; Saxe, Cross, & Silverman, 1988).

Since the 1970s special education has shown increasing interest in professing the relevance of constructivist bases for understanding human growth and learning and has strongly endorsed it as being effective in the treatment of children with learning/behavior disorders (Giordano, 1981; Heshusius, 1989; Poplin, 1988a; Skolnik, 1990).

Being qualitative in nature, constructivism is interested in the kinds of mental operations children acquire as they mature and interact with their environments. Through a process of self-regulated activity, more advanced forms of cognition are constructed anew. An account of these self-regulating processes underlying the construction of these interactions is of crucial importance because it provides the critical vehicle for the application of these concepts to educational intervention (Kuhn, 1981).

---

*The term "learning/behavior disorders" has been chosen to conform to the process approach presented in this book. It incorporates all the traditional labels usually assigned to the motor, sensory, cognitive, and affective problems manifested by special education children. It includes all ranges of disorders from mild to severe as defined by federal law.

Constructivism sees all children as biological systems consisting of gradually developing internal structures that form the architecture for decoding and encoding information. Different levels of cognitive structures underlie the strategies used for problem solving. The systems are open and accessible to structural change regardless of any cause, degree, or level of development of the learning/behavior disorder (Piaget, 1968, 1970b, 1971, 1972).

Children are actively involved in organizing their motor, affective, and cognitive experiences into patterns of behavior that are meaningful to them. They accomplish this organization through a child-environment interaction in which they actively explore and discover the natures of their surrounding worlds. Children come to view themselves as being in charge of their own decisions and choices, and as being responsible for the consequences of these decisions and choices (Kamii, 1975; Henley, 1980).

The processing of knowing prompts children to strive to enlarge the knowledge base in their biological systems. It motivates them to seek changes in the basic structural nature of their cognitive processes that determine functioning. They actively make use of self-regulation, awareness and thinking, contact and dialogue, along with the presently available cognitive organizations, as they select information to be processed. Information is selected based on its relevance and meaningfulness to the individual doing the selection.

The underlying assumption of a constructivistic-developmental approach is that:

> . . . each person has a customary orientation to self and world and that there are stages and transitions (independent of age) along which these frames of reference can be arrayed. (Noam et al., 1984, p. 86)

Children are self-regulating systems and not merely a collection of cognitive, physical, and emotional subsystems. Reality is constantly being reconstructed from an interaction with the environment. All behavior is an active, meaning-making adaptation built on a sequential unfolding of emerging capacities. In any given situation, specific levels of maturity and comprehension differentiate and restructure self and environment. Children thereby gain and/or change insight (Sadler & Whimbey, 1985; Elkind, 1989; Keating, 1991).

Children's perceptions, memories, and problem-solving abilities are determined specifically by cognitive structures. Developmental changes happen through maturational processes stimulated by self-directed exploratory experiences. Actively sought stimulation and problem solutions promote mental growth (Gelfand & Peterson, 1985).

> The developmental approach suggests how a person "organizes" his experience and is in a sense the connection or "experiential pathway" between etiological circumstances and various manifest symptoms. (Greenspan, 1997, p. 416)

Throughout its history, special education has been seriously challenged by the problems of assessing and treating children with academic and emotional adjustment difficulties. It has increasingly and dramatically professed the relevance of developmental epistemology as a basis for understanding human growth and learning as well as frames of reference for explaining the behaviors of children. It incorporated the ways in which the knowledge of developmental concepts enhanced the ways in which treatment is administered to children with learning/behavior disorders (Harter, 1983; Gelfand & Peterson, 1985; Westman, 1990).

When the spectra of difficulties faced by children with learning/behavior disorders are seen from a developmental, constructivist perspective within sociocultural contexts, special implications for prevention and intervention are indicated (Saxe, Cross, & Silverman, 1988).

What is set forth in this book is an intervention model based on the concepts of Piaget's genetic epistemology. Believed to be applicable in educational settings, its focus is on children who experience academic and affective problems. As a learning theory approach, it is designed to help children with learning/behavior disorders actively participate in a fuller integration of their own psychomotor, affective, and cognitive information-processing skills and adaptation. This results in richer meanings of self and environment.

Intervention built upon these principles would:

1. foster acquisition of basic skills necessary for living in a multicultural society including academic, personal, interpersonal, communicative, and economic proficiency;
2. accept the learner's needs and purposes and develop experiences and programs around the unique potential of the learner;
3. facilitate self-actualization and strive to develop a sense of personal adequacy in all children;
4. personalize decisions and practices by including children in the process of their own treatment;
5. recognize the adaptive function of human feelings and use personal values and perceptions as integral factors in treatment;
6. develop a nurturing intervention environment perceived by children as challenging, understanding, supportive, exciting, and free from threat;
7. develop in children both a genuine concern and respect for the worth of others and skills in conflict resolution (Combs, 1981).

CONTENTS

A SELF-REGULATED LEARNING APPROACH FOR CHILDREN WITH LEARNING/BEHAVIOR DISORDERS

Chapter 1

INTRODUCTION

The very nature of life is constantly to
overtake itself.
(Piaget, 1971, p. 36)

Since the turn of the century many children with known learning/behavior disorders were thought to have special personality and/or social needs considered untreatable by traditional psychologies. At the same time, they were described as not being able to acquire knowledge through traditional curriculum approaches. Consequently, psychology and special education have shown gradual but persistent changes in their philosophies and have given serious consideration to the creation and refinement of new intervention models for children and youths whose normal growth and development have gone awry (Sadler & Whimbey, 1985; Poplin, 1988a).

There has been a worldwide movement to reconstruct the social sciences from personal meaning-making and constructivist viewpoints. Separate strands of study from various professional disciplines regarding children with learning/ behavior disorders have been gradually coming together into an accumulated body of knowledge benefiting educators, psychologists, and researchers in their respective endeavors to construct and implement service models. As a consequence of this emerging pattern, new research findings regarding the principles of learning, child development, cognitive psychology, and developmental psychopathology have shaped different instructional and therapeutic approaches for these children. Many reconceptualizations in mental health and learning theory have been motivated by the concepts of Piagetian genetic epistemology. It has become one of the most widely proclaimed exposition of the development of logical thinking. Its general framework for understanding differences in cognitive/affective performance meets the most crucial demands for a theory of human problem solving. The explanation being that such differences could be understood in terms of the developmental capacities a learner brings to the situation (Poplin, 1988a; Beilin & Pufall, 1992; Chapman, 1992). Significant advances resulted in understanding the:

a. biological bases of cognition (Piaget, 1971);
b. developmental, holistic modes of knowledge acquisition (Piaget, 1970a, 1971, 1972, 1991);

  c. adaptive, meaning-making intentions of all behavior (Piaget, 1970a, 1971, 1972, 1991; Greenberg & Safran, 1987);

  d. integration of motor, cognitive, and affective processes as a necessary condition for healthy functioning (Piaget, 1970b, 1971, 1972; Piaget & Garcia, 1991; Greenberg & Safran, 1987);

  e. normalcy as a necessary condition for the study of pathology (Piaget, 1975; Cicchetti, 1984; Gelfand & Peterson, 1985; Kohlberg, 1987);

  f. efficacy of programs that foster social adjustment through social-cognitive problem solving (Spivack & Swift, 1976; Kneedler, 1980; Urbain & Kendall, 1980).

Piaget, in close agreement with other organismic theorists, sought to devise an integrated conceptualization of development through an understanding of the organization and interrelationship of the various ontogenetic domains. This perspective makes a multisystem approach to the assessment of developmental processes and outcomes necessary. It further insists that the ability to adapt and show competence results from the successful resolution of the tasks most salient for a given developmental period (Cicchetti & Beegley, 1990; Jarman, Vavrik, & Walton, 1995).

This view of child development is at the same time, phenomenological and objective. In its phenomenology, the view does not entangle growing children in a content-based theory. Rather, it allows children to make meaning of their existence within the context of their personal experiences. In its objectivity, the view presents an impression that children move toward increasingly more adequate ways of knowing-in-the-world and being-in-the-world. As children progressively heighten their awareness with each advance, they constitute a widening, increasingly more objective perspective of self, other, and world. This perspective optimizes the understanding of an academic or affective disorder in terms of the pattern of elements involved (Rosen, 1991).

Piagetian thinking sees human behavior as a reflection of biological processes, interpersonal experiences, and self-regulation. The incorporation of a biological concept of organismic balance into human psychological functioning explains how self-regulation is maintained and honed. Psychological unfolding, anchored in biological/sensorimotor roots, is governed by interactions between children and their environments. The concern is with how children come to know, how they organize information about their interactions with their environments, and how they form their world views. The pairing of certain biological patterns with certain environmental patterns can intensify each other. Biological factors, rather than acting directly on behavior, influence what children bring into their interactive patterns. Environmental factors, in turn, influence what the culture and family bring into the interactions (Skolnik, 1987; Sadler & Whimbey, 1985).

All behavior, actions, emotions, and interpersonal transactions are infused and enmeshed with thinking. External actions, symbol formation, and language mastery are all coordinated by the same thinking processes. Thinking demands the active participation in the constructing and reconstructing of knowledge concerned with object or social relationships. In normal growth the reconstructed knowledge, in turn, leads to the discovery of the abstract properties of a child's own actions and eventually to objective reality (London, 1990).

Children are born wanting to become aware of, make contact with, and dialogue with information from their environments. They actively organize the information they gain from the moment-by-moment contacts with their worlds and seek excitement, growth, and adaptation. Essentially and initially self-serving biological organisms, children construct their own knowledge by interacting with the environment in a gradually socializing process. Their equilibrated, self-regulated systems seek stability in the changes of daily living. All interactions are governed by the laws of the growing system as a whole. Acquired responses enable children to interpret a wider array of stimuli. The self-regulation process serves as an intermediary for all stimuli that impinge upon it. As the system of behavior becomes more organized and complex, the spiral widens (Piaget, 1971; Reid, 1993). In addition, if children begin from birth to be related and have emotional experiences with cognitive content, consideration must be given to:

> ... the implications of a theory which gives vital intellectual and affective interactions the primary place in the development of a sense of self and loving relatedness with others. . . . (Skolnik, 1987, p. 24)

Persisting throughout Piaget's genetic epistemology are the characteristic themes that (1) all intelligence and thought manifest a logical structure; (2) cognitive structures are one with biological and social realities; (3) reality is partly subjective in that the observer can never be left out in the construction of knowledge; (4) reality is always partly an externalization of action or thought; (5) all knowledge is mediated rather than copied directly; and (6) mental growth is dialectically determined by maturation, physical experience, and social experience (Elkind, in Piaget, 1968).

Prominent in this constructivist, self-regulated learning position is the belief that knowledge is acquired through organizing principles. The acquisition occurs through the individual organization and restructuring of experiential data according to existing cognitive structures. In turn, these very structures are altered and enriched through interaction with the physical and social worlds. Structures underlie and organize all behaviors and are developed, refined, and transformed by the self-regulatory functions. This is an ongoing lifelong process (Sigel et al., 1981; Smock, 1981).

Piaget's developmental epistemology leads to:

> . . . potential transformational [approaches] that could serve emancipatory ends
> for individuals and groups by helping them achieve the highest orders of mind
> and the more adaptable forms or organizational structures demanded by the
> postmodern world. (O'Hara, 1998, p. 154)

Piaget placed the meanings as assigned by children doing the experiencing at the center of his theory. As children organize their personal experiences into specific, meaningful wholes, their subjective existences advance into ontological truths. For authenticity in life, children must be aware of their own needs and desires, and their environments must be aware of opportunities and obstacles to satisfaction of these needs and desires. For authenticity in intervention, educators need to know the way in which children give meaning to their existences (Crocker, 1983; Jacobs, 1992).

Children are predisposed to organize environmental stimuli in a specific manner in immediate experiences. They make meaning of their worlds through evolving systems, and, in turn, the meaning-making systems drive behavior. Perceptual, cognitive, and emotional experiences are organized through acts of differentiation, selection, and construction. Internal, constantly constructing frameworks incorporate experiences into more or less coherent wholes. All action, feeling, and thinking are organized by these systems of meaning-making. The organization, in turn, gives meaning to the experiences. To successfully learn about these meaning-making systems, it is necessary to observe the way the systems actually work (Kegan, 1980).

The developmental programming of cognitive structures is ordered, complex, and selectively vulnerable at a number of stages. Awareness, contact, self-regulation, and dialogue support the capacity to differentiate self from context through the stages. Self-regulatory requirements of various stages of development place serious demands on children at every age. It is imperative that observations be made of how children privately compose life events. Seen through the eyes of children, all behaviors become meaningful and coherent (Kamii, 1975; Kegan, 1980; Wright, 1984; Skolnik, 1990).

Development may be defined generally as a child's organismic, evolving abilities to make sense of and interact with his or her physical and social worlds. Three important aspects of development include self-regulation, construction of social knowledge, and decentration. Self-regulation guides development from a simple, relatively undifferentiated state to states of greater and greater differentiation and integration. The major concern is with how specific models of adaptation at various developmental stages interact with immediate environmental changing forces to produce further adaptation (Pullis & Smith, 1981; Santostefano, 1991).

Furthermore, social constructions are considered to be as integral to epistemology as are constructions of logical development. Children are not born separate essences that later interact with their environments. Instead, they and their environments form a whole from which self-other aspects are differentiated. The part of knowledge acquisition that involves co-constructive interactions between children and other people has serious significance. It impacts how children build a sense of self and become unique personalities as well as how they evolve into societal members. In this light, an understanding of how children construct their behaviors is fully grasped only when seen in relation to society (Chapman, 1992; Furth, 1992; Murray, 1992; Youniss & Damon, 1992).

We learn of children's adaptive abilities by knowing how they privately compose experiences. Adaptation is seen as arising from the abilities to make meaning of the interaction of internal and external environments. Children can explore and discover the nature of their surrounding worlds by constructing their own knowledge directly from feedback from their own experiences and through their own reasoning with these experiences (Kamii, 1975; Kegan, 1980).

Matched appropriately to the data acquired about children's cognitive operations, intervention would:

1. imply that observations of behavior must be evaluated with respect to their meaning in context, not as isolated items of analysis;
2. lead to a shift away from criterion performance objectives to a concern with the processes underlying behavior;
3. emphasize changes in affective (emotional-social) and cognitive structures in growth rather than isolated behavioral changes alone;
4. focus on reciprocal relationships between children and their environments rather than only on the actions of the environments on the children;
5. believe that development is organized and complex, not merely segmented and simple (Kreger & Kreger, 1981, pp. 3–4).

This stance challenges and encourages educators to design and implement intervention strategies that are matched to the level of an emerging stage of cognitive ability, self-regulating balance, meaning-making abilities, and sociocultural context (Sadler & Whimbey, 1985). This is especially relevant for children with learning/behavior disorders.

What is needed to deal adequately with the complexities of learning/behavior disorders is a comprehensive theory that portrays development as emerging from the striving of children to understand and control their worlds and their relations to them. A theory is needed that is interested in human psychological growth in all its aspects, and the developmental sequences that various types of problem solving, planning, language skills, and self-regulation undergo. Not only implying a structured mind interacting with a structured world, this theory would suggest that children's judgments and actions are neither direct products of biological inheritance nor simple passive absorptions of the examples encountered in the environment. Rather, these behaviors are something children arrive at through an ongoing, shared interaction with these and other facts about self and world (Child, 1973; Gelfand & Peterson, 1985).

Learning/behavior disorders can be better understood by grasping the integration of the developmental inherent processes within children at the biological, psychological, and social levels. The proficiency of the resolutions made by children to developmental hurdles influences how particular issues are incorporated into their systems as reorganization occurs. Positive adaptation is advanced when internal resources are refined and extended to hierarchically integrate the challenges of each issue throughout the life span (Cicchetti & Toth, 1998).

The attention being directed to the application of research findings of developmental epistemology within systematic intervention models allows for the assessment of both the degree and the form of a learning/behavior disorder. Behaviors can be evaluated in terms of the development of quantitative delays and/or qualitative deviations.

The purpose of intervention becomes the facilitation of the emerging capacities and of meaning-making. It is based on some conception of the knower (structure), the known (content), and the knowing process (function). Learning comprehension is best understood when examined from the interrelation of all three. Structure refers to the organization and logical combinations of elements. It represents a set of concepts and the premises that relate these concepts. Therefore, the structural elements and the rules that combine them need to be identified. Content refers to the individual characteristics and special information of a particular setting. Function refers to how children identify and use sequences of events within situational context as well as how they alter and expand their structures and content (Thorndyke, 1977).

The individual organization and restructuring of experiential data takes place according to existing cognitive structures. In turn, these very structures are altered and enriched through interaction with the physical and social worlds. The structures underlie and organize all behaviors and are developed, refined, and transformed by the self-regulatory functions. This is an ongoing lifelong process (Sigel et al., 1981; Smock, 1981).

Because schools see children over most of their formative life, it is imperative that educators become aware of the critical growth points in the cognitive-affective domains of children. They must also become alert to the signs of these growth points when they appear and constantly have in mind the mental health as well as the cognitive potential of any change at these growth points. Teaching from this stance can provide children with the best chances of experiencing all kinds of important motor-cognitive-affective connections in order to advance a separation of self from environment (Bower, 1972; Kreger & Kreger, 1981).

The efficacy of intervention techniques is optimized when stage-salient correlates are used as departure points for evaluating emerging, present, and future significance of a given maladjustment. These departure points highlight the degree of sophistication reached in the development of the self, cognition, and interpersonal relationships. They can help address those learning/behavior disorders that can possibly be outgrown as opposed to those that have more lasting and serious implications. A developmental model would describe learning/behavior disorders as stage-salient appropriate behavior that is either exaggerated, deficient, or absent. Determining when a behavior is stage-salient and age-appropriate or significantly excessive or deficient is of key importance in delivering effective intervention (Wenar, 1982). As a result, children with learning/behavior disorders can be brought closer to their own reality by learning how to:

1. conceptualize behavior as a search for meaning;
2. monitor comprehension to ensure that meaning indeed is derived;
3. engage in strategic behavior to bring meaning to behavior when there has been a break in comprehension;
4. modify choice of strategies to meet the various demands of adaptation. It strives for each child's achieving that amount of integration which facilitates his or her further development (Bower, 1972; Kreger & Kreger, 1981).

Cognitive functions develop in dialogical contact with the demands made on it by the environment they create. When challenged, the functions are stimulated to respond. Any response made to meet the demands might be either a transformation toward a higher level of development, a regression to defensive behavior, or a fall into misunderstanding. Therefore, it is a major responsibility of education to see that children with learning/behavior disorders not only gain new knowledge but also learn how to organize it. Children who are experiencing academic and/or social-emotional problems exist in fields consisting of disordered organisms and environments. The very meanings that children give to their experience exist within these contexts. However, even within these disordered children, there are innate self-regulating abilities to cope with, attend to, and experiment with personal phenomenologies (Resnick, 1997; Skolnik, 1990; O'Hara, 1998).

Children with psychomotor, affective, and cognitive disorders manifest special difficulties with adaptive processes. In Piaget's terms, these children consistently show severe structural delays in at least four important conceptual abilities: object permanence, symbolic formation, decentration, and conservation. They can also suffer from faulty modes of self/environmental contact, either being invested too much in the self or too much in the environment. Attending to these difficulties can bring children with learning/behavior disorders closer to their own adaptive, shared realities. Further explanation of these concepts is found in later chapters.

A constructivist approach would help children with learning/ behavior disorders attend to and experiment with personal meaning-making. It would lead these children to carefully look at how self and others are experienced. It can guide them toward and through active participation in a fuller integration of their own psychomotor, affective, and cognitive information-processing skills and adaptation. What they can arrive at is richer meanings of self and environment.

Important concerns are:

1. how disruptions and delays in development affect the domains of information processing;
2. how educators can help children with learning/behavior disorders integrate the different levels of processing into the construction of adaptive experiences;
3. how positive change in one behavioral domain can bring about positive change in another (Goldberg et al., 1983).

Chapter 2

DEVELOPMENTAL CONSTRUCTIVISM

The mind at any point in development is the
unfinished product of continual self-construction.
(Smock, 1981, p. 56)

Until the early 1900s, explanations of the hierarchy of concepts was the task of logicians. From that time, structural developmental theory was gradually extended from the realm of intellectual development into the realm of interpersonal and intrapersonal evolution. The stage model of psychosexual development put forth by Freud resulted in viewing all cognitive and social-emotional aspects of human growth from a developmental framework. Human behavior was subjected to close study couched in terms of internal dynamics beginning from early infant behavior and evolving through and culminating with maturation of the adult personality (Welch, 1940; Cooney, 1977; Harter, 1983).

> Freud . . . concluded that knowing was a kind of experiencing that involved personality or ego processes as information selectors, as differentiators of knowledge, and as integrator of new thoughts, new levels of feelings and new modes of behavior. (Bower, 1972, p. 4)

Freud's ideas began to influence education as the scope of mental health services to children broadened to the growth of child guidance clinics. The founding of the American Orthopsychiatric Association in 1924 brought together a variety of mental health disciplines focusing on the educational problem of children. The pendulum then swung toward the emotional aspects of learning difficulties. At this time Anna Freud was stressing the interrelationship of psychoanalysis and education, writing and lecturing extensively on how and why the two should be connected and applied (Westman, 1990).

Interpretations of development originally stemming from this closed, deterministic framework gradually came under the influences of the more open perspectives of both existential phenomenological and cognitive psychologies. Consequently, a systematic examination was made of the ways in which knowledge of developmental concepts may enhance the administration of intervention (Harter, 1983; Westman, 1990).

In 1948, Hilgard identified Gestalt field theory as one of the major learning theories. Generating from this theory were three prevailing subgroups:

(1) phenomenology, with its stress on perception and cognition; (2) cognition-neurology, with its stress on the use of neurophysiological knowledge to enrich an understanding of cognitive and social behavior; and (3) epistemology, with its stress on an explanation of the structures and functions of knowledge acquisition.

As professionals from education embraced field theory doctrine, they turned away from the trend of analyzing phenomena into bits and pieces, and phrased their thinking in constructivist, configural terms. The focus was put on an analytic method for comparing and reordering systems of self-regulating relations composed of continuously changing patterns or gestalts. This movement revolutionized traditional models of cognitive development and knowledge acquisition. It endorsed an underlying method for collecting, perceiving, organizing, and interpreting variables viewed and treated within the context of all the interactions that form a particular experience. It offered a pedagogical approach based on an understanding of cognitive development, that is, how learning happens (Rhyne, 1980; Kuhn, 1981; Smock, 1981; Rogers & Kegan, 1991).

This holistic paradigm reached out:

> . . . to the entire web of ultimate beliefs, values, needs, practices, interests, thought, and action from which we br ing forth (often unconsciously) a picture of being and knowing in the world, and which gives rise also to method. (Heshusius, 1989, p. 595).

The manner in which cognitive-developmental viewpoints was interwoven into many psychoeducational theories followed two predominate and separate paths. The first involved characterological theories and was basically psychoanalytic and focused on rather basic immutable characteristics. The second, involving transformational learning theories, focused on the development of rational consciousness defined as an accurate awareness of one's real nature as a person, of one's natural and social environment, and of one's connection with the outside world (Johnson, 1985; Sherrill, 1986; Reid, 1993).

A gradual shift from psychiatry's focus on the unconscious to the problems and phenomenology of awareness occurred. The study of creative adjustments between the individual self and the environmental ground was advocated. Consequently, difficulties were seen to occur when the course of normal adjustment is interrupted or inhibited. Since the agency of growth was defined as awareness, emphasis began to be placed, not just on the content, but on the evolving processes of behavior throughout a life span.

As the American educational scene became more strongly influenced by cognitive/developmental theories, it turned its focus to both the structures and processes of human ability and on how the nature of behavior was altered by learning and development. The goal of the cognitive/developmental theory that emerged at this time directed its attention to the structuralistic basis of its theory. Piaget serves as one of the most prominent figures of this stance. His fundamental teaching that form and function coexist gives an adequate account of logical and rational thought within a developmental framework. It embraces both logical form and semantic content functions. His concepts concerning the generativity of intelligence and the progressive rigor of intellectual development still maintain all their importance and his constructivist theory of equilibration as self-organization holds strong authenticity (Schmid-Kitsikis, 1973; Glaser, 1990; Beilin & Pufall, 1992; Chapman, 1992).

> The increased research in cognitive psychology, infant development, and special education going on all over the country is stressing a structuralist epistemology. (Skolnik, 1987, p. 7)

Piaget's studies provided special example and guidance for understanding the development of cognition. He articulated his epistemology in structuralist terms while fully incorporating the concepts of wholeness, transformation, and self-regulation into his theory. In centering on the ability of children to organize their present experiences into meaningful wholes, Piaget offered powerful explanations of the overall human experience in constructivistic terms. For him, children are driven to explore new knowledge and are open to new possibilities, taking roles in their own developmental processes. They generate and construct individual realities with self as the central referent and director of those realities (Child, 1973; Silverman, 1980; Furth, 1983; Rhodes, 1988).

Much importance is placed on the manner in which information is processed and turned into psychologically meaningful knowledge. Piaget's principles of knowledge acquisition are based primarily on a biological organization and propose that mental growth follows the same laws as biological growth. The same processes occur in intellectual organization and adaptation as well as in biological organization. Nourishment for both the biological and mental structures is provided by the environment. Environmental situations and stimuli are offered that can "free any given child to realize his/her capacities within his/her own time and space" (London, 1990, p. 83).

Since human thought and affect interact with the physical world, the development of self is inseparable from the development of the construction of the environment. Matter and mind are seen as coexisting within the wholeness of any particular acting self. All behavior is motivated by a need for self-realization. Given the opportunity to think out, or play through, cognitive and emotional challenges, children will eventually arrive at a constructive solution (Furth, 1983; Rhodes, 1988; Child, 1973; Silverman, 1980).

Children personally construct and coordinate experiential data and subsequently project these structures into the environment (Smock, 1981). For Piaget

. . . the problem of knowledge is the problem of the relation between the subject and the object–how the subject knows the object. If you translate this into
biological terms, it is a problem of the organism's adapting to its environment.
(in an interview with Hall, 1970, p. 25)

In the constructivist framework, there is an inherent motivation to understand and give meaning to the self and to the world as well as to extend knowledge. The gradual internalization of social interactions effect the restructuring
of cognitive development (Sigel, 1969; Gordon, 1988; Cicchetti et al., 1990;
Keating, 1991; Inhelder, 1992).

There is an inveterate need for all children to make meaning of themselves
and their worlds. The very nature of each child's system is to self-organize
and what is organized is meaning. Meaning is defined in terms of each child's
ability to organize, structure, and restructure experience in accordance with
existing and ever expanding cognitive structures (Rosen, 1985).

Developing through an evolving system, meaning-making is not so much
what one has, but what one is. The meaning-making systems shape one's experiences and give rise to one's behavior. It is responsible for organizing one's
actions, feelings, and thoughts over a broad sphere of human functioning. To
arrive at how children make meaning, it is necessary to observe how their systems actually function. The study of the development of meaning-making activities demands that children's immediate behaviors be seen as coherent and
meaningful. It must focus on their construction of reality, that is, on how they
bring reason to their existence. Of greater importance than an actual experience is what one makes of that experience. To know how children privately
construct their experiences is to learn their ability to adapt (Kegan, 1980).

Cognitive development is the growth of the following competencies:

1. mental reversibility and comparison of events that change form, disappear, or
   vary in relation to other events;
2. recognition of the point when the environment does not provide adequate
   information;
3. invention and discovery of more and more possible ways to go about achieving goals and resolving problems when the environment does not offer
   direction;
4. and selection, use, and thought about information derived from personal actions in qualitatively more complex ways (Moses, 1981).

Children construct reality in versions that develop over time in predicable
patterns and are markedly different from those of adults. As they grow older,
children can construct and retain more complex cognitive patterns, which
then allow more varied opportunities for interacting more objectively with the
environment. Essential to this construction of meaning are two basic principles: (1) intention, which refers to transformation; and (2) significance, which
refers to self-regulation (Piaget, 1973).

To explain how the knowledge acquisition strategies evolve as children adapt to their environments, Piaget derived the concept of equilibration. Equilibration represents a balance between the functions of assimilation and accommodation. Through interactions with their environments children integrate new experiences with already existing ones (assimilation) while at the same time responding to external circumstances with novel and more sophisticated behaviors (accommodation). It is an early instance of self-regulation (Henley, 1980; Chapman, 1992).

Development is a progressive equilibration from a lesser to a higher state of equilibrium. In addition to assimilation and accommodation there are the variable structures that are the organizational forms of mental activity. They are organized along both intrapersonal and social dimensions. The structures are motor or intellectual on the one hand and affective on the other (Piaget, 1968).

The tendency toward self-regulation is the propelling force with which children organize physiological maturation, physical experience, and social experience into coherent, meaningful wholes. Hence, the goals of self-regulation are meaning-making and adaptation. These, in turn, are always constructivist activities. Meaning-making and adaptation are guided by the inner logic of any given child's achieved developmental level and further transformed by interactions with others. The internal dynamics of the subsystems of the psyche as well as the structure of the psychological environment demand particular attention (Furth, 1983).

It is extremely important to remember that cognitive development refers to the ability to make more complex meaning of self and surroundings. Qualitatively different kinds of thinking and adapting become available with the accomplishment of issues that have salience at different stages of development. Each stage represents a fundamental change in cognitive processing and knowledge acquisition, and therefore, in meaning-making.

Human development occurs as a function of personal experiences and, at the same time, those experiences are a function of development. Selfhood is always in the process of its own making. Self-configuration is formed from influences with which children identify and interact. Children are not solely dependent on either external environmental fields or on their own innate mechanisms, but on their own histories (Piaget, 1973; Sherrill, 1986).

Discoveries about the objective and interpersonal world cause the development of cognitive structures. As development proceeds, the underlying mental structures of children undergo constant modification and become coordinated into more and more complex units. Active discovery along with the intercoordination of reasoning across domains promote changes in thinking (Pullis & Smith, 1981; Gordon, 1988).

Piaget saw no fundamental split between reasoning and action. Since thought is praxis-based, it emphasizes a form of action but with the capacity to operate on all strata of mental representation. Thought can focus on modes of action that are practical and closely attached to real life or those that are theoretical and hypothetical contexts of behavior (Youniss & Damon, 1992).

Cognition moves from dependence on one's actions to a greater control of symbolic signifiers. Meaning-making advances from a trial-error level, through a symbolic representational level, to conceptual thinking about thoughts themselves. As children strive to adapt to each new developmental challenge, they must constantly negotiate the balance between independence and autonomy and being connected to others. Autonomy comes about by an emerging awareness of one's capabilities, goals, activities, feelings, and actions (Furth, 1981).

The study of normal intellectual development and healthy adaptation is not a detailed assessment of the various forms of behavior. Rather it is an uncovering of the underlying structural mechanisms attained through an analysis of self-regulation. In order to achieve this self-regulation, children must take an interest in both the self and the external world. Cognitive structures arise along the continuous states characterized by little or no differentiation between self and other to states of self–other polarity. This self–other polarity is essential for the construction and maintenance of personal and social realities. Within this polarity children can bring consistent order to experiences. Clear distinctions of internal-external, subjective-objective, and imaginary-real can be established (Rogers & Kegan, 1991).

The intellectual process is explained in terms of the ability to organize and reconceptualize experiences in accordance with existing cognitive structures. In turn, the course of interaction with the physical and social environments modifies and enriches the structures. It is through self-directed or self-regulated activities that more advanced forms of cognition are reconstructed (Rhyne, 1980; Kuhn, 1981; Smock, 1981; Sadler & Whimbey, 1985; Rogers & Kegan, 1991).

Self–other unity is another basic assumption of Piagetian theory. Neither self nor other singly give rise to knowledge. Rather, it is from their interaction that cognition develops. Children do not take in a preexisting reality but expand and refashion personal reality out of each experience. The meaning of things is continuously modified as new data are received (Smock, 1981; Westman, 1990).

The interactions between internal organizational factors and external environmental influences are absolutely necessary for change to occur in children. These interactions follow a step-by-step process of self-regulation. Whether intraindividual or interindividual, all coordinations follow the same laws. A problem solution creates within children a sense of adequacy and power that, in turn, generates its own structure. New possibilities are often realized and things surprisingly seem to fall into place.

Over the years developmentalists have found more and more support for the concept that the acquisition of behavior in any one area (cognitive, social, motor, or play) is dependent on the acquisition of behavior in the other areas. They also assume that certain mental structures within children's internal systems must be intact before they can efficiently adapt (McNutt & Mandelbaum, 1980).

Structures are not extemporaneous patterns but derive one from the other by a progressive relation during a continuous construction. The whole is arranged hierarchically into subsystems. As each subsystem grows in complexity, it gains in autonomy and independence. It is in terms of structure of logical transformations that a cognitive definition of stages is given. The structures in turn are constructed and modified through the dynamic mechanisms of the functions of assimilation and accommodation. Children make meaning of, and organize, their experiences through structures (Piaget, 1973; Sigel, 1981).

Cognitive structures:

- embody dynamic self-regulations that include interchanges with the environment.
- are open systems of energy exchanges intrapersonally and interpersonally.
- experience temporary states of closure so that consideration can be given to the relationships among the elements and to the relationship between elements and whole.

What results from the interaction of children's natures and the aspects of their experiences is the appearance of qualitatively different characteristics. The distinctiveness of these different characteristics is referred to as a stage. Piaget's model considers and makes use of all aspects of children's physical and social environments as these aspects interact with their continuously changing intellectual, affective, and motivational characteristics (Furth, 1991; Reid, 1993).

Development proceeds through differentiation of the self. Piaget often wrote that he sees ". . . development as a process of successive 'decentrations' or 'triumphs over egocentrism'. . ." (Rogers & Kegan, 1991, p. 104).

> . . . the organism selects its environment while being conditioned by it. What this means is that the notion of structure as a self-regulating system should be carried beyond the individual organism, beyond even the population, to encompass the complex of milieu, phenotype, and genetic pool. Obviously, this interpretation of self-regulation is of the first importance for evolutionary theory. (Piaget, 1970b, p. 50)

The aim of cognition at every stage is to incorporate the world into itself. All mental life tends progressively to assimilate the surrounding environment. The mode of incorporation varies beginning with movement and perception and continuing to those of the higher mental operations. This is effected through more and more extended movement and perception at first concerned with objects that are close and viewed statically. Following this, representations, anticipation, and transformations of these objects are possible through memory and practical intelligence. Memory and practical intelligence are subsequently reinforced through intuitive thought. Further progress through logical thought and ultimately abstraction reaches a conclusion when children master events that are remote in space and time (Piaget, 1968).

Behavior manifested in any given situation is best illustrated by a constructivist perspective that suggests neither a health-and-illness model nor a learning-deficit model but rather a meaning-making paradigm. While remaining interested in the motoric and the affective as well as the cognitive, it does not reduce one to the other. It seeks to include an adaptive orientation to human motivation, which results from a child's ability to make meaning of the interaction of his/her internal and external environments. Action, emotions, and cognition hold equal prominence. One does not become subjugated to the other (Kegan, 1980).

A developmental-constructivist approach holds these fundamental priciples:

1. Children construct experiences of the objective world by viewing them through logical frameworks that transform, organize, and interpret experiences.
2. Constructions result from interactions between interpretations of new information according to already existing cognitive structures and the formation of new structures to resolve any given cognitive conflict.
3. Learning is a process of invention.
4. Meaningful learning occurs through reflection and resolution of cognitive conflict and serves to negate earlier, incomplete levels of understanding.
5. Learners are actively involved and responsible for what they learn.
6. Organization and integration of new information are critical to learning and memory.
7. Learning is holistic; focus is on part-whole relationships.
8. Self-regulatory functions are biological factors.
9. The process of equilibration refers to the balance achieved when new information is integrated into the internal structures of the child, who then modifies new understanding in accommodation to environmental demands.
10. Whatever experiences and content get into personal construction of the knowledge process are internally regulated by feelings, interests, and values. (adapted from Jacobs, 1984; Wadsworth, 1997)

A developmental-constructivist approach has not designed new intervention techniques or materials. Rather, it emphasizes naturalistic learning, discovery by the learner, and motivation via interest and/or meaningfulness. It guides us in understanding the broad organizing principles of the human mind. The capacity to gain and to use insight changes with development (Rogers & Kegan, 1991).

The wider application of these concepts to learning and instruction has resulted in an increased acceptance of the importance of developmental changes for the learning process and a greater recognition that children are active learners. With the emphasis on the interaction between developmental status and the components of academic/adaptive performance, the focus has shifted from the importance of materials and tasks to the roles of learners and their specific activities (Reid, 1988; Meltzer, 1993).

All children would be placed on a continuum of cognitive abilities without undue emphasis on age or etiology. Within this framework all children would be expected to change and learn. Educators would direct their efforts to promoting the emerging structures of children with learning/behavior disorders by including the following:

1. adherence to theoretically based lines of development;
2. attention to processes of development common to all areas of growth;
3. focus on the interrelated areas of development particularly affect and cognition; and
4. emphasis on helping children negotiate earlier stages of development that may have remained unfulfilled. (adapted from Kreger & Kreger, 1981)

RELEVANCE FOR CHILDREN WITH LEARNING/BEHAVIOR DISORDERS

Neither normalcy nor deviancy can be understood in isolation. Indeed, an understanding of normal development is crucial in judging behavior that may be characteristic of overmanifestation, deficiency of structure, or unresponsiveness to sensory input. Exploration of atypical psychological and academic disorders results in a keen awareness of the significance and merit of a developmental perspective. The study of normal development is a necessary condition for the study of pathological cognitive and/or affective conditions and, correlatively, the study of pathology increases the understanding of normalcy (Gelfand & Peterson, 1985; Furth, 1987).

It is possible to order symptoms as they are manifested along a developmental sequence of progressive differentiation and integration. Because maladaption, like adaption, is shaped by the developmental transformations of cognitive structure, it too can be analyzed according to developmental criteria. It is the form of symptom expression that changes with development.

Structural change is a normative dimension that interacts with such individual differences as psychopathology in a number of ways. Symptoms of a given problem predictably change with developmental level. A full understanding of an in-

dividual child therefore requires the assessment of his or her level of development. Similarly, intervention strategies must be determined in part in terms of
developmental level. (Breslow, 1988, p. 161)

As the genetic development of abstract thinking began to be actively in-
vestigated, especially in its relationship to certain clinical types of learning/
behavior disorders, significant changes occurred in the creation and implementation of intervention for children with such disorders (Harter, 1983;
Westman, 1990; Cicchetti et al., 1991; Rogers & Kegan, 1991).

Research in development that has gone awry evolved into a separate discipline, developmental psychopathology, in the early 1970s. Currently, it seeks
to clarify two important questions. First, it asks whether disturbances of early
experiences and biological disposition change in their effect and meaning
throughout life. Additionally, it questions whether different stages bring out
new symptom patterns, maladaptive behaviors, and pathologies, as well as
new possibilities for their resolutions.

> The conceptualization of psychopathology as "normal behavior gone awry"
> stands in contrast to, but is compatible with, the two current approaches to psy-
> chopathology: psychiatric diagnosis and factor analysis. (Wenar, 1982, p. 199)

Establishing links between a current academic or psychology disorder
and earlier life situations is a fundamental purpose of developmental psychopathology. Of more importance is the discovery of how patterns at different developmental periods interact with both changing physiology and changing external environments to produce subsequent adaptations. Consideration
must be given to mechanisms that result in certain adaptive patterns that are
relatively impervious to change, while other patterns are readily changed. The
amount and kind of changes taking place in the adaptive mechanisms due to
development need to be carefully noted (Sroufe & Rutter, 1984, as cited in
Santostefano, 1991).

Developmental psychopathology is surprisingly congruent with Piaget's
theory. Continued comparisons reveal that there is not so much a change in
any basis tenets of either, but rather a more inclusive incorporation between
them. Throughout the years research findings have seen both approaches sup-
plementing each other (Rogers & Kegan, 1991).

Piaget was well acquainted with the early writings of modern abnormal psychology, having full exposure to the ideas of Freud, Jung, Binet, and Simon.
This knowledge was reflected in his conceptualization of the *methode clinique,*
which he applied to the cognitive rather than affective processes (Cowan, 1978).
Learning situations are set up in ways that offer challenges to the existing
cognitive abilities of a child with sufficient vigor so as to provoke higher order
problem solving without being overwhelming.

Piaget (1975) provided a major impetus by cogently suggesting an integration of cognitive psychology within other points of view to form a study of individual human development. This goal would lead to the constructing of common concepts that would help define a psychological disorder in terms of the "ensemble of elements involved" (p. viii). The application of his theory to developmental anomalies:

> . . . should go beyond juxtaposing findings from different diagnostic groups, or from assessment of family conflict, emotions, and intellectual performance, and pursue the goal of integrating cognitive psychology within other points of view to form a science of ontogenetic development. (1975, p. vii)

Developmental psychopathology has more to offer than the establishment of links between pathology in earlier and later stages of growth. Any behavior or thought pattern expresses a meaningful response, maladaptive or otherwise. It plays a role in a child's interactions with ever-changing environments. Behavior must be interpreted with reference to both past and present developmental responses or structures (Furth, 1983; Rogers & Kegan, 1991).

Piaget's brilliantly outlined structural activity can be embedded within the larger theoretical construct of the developing self.

> Freed from the confusion of viewing self-complexity as psychological health, we can now propose a radical aim for clinical developmental psychology: that the ultimate definition of mental health is not the person who can love and work, but the person who can continue to develop throughout life. The ability to function in love and work is a necessary but not sufficient condition for developmental maturity. The aim of therapy [and education] is the person who can create ever new meanings in work and love by taking constructively the hurdles and opportunities, as well as disappointments, created by life. The enemy of development is stagnation and disintegration. (Noam, 1988, pp. 118–119)

Piagetian research in psychopathology focused attention on cognitive discordances, cognitive instabilities, and absence of certain cognitive concepts as well as on the problems of the developmental stage hierarchy (Bauer & Modarressi, 1977). Development can no longer be seen as a series of unfolding tasks that must be accomplished and then decreased in importance. Rather it consists "of a number of important age- and stage-appropriate tasks that, upon emergence, remain critical to the child's continual adaptation" (Cicchetti et al., 1988, p. 127).

A correspondence exists between psychological integration and levels of cognitive development. A constructive-developmental perspective looks at academic and affective disorders relative to the self-regulating structures and transitions of the self occurring throughout the life span. This orientation is not age related. It places transitions in a sequential array. Any developmental sequence of critical masteries such as infantile self-other differentiations (first year of life), separation-individuation (second year), empathy and identification (third-fourth year), Oedipal conflict resolution resulting in a stable organization of impulses and identity (fifth year) that have gone awry; can be specified. A stage of mental development can be conceived as a distinct state of self-other differentiation. Focusing on stage-salient developmental issues and assessing the processes of integration and differentiation of social, emotional, cognitive, and linguistic development in concert with biological growth will result in a more comprehensive understanding of normal and abnormal development (Noam et al., 1984; Cicchetti et al., 1991). Stage-salient issues are:

1. homeostatic regulation and the development of a reliable signaling system,
2. management of tension and the differentiation of affect,
3. development of attachment,
4. development of an autonomous self,
5. symbolic representation and self-other differentiation. (Cicchetti et al., 1988, p. 128)

The underlying concepts argue that behavior is holistic, goal-directed, and differentiated by mobile and ever-changing modes and goals. A longitudinal investigation of both normal and deviant behavior is essential. Since the present is regarded within the context of the past and the future, all behavioral processes are seen as extended through time and must be understood within their temporal contexts. Any deviation is conceived as a disturbance, distortion, or degeneration of normal functioning; that is, normal development that has gone awry (Sigel, 1969). Deviations may be seen as:

1. exaggerated behaviors or overmanifestations of age-appropriate behaviors;
2. actual lacks in the internal structures of the child;
3. an absence or unresponsiveness to sensory input.

Any behavior reflective of diminishment of sensory input, overmanifestation, or deficiency must be judged in contrast to normalcy (Gelfand & Peterson, 1985). A comprehensive understanding of normal and abnormal behaviors will evolve if focus is placed on stage-salient developmental issues. Necessarily, assessment would consist of how the child integrates and differentiates social, emotional, cognitive, and linguistic development in concert with biological growth. Intervention would help a child learn those tasks needed to coordinate cognition, affect, and behavior and on multiple ontogenetic systems.

> If we follow a developmental view of the world, we would embrace a genuinely integrative framework which considers both normal and atypical [forms] of ontogenetic growth within and between psychophysiological, cognitive, and affective systems. (Cicchetti et al., 1991, p. 72)

Recent research confirms the validity of a developmental-constructivist view of cognitive and social adjustment to teach or modify children's problem-solving strategies. In addition, its use can be optimistically advocated for children with learning/behavior disorders (Spivack et al., 1976; Kneedler, 1980; Urbain & Kendall, 1980).

Eschewing chronological age or social timetables as major developmental variables studied by most developmental psychologies, constructivism offers different developmental markers. It contends that the study of human development can be organized around the concepts of structural organization and functional balance independent of age. The acquisition of specific structures and specific functional balance must each be considered in terms of their adequate implications for psychological adaptation, dysfunction, and intervention (Noam, 1988).

The roots of constructivism affirm that cognitive, affective, social, and moral aspects of life play co-equal roles in development and meaning-making. They can offer a strong basis to serve emancipatory goals for children with learning/behavior disorders. Intervention techniques emerging from this theory can help such children realize their highest order of mind as well as attain their most adaptable forms of structural organization. In turn, they will be better equipped to make meaning of, and to meet the demands of, their worlds (O'Hara, 1998).

A developmental-constructivist approach must adhere to the consideration that children who experience academic and/or social-emotional problems exist in fields consisting of disordered organismic and environmental aspects. Their very meaning exist within this context. However, even within disordered children, there is an innate self-regulating ability to cope. They too, will replicate the stance that they hold in the world in many of their encounters.

Since the field of special education has been articulating a more constructivist viewpoint toward learning and teaching, professionals in this discipline have been led to view the process of intervention in more holistic terms; to understand the knower as a meaning-maker; and to see knowledge as deriving from an interaction of learner and environment (Poplin, 1988b; Glaser, 1990).

Both the functional and the content aspects of cognition are needed in order to obtain a more useful explanation of individual differences. The former aspects include the various information-processing faculties (such as memory, attention, and perception), biases, strategies, algorithms, regulatory processes, and emotional factors (such as motivation). The latter includes learning, specific nonstructural knowledge, and skills.

> A major contribution from constructivism to the practice of psychotherapy is the importance of matching communications, strategies, and programs to the cognitive-structural level of the patient. (Breslow, 1988, p. 165)

Children with learning/behavior problems are likely to have experienced faulty resolution of stage-salient issues. Developmental psychopathology seeks an integrated conceptualization and understanding of how various ontogenetic domains are organized. It provides valuable insights to understanding:

> . . . how the varying capacities of children at different developmental levels influence their capacity to utilize various therapeutic strategies. (Cicchetti & Toth, 1998, p. 236)

Various forms of learning/behavior disorders manifest atypical patterns such as delay in the emergence of communication skills, thought disorder, and inability to focus and maintain attention on relevant task demands. They are best viewed in a developmental perspective. In addition, cognitive development affects social perception and adaptation. Children at different developmental stages have differing abilities to explore past patterns and to construct new ones. They experience and make use of such explorations and constructions very differently. Continued development does not necessarily protect a child from psychological distress, but it can change the form of distress. Intervention can not only facilitate mental growth, but it can also enhance that child's developmentally determined capacities to explore and construct (Cicchetti et al., 1991; Rogers & Kegan, 1991).

Since each developmental stage includes a child's behavioral, social, psychological, and cognitive changes, it deserves special scrutiny in light of the many problems and unsolved conflicts that affect it. Confusion, difficulty with meaning-making, increased peer competition, and the challenges of autonomy are all characteristics that may overwhelm some children in any stage (Sabornie & deBettencourt, 1997).

In normal circumstances the earlier structures become transformed and integrated. However, there are times when usual transformation and integration fail to arise. Situations can occur in which earlier self-systems coexist rather than coordinate with later ones. Early internalized structures can continue to shape experiences in an unconnected way even though more complex structures have been developed (Smock, 1981; Noam, 1988).

Certain stage salient behaviors must be allowed and encouraged so that a child does not end up with patterns that are inappropriate direct discharges of behaviors or rigid, fixed belief systems (Greenspan, 1997). Deficits, constrictions, and instabilities in each area must also be identified. This then leads to an exploration of how the biological system as well as the environmental system contribute to the pattern of strengths and weaknesses.

> When [types of structures] have not been formed because certain patterns got set into place and new experiences are not of sufficient quality to alter the early patterns, a structural deficit arises. (Greenspan, 1997, p. 61)

These considerations must be taken into account when treating children with learning/behavior disorders. Meeting a child at his or her level of ego structure development is imperative. This involves both dealing directly with a child's regulatory patterns as well as creating, within each intervention session, a regulatory environment.

It should be kept in mind that any child can continuously fluctuate between different structural levels. Early internalized structures certainly continue to shape the child's experiences even though more complex structures have been developed (Smock, 1981; Noam, 1988).

It is possible for simpler logic of earlier internalized relationships to continue to shape a child's experience even though that child has developed more complex meaning-making structures. If the old structure does not become transformed into a higher level one, it becomes encapsulated and can coexist with later, more sophisticated ones. Different developmental stages allow for differing abilities to construct new patterns of behaviors and to explore past patterns. Yet, because these abilities may actually change in the very process of intervention, intervention itself may facilitate mental growth (Noam, 1988).

Each stage deserves special scrutiny in light of the many problems and unsolved conflicts that affect it.

> . . . one cannot properly either understand, analyze, or alter a drama without also taking into account the stage upon which this drama is being played out (Greenspan, 1997, p. 48). It is easy to focus on only one perspective, such as the dynamic, and lose sight of the fact that every dynamic drama must take place in the context of a particular structure or set of structures. (Greenspan, 1997, p. 51)

Within any diagnostic category there are children at different developmental levels. The forms that symptoms of a diagnostic category take are related to developmental conditions. For example, children with the same DSM diagnosis may still be at different stages of development. This profoundly influences what the disorder means to any individual child. A child's response to and capacity to relate to any disorder vary greatly.

Piaget's model provides a relatively comprehensive description of both the stages and dynamics of cognitive acquisition. It also lends itself to understanding the link between cognitive dysfunction and adaptational difficulties. The developmental perspective provides a model of positive mental health. It subsumes a pulsatory movement of expansion and contraction within children. This fundamental movement directs them toward meeting their needs and affirming independence. The extent to which the needs are met by the environment and the strength of the expression of independence vary with personal development. Frustration or growth delays may interfere with attempts at self-fulfillment (Johnson, 1985; Gordon, 1988).

Chapter 3

DEVELOPMENT AND MEANING-MAKING

The importance of Piagetian stages lies in their capacity
to direct children toward making meaning of
self and environment.
(Gordon, 1988, p. 60)

In recent interpretations of Piagetian stage theory, salience has taken precedence over stage sequencing. Development goes through a process of successive embeddedness, disembeddedness, and qualitatively new embeddedness. A prior system emerges into a more complex system. With the emergence of new tasks, old issues may decrease in relative salience. Each issue represents a life span developmental task that needs to be continually coordinated and integrated both to adaptation to the environment and to stage-salient developmental issue of the period. Increasing the probability of any child's successfully resolving each stage-salient issue is crucial. Development can no longer be seen as a series of unfolding tasks that must be accomplished and then decreased in importance. Rather it consists ". . . of a number of important age- and stage-appropriate tasks that, upon emergence, remain critical to the child's continual adaptation . . ." (Cicchetti et al., 1988, p. 127).

> Salience often becomes the basis for introducing activities. For example, the salient action or movement of the sensorimotor individual; the salient symbolic formation of the preoperational individual; the salient transformation of the concrete operational individual; and the salient ideation of the formal operational individual. (Gordon, 1988, p. 65)

According to Piaget's stage theory, one can see that action and movement is most salient for the sensorimotor child; symbolic formation, for the preoperational child; part-whole transformations, for the concrete operational child; and abstract ideation, for the formal operational child. These defined developmental stages do not exist in a void but are prompted by constitutional, maturational, and environmental factors. Each stage results from specific self-other interaction patterns (Sigel, 1969; Gordon, 1988; Cicchetti & Beeghly, 1990; Keating, 1991; Inhelder, 1992; Greenspan, 1997).

Cognitive development is the growth of logical structures that must be acquired through action within a meaningful environment. It is through these structures that children organize their thoughts and behaviors. Structures are organized patterns of physical and/or mental action providing children with systemized frameworks to make experience meaningful. Being neither innate nor instinctual, the substance of the structures comes from the action coordination itself and not from the external object. That is, they are derived from within (Piaget, 1973).

As this organizing interaction is taking place, children evolve through progressive stages of intellectual and emotional reconstruction. Each stage has exclusive milestones that must be reached for its completion. Meaning-making is directed by each stage's own particular proficiency. A lower level stage becomes incorporated into the next developing stage, which then has more flexibility and proficiency to adapt and can hold more energy. As each stage emerges, it allows the creation of more complex figures that absorb the stage energy to a spontaneous closure (Child, 1973).

In theory, the presence of organized cognitive structures mark psychological adaptation as they vary in form according to a child's stage of development. Advancement through developmental stages allows children more elaborate differentiation and more complex methodology in viewing the world. The ability to adapt and show competence results from the successful resolution of the tasks most salient for any given developmental period (Sigel, 1969; Gordon, 1988; Cicchetti & Beegaly, 1990; Keating, 1991; Inhelder, 1992).

There are two necessary conditions for stage development. First, the stages must be defined in a way that guarantees a constant order of succession. Second, the definition for each stage must allow for progressive construction without entailing any total pre-formation (Piaget, 1971).

Essentially, growth stages arise from the meaning that children make of their intrapersonal and interpersonal worlds. As children form structures of thinking by a progression through a succession of stages, points of difficulty or conflict are likely to arise. If children achieve the requisite transformation of thought-structures, they are then prepared to encounter the difficulties occasioned in interaction with the world. This evolutionary cycle affords children the possibility of moving on to structures that will allow broader, more objective meaning-making skills to resolve those difficulties (Elkind, 1970; Piaget, 1968, 1971, 1973; Child, 1973; Gordon, 1988).

Fully self-regulated structures are characterized by reversibility and are self-regulated only to the degree that they allow active compensations for all intrusions.

> For every structure of experience in the given situation that we perceive and describe, there is another vantage point, another possibility of being conscious of the situation next to or beyond where we are. (Miller, 1989, p. 37)

Structures are built in step-by-step processes as part of an evolving, dynamic organization. They strive toward a self-direction that is patterned at different levels by rhythms, regulations, and cognitive operations. Each structure is "a system of transformations, not a mere collection of elements and their properties" (Piaget, 1970b, p. 18).

Cognitive structures are characterized by laws of organization outdistancing particular situational figures. They are the result, not the cause, of an evolutionary operation. While partly dependent on practice and experience, their elaboration stems from the actions of children. Structures become coordinated when new goals are sought that require actions that have not been combined before. They are made stable and consistent through the use of overriding logical categories, which Piaget calls operations. Provided these operations have been acquired, movement can occur from one point within the system to another based on the internal logic achieved. The most valuable function may be the ability to construct and reconstruct personal intelligence (Piaget, 1973; Furth, 1987).

Structures that are observable are in a stable state, that is, they are temporally ordered in a relatively autonomous state. However, they are not separately existing entities but are components of a larger, higher-energy order. The higher-energy order is an undivided whole made up of interrelated parts being woven together into a unified pattern. By definition, the pattern itself is always in the process of growing and expanding (Gordon, 1988).

In order for the critical developmental structures to evolve, a tension must exist between the conserving and transforming energy patterns of their activity. As structures extend and reorganize their form, disturbances may emerge. If newly formed structures are stable enough, the disturbances will be faced and reality will be redefined. If sufficient stability and tension needed to sustain the process of change is lacking, reality will not be transformed. Should activity be interrupted by disturbing interactions with the environment, the structures will dissociate and then reorganize. Beginning with simple structures, this reorganization gives rise to more complex structures transforming children and their environments as they interact. The activity generated from the disruptions cause the structures to expand and extend their form, which in turn creates a need for nourishment from the environment. As the structures expand, they change in a spiral fashion, rather than in a linear way. As the structures become more integrated, it is expected they will lead children to more objective meaning-making (Grobecker, 1998).

Organized cognitive structures vary relative to the particular stage of development and are fundamental for optimal psychological adaptation. Qualitatively different cognitive and affective characteristics appear as children conquer the salient challenges demanded of each developmental stage. According to Piaget, as children are afforded increasingly differentiated and complex perspectives of the world, they advance through the sensorimotor, preoperational, concrete operational, and formal operational developmental stages (Gordon, 1988).

During the sensorimotor stage, young children move from complete egocentrism and no self-concept to nascent internal experimentation and a basic self-concept. Meaning-making is related to actions that gradually become goal-directed and eventually lead to the formation of object permanence. Preoperational children can represent their thoughts through symbolic functions such as play, imitation, drawings, fantasies, dreams, and referential language. Physical action now becomes mental action. At the concrete operational stage, the child can coordinate part-whole relationships with basic logical thinking such as classification, seriation, decentration, reversibility, and conservation. However, at this point these meaning-making abilities can be carried out only in immediate time/space situations. The formulation of hypotheses, the carrying on of arguments to logical conclusions on an abstract level, and the ability to handle second order operations are indices of formal operational thinking. The formal operational thinker can classify all possible categories and can form an operation on other operations. This means true "reflection" in a cognitive sense Rogers & Kegan, 1991).

MAKING MEANING WITH SENSORIMOTOR INTELLIGENCE

Knowledge is constructed through the process of acting on and interacting with objects, actions, and others in one's world. Biological constitution, maturity level, motivation, and personal discipline are brought to the construction of structures (Johnston & Johnston, 1984).

The primary function of sensorimotor meaning-making is the assimilation of sensory information into the cognitive processes. Meaning-making is connected to sensory input and evolving motor abilities. Organismic/sensorimotor behavior provides the primary building blocks of true knowledge. There is a lack of knowledge beyond actions. Children engage in movement to bring meaning to their worlds and to find solutions to problems. Awareness evolves slowly from neonatal reflexes to an external world apart from a child's personal existence. The coordination of sensorimotor actions is of major importance and is the derivation of all knowledge and intelligence (Piaget, 1968; Henley, 1980; Morozas, 1983; Furth, 1991; Rosen, 1991).

The four relevant early stage-salient issues marking sensorimotor adaptation are:

... (a) the development of homeostatic and physiological regulation, (b) affect differentiation and the modulation of attention and arousal, (c) the development of a secure attachment relationship, and (d) the development of the self-system. (Cicchetti & Toth, 1998, p. 227)

Initially, the processes of self-regulation allows infants a sense of confidence in their ability to be calm, regulated, and interested in the environment. The challenge to early infants is to maintain self-regulation of internal physiological states such as object permanence, object relations, causality, and spatial relations. The innate motor reflexes serve to reduce any tension in the biological systems that may exceed optimal levels. As the inhibitory tracts and neurotransmitters develop, infants grow increasingly more self-sufficient in regulating tension. Self-regulation is enhanced by interhemispheric connections that allow infants to more carefully attend and respond to the physical environment.

This level of ego development has particular structural features and themes. The processes of self-regulation allow sensorimotor children a sense of confidence in their abilities to be calm, regulated, and interested in their surroundings. They gain a feeling of basic security in their perceptual and motor abilities (Piaget, 1968; Greenspan, 1997; Cicchetti & Toth, 1998; London, 1990).

Sensorimotor children deal with ". . . basic issues as regulation and security, the depth, range, and stability of relationships, and the formation of drive and affect . . ." (Greenspan, 1997, p. 37). Differentiation of a sense of self and of early character patterns are formed. A child comes to a sense of who he or she is, what he or she wants, and how he or she will be treated by others.

> Understanding the structural development of the mind provides us with a way of comprehending how an individual learns to regulate the intensity of sensations, and later, the intensity of internal wishes and affects. It also provides us with a way of understanding how individuals process, that is, comprehend and organize sensations, wishes, and affects and organize both motor and communication patterns. (Greenspan, 1997, p. 53)

The first task of the infant is to begin to establish ego boundaries, that is, some sense of where he or she leaves off and the environment begins. As the infant progresses in organizing space and time, knowledge and awareness of intentionality begin to appear. Initial construction of object constancy, coordinated space, causality, and temporality emerges. Cognitive and affective states at the behavioral-gestural level must be experienced before infants can give symbolic representation to them (Johnston & Johnston, 1984).

Initially, infants fail to recognize where their own bodies end and the outside world begins. They lack any clear differentiation between an external environment and an internal or subjective world. As they progressively expand their worlds, they gain greater meaning to what they see, hear, and touch. How much, and in what manner, infants reach out and explore their worlds will be a combination of their physical abilities and their learned feelings about their environments as they interact with them.

Children are born with no sense of separation between themselves and their external worlds, that is, impressions that are experienced and perceived are not attached to a personal consciousness sensed as a "self," nor to objects conceived as external to the self. These impressions simply exist in a dissociated block or are spread out on the same plane, which is neither internal nor external but midway between these two poles. These opposing poles will only gradually become differentiated. In other words, consciousness starts with an unconscious and integral egocentricity, whereas the progress of sensorimotor intelligence leads to the construction of an objective universe in which the child's own body is an element among others and with which the internal life, localized in the child's own body, is contrasted (Piaget, 1968).

The initial exploration of sensations forms the foundation to building a meaningful alliance. At this time opportunities can be created in which the caregiver's nonjudgmental attitude can lead children in nonthreatening interaction (Matzko, 1997).

Expressions of sensorimotor affect are adjustments to caregivers. Infants, with repeated interactions, attach interpretations and reactions to the external events that become the basis for evaluating the environment. Very young infants do not experience separation between the self and the external world. Perceived motor impressions and/or sensory perceptions are not attached to a personal consciousness sensed as a "self," nor to objects conceived as "other." At this time the impressions exist either in a dissociated state or in a plane, which is neither internal nor external but midway between these two poles. A gradual differentiation emerges between these opposing poles. Self-other separation is progressive. At first, very young infants experience little differentiation between the perspectives of the self and other. This is the beginning of self as actor. Following this, infants can observe certain characteristics in another and can engage in a primitive form of perspective taking. This is the beginning of self as observer. Yet they can not mentally step outside to observe this perspective (Piaget, 1968; Greenspan, 1997).

Through action on objects in any immediate situation, plus feedback from movement and body sensations, infants make meaning of self and other. Preverbal, presymbolic gestural interactions encompass the meanings they attribute to themselves and to the objects and other people they come into contact with. The gestural interactions lead to a definition of oneself and to "a core sense of what is 'me' as it interacts gesturally with 'you'." Boundaries defining gestures help them distinguish where their personal selves begin and end. Sensorimotor self-other separation is established through the construction of closure of actions. As children come to understand characteristics of, and relations among, object, they extend their knowledge to people, relations among people, and their own relations with other individuals. There is a progressive awareness of the self as the agent of its own actions and of others as agents of their own actions. This provides a framework for a realization of logic in the actions performed (Piaget, 1968; Morozas, 1983; Furth, 1991; Rosen, 1991).

Focus on awareness of the logic of action culminates in the establishment of object permanence. In their simplest forms these cognitive changes are perceptual, sensory, and motoric, for example, kinesthetic sensations, sensori-motor learning, eye-hand coordination, perceptual attention, and perceptual processing (Johnston & Johnston, 1984).

Beginning with its pure reflex behavior, an infant repeats actions for their own sakes. During the first six months of life, the reflex patterns become real play as they come under an infant's conscious control. The infant uses all motoric elements of the communicative context at his or her command. When vocalization is added to these acts, the infant begin to form concepts of identity and mutual reference. As infant/other dyads develop, a reciprocal social interaction occurs resulting in the development of a knowledge of referents. From six to twelve months of age infants become aware that personal cognition is in some ways independent of personal actions. Purposeful behavior occurs. The ability to anticipate beyond the motor act extends into the affective realm. The infant becomes less interested in his or her own actions and more conscious of the various objects toward which those actions are directed. The meaning of a situation is grasped and not just reacted to. Novel situations are sought out and explored with great interest. A very primitive sense of the world is established. Events are conceived as collections of motor and/or perceptual stimuli. Short-term future goals can be anticipated. A vulnerability to new feeling states emerges (Piaget, 1968, 1971; Emde & Sorce, 1982; Johnston & Johnston, 1984).

At this time attachment relationships form the primary benchmarks of child development. Evolving affect, cognition, and behavior is organized according to the quality of physical and emotional support available from the caregiver. The regulation of arousal and the maintaining of internal security are facilitated from a dependable support base. Intentional gestures and affective communication help to construct more defined affective states and contribute to the most fundamental sense of reality, mastery, and partial self-differentiation. Establishing and maintaining intimate relationships follows and builds the foundation for warmth and security with others. A sense of positive nurturance is cultivated (Greenspan, 1997; Cicchetti & Toth, 1998).

> Although a few words are used here and there during this phase, an infinite number of gestures and nonverbal patterns are being displayed. These gestural interchanges reveal how the child is dealing with such major psychological issues as dependence and independence, closeness and warmth, pleasure, asser-

tiveness, anger, approval and disapproval, pride and admiration, and envy and competition. (Greenspan, 1997, p. 190)

OBJECT PERMANENCE

When children can detach their thinking processes from the actions they perform on objects, they have established sensorimotor intelligence. This is accomplished at first when children visualize and imagine the objects as they actually are experiencing them in their immediate sensory experiences. They are able to differentiate among their own acting, their sense of agency, and the object that they act on, they have reached conscious awareness (Selman, 1980).

With the progression of sensorimotor intelligence comes the construction of an objective world. Any symbolically represented and theoretically known information is based on the construction of object permanence. This symbolic representation and information require a medium or modality such as action, vision, sound, or speech. The development of sensorimotor abilities leads to the establishment of the prerequisites of language and a desire to communicate to others. The evolution of those abilities necessary to construct and reconstruct objects is the primary focus (Piaget, 1968; Furth, 1991; Rosen, 1991).

Children have grasped object permanence when they are able to integrate perceptive-proprioceptive functions and motor-muscular functions with organic needs as well as view an object as persisting in the absence of all perceptual contact (Piaget, 1968).

With the ability to internalize and associate actions with objects, children are able to anticipate the consequences of their actions. They are freed from dependence on the trial and error. Cognition becomes independent of actions in some ways. Children move from complete egocentrism and no self concept to a grasp of the permanency of objects and a basic self concept. It is the differentiation of what is "I" and what is "NOT-I" (Inhelder & Piaget, 1964; Emde & Sorce, 1982).

Object permanence, coordinated space and time, and intentionality are built with sensorimotor intelligence. Boundaries need to be established in order to understand in some sense the dimensions of self and environment. Space and time become organized through interactions with environmental objects. Space must first be organized before the localization of objects. When space is organized, it becomes possible for the child to combine movements, reverse movements, and take detours leading back to the starting point of a motor pattern. Objects can then exist in their own independence. With the attainment of object permanence children realize that objects have a stable existence apart from themselves and continue to exist when not in their immediate presence.

When young children can coordinate how they relate to objects and other people in space, they can also understand the prepositional constituents of language. An understanding of temporality gives children a growing understanding of continuing activity and hence the elements of verb tenses (Johnston & Johnston, 1984).

Intentionality begins to evolve when a child understands cause as something beyond reflexive or repetitive of immediate stimuli. Intentionality marks the initial step of the child's emerging cognition (Henley, 1980; Johnston & Johnston, 1984; Rosen, 1991; Piaget, 1968; Piaget, 1981; Greenspan, 1997).

With causality children can think in terms of agent, action, and receiver of action. They can generate words such as because, until, and before that refer to coordinations and subordinations in language.

The permanent object endures in the absence of perceptual contact. Object permanence allows a child to mentally conserve an object in space and time even though it is no longer in the present perceptual field. Additionally, it allows a child to conserve the integrity and consistency of the self. The culminating task of this stage is the ability to create mental images of objects and people. By the age of two, sensorimotor intelligence reaches a remarkable state of self-regulation (Piaget, 1981; Furth, 1987).

Attachment has long been attributed to levels of the development of object permanence. Children who have an unstable concept of object permanence, who achieve only rudimentary object permanence, or who have difficulty in predicting the object states, may be severely handicapped in their ability to establish healthy social interactions. Rigid behavior may develop that interferes with the development of more advanced cognitive activities, such as symbolic functions that are necessary for normal social development. Symbolic functions serve as a means for the development of personal expression, the concept of the self, and ways of interacting with others. Further social interactions may be impaired because of some cognitive defect in dealing with social and emotional cues (Morgan, 1986).

EVALUATING SENSORIMOTOR MEANING-MAKING

Sensorimotor structures are for the most part unconscious. Emotional excitement and investment in body experiences characterize the first months of life. Nonverbal experiences receive meanings from an infant's initial psychic reality. In order to receive further meaning they need to be translated into symbolic forms. If repeatedly revised they facilitate psychological growth. Although actions are subordinated by and integrated within the symbolic functions mode in the course of development, they are not replaced but remain potentially active (Piaget, 1981).

When language is analyzed from pragmatics principles, the intentions that children have are the major foci. Pragmatics is the extralinguistic communication that guides the use of language. It is seen in the basic gestural communication of infants as it forms the foundation of not only language but of interpersonal activity. Pragmatic appropriateness begins when infants first begin to use correct gestures and vocalizations for a communicative purpose. Pragmatics is concerned with the communication conventions used.

The mode used to present the relations between referents and the sound system that represents them is phonology. During the time children are developing sensorimotor abilities, they should be acquiring the other prerequisites of language:

> . . . linguistic experience, nonlinguistic experience, and a desire to communicate to others. There must be some notion of object permanence, realized as nouns in the language; coordinated space, realized as notions of relationship and of prepositions; causality, realized as the concept of agent and the words that show this; and temporality, as reflected by ideas of verb tense and designations of various ways of representing time. (Johnston & Johnston, 1984, p. 41)

Evaluation of sensorimotor meaning-making gives evidence of the following functions of ego development:

1. how regulation (sensory reactivity and processing) occur;
2. how early engagements and relationships are formed and elaborated;
3. how early simple and complex, intentional, gestural communication becomes a part of prerepresentational pattern of mental organization;
4. how experience is represented and how representation is elaborated;
5. how representations are differentiated. (adapted from Greenspan, 1997)

How an initial difficulty with gestural communication is related to a child's inability to get certain needs met, that is, how it relates to self-regulation, must be determined. Then, how a child has elaborated gestural patterns that are connected to the original state of mind must be established. A child, by learning to separate these two components, comes first to identify and tolerate the somatic states associated with the need for self-regulation and, secondly, to read more correctly the gestural signals of other people (Greenspan, 1997).

There are four considerations relative to the gestural system:

1. Does the gestural system exist in a complex form?
2. Do the breadth and range of gestures express affects and themes?
3. Are the countergestures occurring in which the educator responds nonverbally to a child's initiatives, and vice versa?

4. When a child experiences intense affect or stress, does the gestural system remain stable? (adapted from Greenspan, 1997)

EVALUATION OF SENSORIMOTOR PROCESSING

1. Does the child have any sense of separation of his or her actions from his or her self?
2. Does the child have any recognition of others and their actions? Does the child have any sense of separation from them?
3. Does the child see objects as sharing a common physical space?
4. How does the child select actions from his or her repertoire?
5. How does he or she incorporate actions received from others?
6. How does he or she use available objects as means to achieve a goal?
7. How does he or she understand spatial arrangements between objects located in his or her immediate environment?
8. How does he or she understand spatial arrangements between objects moving through familiar space?
9. Does he or she cause a reoccurrence of various events and thus reveal his or her concept of the cause of these events?
10. Does he or she have evocative memory, i.e., permanent object?

MAKING MEANING WITH PREOPERATIONAL INTELLIGENCE

The ability to internally represent the external world allows for the emergence of the preoperational stage. Early concepts of time, space, and causality emerge to provide a base for a meaning-making level that deals with symbolic meanings. The conquest of symbols is the stage-salient challenge for the preoperational child. Meaning-making with preoperational thinking begins between eighteen and twenty-four months of age. A symbolic, representational experience occurs when children can put feelings and gestures into words. Sufficient sensorimotor structures exist allowing young children to form verbal symbols to represent them. What children have learned by sensorimotor interaction with objects is now destined to lead to knowledge of the qualities of objects. With the capacity to form mental images, they can now move from a gestural release mode to a representational one. The ability to represent and use symbols initially involves becoming aware of a behavioral pattern, staying with it, and reflecting upon it without needing to immediately satisfy the goals of that behavior pattern. As these patterns come into awareness, children learn to describe thoughts and feelings that precede and/or accompany them.

The moment of separation of the motor-muscular and perceptual-thought functions is a critical point in child development. Children experience a new phase of self-regulation. Actions are gradually organized, through the use of symbolic functions, into semilogical structures. Mental representations evolve that can be internally imagined in a series of actions without motoric components. The symbolic functions, the means through which self is represented and needs and emotions are communicated, consist of deferred imitation, pretend play, imagery, graphic imagery, and language.

The ability to understand, use, and produce symbols is a critical cognitive achievement. It is through the power of symbols that children are able to communicate with others and with self. Symbols permit children to simplify, generalize, and abstract information. They also allow this information to be manipulated, transformed, and used to produce and consider several possibilities. Through the symbolic functions, information is to be carried far from the referent.

With preoperational intelligence, children can reflect on the past, take the role of another, and make inferences. Reflection on their own past behaviors brings them to the realization that they have a choice with respect to a prior action. The problems of adaptation are no longer measured by practical, physical success alone. In addition, with this quality of thinking children learn to form an internal representation of the availability of the self and on the self in relation to others. They gradually come to recognize the self as the agent of their symbols and representations just as they come to recognize others as persons with their own symbols and representations (Piaget, 1971).

These cognitive changes involve memory, discrimination of similarities and differences in all sensory modalities, classification, concept building, receptive language, use of objects, recognition of details in pictures, and basic concepts of numbers. With the emergence of evocative memory, children can remember past actions and can relive past experiences mentally without the actual sensory experiences. This beginning of interiorized mental activity creates some problems because objects and events are assimilated to personal viewpoints. In addition, possible accommodations are still fixations on perceptual aspects of reality.

With development reaching the point where language becomes an available vehicle, it is used to speed up and expand cognition.

In Piagetian terms, "(1) verbal behavior permits representation of many acts very quickly, (2) language behavior may range beyond the here and now, and (3) language permits the child to handle several elements and actions at once." (Wadsworth, 1978, p. 68)

There is a close parallel between the development of referents and the construction of the cognitive system. Children who generate the expected relations build positive connections with the family cultural group. Failure to use a variety of referents may reflect problems in the psychosocial aspects of development (Johnston & Johnston, 1984).

With this kind of meaning-making, children have the ability to act on the states and conditions of their environments. An awareness and understanding of many scripts is now possible. Yet to come, however, is the ability to incorporate self scripts and those of others into part/whole relationships. Thinking tends to be "all-or-nothing," one-way mappings. Although involving a recognition of things as separate from self, children are not yet able to distinguish their perception of a thing from the thing itself. They are restricted to static imagery and to personal perspectives. Using personal perspectives as ultimate standards, they have little ability in anticipating how things might appear to someone else. Objects and events are assimilated to the personal actions and viewpoints. Accommodations are incomplete because they still consist only of fixations on figural, qualitative aspects of reality as opposed to operational transformations (Piaget, 1971; Loevinger, 1976; Rogers & Kegan, 1991; Liben & Downs, 1993; Cicchetti & Toth, 1998).

The psychological life of children is fundamentally changed with the appearance of the symbolic functions. Children achieve mastery over cognitive and affective conflicts by keeping them within an adaptive range of behavior. Their symbolic style and the flexibility of the fit between meaningful experiences and expressive behavior used to express that meaning demands cognitive coordination (Piaget, 1981; Furth, 1983).

The first of the symbolic functioning is imitation, which is basically an accommodative process during which children repeat what has been witnessed from personal experiences. The symbols used in imitation represent environmental events. What children strive for is bringing their structures into agreement with the external referents (Piaget, 1954; Voyat, 1983).

Children by the age of two imitate themselves doing something they actually are capable of doing. Following this, they can imitate another's actions if they themselves can perform those actions. Finally, they can imitate entire episodes (Johnston & Johnston, 1984).

Imitation embodies practice. Children imitate what they are in the process of learning. They perform the actions done by others but that are not yet a part of their own repertoires. They determine what and when to imitate and how much use to make of imitation as a learning technique. As the mental representations of the behaviors of others are encoded in children's long-term memories, a sense of psychological relationship between self and the person who performed the original action unfolds (Furth, 1983; Johnston & Johnston, 1984).

Imitation varies along three continua: content, spontaneity, and time. Relative to cognitive content, children develop from rote imitation to cognitive mediated imitation. Concerning spontaneity, children develop from elicited imitation to spontaneous imitation. Regarding time lapse, children develop from immediate to deferred imitation. Deferred imitation occurs when behavior is imitated at a later time and/or in a different context. At this point children cannot only master the behavior involved, but they can do so in other frames of reference (Inhelder & Piaget, 1964; Furth, 1983; Johnston & Johnston, 1984).

The second of these symbolic functionings is pretend, or symbolic play. Symbolic play, primarily an assimilative process, allows children to mentally enact experiences in which they attempt to fit the environment into their already existing structures. Play allows children to bring the outside world into agreement with internal meanings. The symbols used in symbolic play, in contrast to imitation, have internal referents (Voyat, 1983).

Symbolic play initially is the projection of children's personal wishes, impulses, and so on onto the environment. However, in thinking at the preoperational level, it is the object that does the wishing and has the impulses, not the self. Children use their own bodies as symbols for what they are pretending at any given moment. Both real and fantasized events are reproduced through dramatic play. As play becomes more integrated into cognition, children become better adjusted. When they have assimilated and organized sufficient stimuli to the point that they can pretend in an "as if" manner in the absence of an object, children have reached the crucial development of the preoperational stage (Anthony, 1956; Piaget, 1962).

In early preoperational thinking, symbolic play centers on role playing, which allows opportunities for exploring and widening the parameters of the environment. Children's egocentricity and inability to operate with rules mitigate against their playing in a truly cooperative way. When children have indeed reached these milestones, they are ready to truly cooperate in rule-governed play. Most four-year-olds are able to operate within a rule system and creative games. Kindergarten-age children are ready for the collective symbolism of group games.

Play is purposeful and not a random activity. It develops over the life span from very simple to the more formalized and abstract play of adults and can take many forms. It becomes both systematic and rule governed as well as parallel to cognition and language (Johnston & Johnston, 1984).

Another symbolic function, imagery, permits children to mentally put together a sequence of symbols that has a beginning, middle, and end, and which indicates cause/effect relationships. The anticipation and fantasy of imagery also serve the emotional needs of children. Imagery may be the first awareness of emergent and previously hidden ideas or feelings. It creates the symbolic formation of reality as well as the neutralization of conflict and feelings.

A symbol is constructed as an internal image that may be a tool of thinking and expressed behaviorally or verbally. Along with the strong communication function of imagery, children eventually become able to graphically depict their images through drawings (Anthony, 1956; Inhelder & Piaget, 1964; Selman, 1980; Gordon & Cowan, 1983; Westman, 1990).

An important factor in preoperational intelligence is language development. Deficiencies in language can hinder advancement to higher levels of reasoning. Social interaction is hindered in this stage if limited language abilities and egocentric thought processes prevail. Language must go beyond merely playing a supportive role in the workings of the other symbolic functions. Challenged by the conquest of the symbol, preoperational children must differentiate words from their referents and self-created play and dream symbols from reality. They must avoid concluding that words carry more information than they actually do (Voyat, 1983).

Language frees children to move from symbols with very private meanings to social communication. For social life to have permanence, it must have thought expressed in universal language symbols. If this is to happen, a child's thinking can no longer be represented predominantly in terms of personal symbols. They must gradually come to recognize the self as the agent of personal symbols as well as recognize that others have agency over their own representations.

Language during the preoperational stage evolves from a very private meaning system to one in which relationships among symbols and what they signify reaches the point of social speech. The social enforcement of universal language symbols plays a large part in the development of cognitive structures and will lead to analogous transformations in the affective domain (Voyat, 1983; Selman, 1980 in Sabornie & deBettencourt, 1997).

Children gradually become more adaptive to reality as social symbols replace private ones. Values and feelings from isolated situations are remembered over time and become increasingly permanent as constructed values. The ability to take a true social perspective provides children with the ability to distance themselves from objects in their environments. Personal knowledge can now be expressed in symbolic forms that convey meanings in shared language as well as shared actions (Anthony, 1956; Gordon & Cowan, 1983; Cicchetti et al., 1988; Wadsworth, 1997).

As the representational system then begins to form around the polarities of self and other, children move into a shared experience around a particular thought or feeling. Behavior patterns that have never before reached the representational level come to realization. Categorization can form around

(1) what is "me" and what is "not me"; (2) such emotions as dependency, pleasure, and aggression; (3) what is subjective and objective; and (4) what is fantasy and what is reality. Along with a representational self-other separation exists impulse control, mood stabilization, focused attention, and an ability to plan (Greenspan, 1997).

The acquisition of evocative memory allows the recall of absent situations by means of arbitrary signifiers. Feelings take on a stability and duration they have not yet had before and can now be conserved into interpersonal and moral convictions. The simplest form of these feelings resides in liking and disliking others.

Feelings can be reconstructed. What is conserved is not the feeling per se but the structure of interaction with other people.

> Feeling, properly speaking, appears, disappears, and oscillates in intensity not because it sinks into or emerges from the unconscious but because it is created, then dissipates, then is recreated. In other words, it is constructed or reconstructed on each occasion. (Piaget, 1981, pp. 50–51)

A strong correlation exists between symbolical functions and mental age. Although children with learning/behavior disorders often follow a developmental course of symbolic functioning similar to that of normal children, they tend to be more rigid and repetitive in their application of symbolic structures. They lack a subtlety and diversity of symbolism.

Intertwined structures about self and other render a child deficient and impoverished in symbolic play. This can lead to a distorted view of the objects in their environments. A child in such a situation will not have appropriate symbolic functions at his or her disposal for mastery of cognitive or emotional conflict (Kim et al., 1989; Gordon & Cowan, 1983).

EVALUATION OF PREOPERATIONAL PROCESSING

1. Does the child have any sense of separation of his or her symbols from his or herself?
2. Does the child have any recognition of others and their symbols? Does the child have any sense of separation from them?
3. Does the child see symbols as sharing a common psychological space?
4. How does the child select symbols from his or her repertoire?
5. How does he or she incorporate symbols received from others?
6. How does he or she use available symbols as means to achieve a goal?
7. How does he or she understand sequential mental arrangements between symbols located in his or her immediate psychological environment?

8. How does he or she understand sequential mental arrangements between symbols moving through familiar psychological space?
9. Does he or she cause a reoccurrence of various symbolic events and thus reveal his or her concept of the cause and sequence of these symbols and what they represent?
10. Can he or she differentiate between symbols and their referents?
11. Can he or she differentiate between self-created symbols and reality?

MAKING MEANING WITH CONCRETE OPERATIONAL INTELLIGENCE

The integration of symbolic functions provides the foundation for operational, inferential processing needed for the concrete operational period. What children construct from their mental activity will become logicomathematical knowledge, and what they learn from interactions with other people will become socioemotional knowledge (Johnston & Johnston, 1984).

In their most complex forms, cognitive changes are abstract operations such as expressive language or idea production, as well as the use and evaluation of the rules of problem solving. Advanced cognition is essential to understanding cause and effect relationships, reality consequences, right and wrong, values clarification, and social knowledge. It is also needed for academic achievement, personal enrichment, managing feelings and anxieties, effective social behavior, and creative interpersonal problem solving. True mental operations begin with concrete operational intelligence and continue throughout formal operational thinking. It is attained when children have the capacity to anticipate and reflect, that is, to internally (re)construct reality, which is dependent on referential as well as inferential thought processes. Cognitive progress is not only assimilation of information; it also entails a systematic decentration process that is a necessary condition of objectivity itself (Inhelder & Piaget, 1964).

The awareness of logical necessity and the implicative rational connections among notions is a landmark for the integration of cognitive operations. It defines concrete operational thought. This kind of awareness evolves along with progressively reversible thought (Piaget, 1954; Voyat, 1983; Montangero & Maurice-Naville, 1997).

At this point structures go beyond mere figural arrangements to conclude in compositions of relationships proper. They comprise a system of balancing interchanges and alterations that are constantly being compensated for. The conditions are discovered by observations and by mental experiments. They constitute the causes and laws that explain the mechanisms of intelligence. They demand logical necessity. Necessity is the ". . . satisfaction of arriving at a system which is both complete in itself and indefinitely extensible" (Piaget, 1981, p. 139).

Concrete operational thought allows meaning-making from transformations of knowledge with basic logical operations. Its quantitative capacity eventually leads to the ability to classify, seriate, reverse, and conserve part/whole relationships.

Operations indicate the sudden ability to coordinate elements in a whole pattern. With operational thinking children can disengage from focus on particular states of element and follow a succession of changes that coordinate opposites and different viewpoints within a system of objective mutuality. They enable children to realize adaptations that are both unlimited and mutually balanced. They extend the scope of action by internalizing it. The operatory functions characteristic of concrete operational thinking involves a progression, that is, a step-by-step balancing of positives and negatives. They allow children to (1) understand the relations of elements and events at the outset, (2) simultaneously take into account two dimensions of an element or event, (3) see many possible exchanges among elements, and (4) predict advantages and disadvantages of each exchange (Malerstein & Ahern, 1982; Piaget, 1981; Piaget & Garcia, 1991; Beilin & Pufall, 1992).

Operational reasoning means knowing in advance that a whole pattern (field) can be observed independently of its parts. Being able to coordinate part-whole relationships with basic logical thinking makes it possible for children to extract relevant information through a simultaneous account of a situation. They can distinguish between their own regulations and transformations and assumptions on the one hand, and empirical evidence on the other. Furthermore, they can easily compensate for any distortions caused by perceptual changes (Johnston & Johnston, 1984; Cicchetti et al., 1988; Grobecker, 1998).

Children at this level of intellectual functioning are no longer fooled in a problem that involves a conflict between logic and perception. They can now attend to all aspects of transformations and can see correspondences between various transformed states, that is, part/whole relationships (Inhelder & Piaget, 1964).

When children can use the underlying abilities of basic logic, they can conduct mental interactions between two dimensions. The construction of a framework of logical, part-whole transformations begins when children have acquired the ability to form simple conjunctive classes through the transformational functions. The underlying abilities of concrete operations are:

1. classification: ability to sort according to likes and differences;
2. seriation: ability to dissect wholes into component elements, to keep the elements in proper sequence according to specific criteria;

3. reversibility: ability to turn a whole situation around; to consider the whole arrangement of elements that could be represented by the one element;
4. decentration: ability to take into account and simultaneously coordinate several dimensions of a situation in order to extract the relevant information;
5. conservation: ability to realize that substantial changes may take place in a system without altering its fundamental characteristics (Johnston & Johnston, 1984; Cicchetti et al., 1988; Grobecker, 1998).

Classification

Classification is the systematic combining of elements according to shared properties. It is the fundamental act of the logic of classes. It is the systematic combining of elements according to shared properties. It involves combining elements by considering them in some way equivalent. Based on a primary, fundamental operation, namely, the combining of elements in classes and of classes with other classes, it leads to the recognition of groupings of similar elements as well as their mutual connections. Elements can be joined together into progressively more inclusive patterns (wholes). Class inclusion infers the understanding that the members of a subclass are members of a class but the reverse is not true.

The systematic arrangement of elements into classes and subclasses with the understanding of the relations among these sets of elements constitutes hierarchical classification. In multiplicative classification, the construction of elements are based on combining elements according to more than one variable (e.g., red and square; tall and thin, etc.) (Gruber & Voneche, 1977; Piaget, 1981; Piaget & Garcia, 1991).

Seriation

Thinking in terms of relationships is not possible unless and until the ability to seriate is present. Seriation is the primary reality. It is the systematically arranged collection of elements according to some dimension along which they differ. The concept involves keeping in mind an overall dimension of a group of elements while focusing on the relationship between the elements in the series. Seriation is the product of a set of asymmetrical transitive relations connected in a series, that is, the combination of elements is made according to an asymmetrical relationship. Although the units are at the same time equal to one another, the construction of the array takes place through the equating of differences. The differences are defined by order (Gallagher & Reid, 1981; Piaget, 1981; Malerstein & Ahern, 1982).

Reversibility

The task of intellectual development throughout the life span depends on the ability to imagine the possibilities of an opposite for any idea. To do this, children must undo the property, event, or action, or must invent another idea that cancels the original idea. Logic depends on the ability to form and discriminate a possible whole pattern, imagine its being undone, and invent another way to cancel it. All of this while being aware that the two undoings are also bound together in a system of mutual implication (Beilin & Pufall, 1992).

Reversibility is ". . . the most clearly defined characteristic of intelligence. . ." (Piaget 1981, p. 41). It characterizes the final states of assimilation and accommodation balance as well as the very processes of development. It enables children to construct hypotheses, discard them, and return to a starting point (Beilin & Pufall, 1992).

Reversibility is the recognition that an original part/whole relationship can be readily reconstructed. Being able to anticipate what will happen to an element under various conditions enables the appreciation that an element can at once have different roles.

Reversible operations establish a foundation for harmony between assimilation and accommodation. This balance is indicated because children can distinguish clearly between what they think and what they perceive as well as between personal assumptions on the one hand and empirical evidence on the other. Children can at this point cooperate in society with greater cognitive and moral insight.

It is the process that makes it possible to pass from element to element, and element to whole without destroying either. This is so because the elements are always exactly compensated by inverse operations. An inverse operation initiates a change in an opposite direction. The knowledge of a relation establishes the possibility of an inverse and eventually to a coordination of various points of view (Inhelder & Piaget, 1964; Piaget, 1971; Cicchetti et al., 1988; Grobecker, 1998).

With reversibility, children are able to go back and forth along the path of their thinking and are able to construct the inverse of a property of a relation or find the reciprocal of a relation. They can simultaneously transform an element in various ways; keep its identity; bring it back to its original state; and create counter positions.

Decentration

An emerging capacity to reflect upon one's own behaviors distinguishes concrete operational thought. The self as actor can engage in the observation process itself. This allows for the decentering of the self from others. Children develop self-cognitions that allow a self-view in terms of concrete terms such as appearance, possessions, and preferred activities. In interactions with others, concrete operational thought enables children to assimilate different viewpoints, achieving a set of mutually agreed-upon rules. They are capable of attending to their own communication and that of others in order to negotiate. Children come to recognize the self as the agent of their part-whole transformations and can acknowledge others as agents with their own transformational structures. Closure of logical, part-whole transformations is ultimately attained (London, 1990; Sabornie & deBettencourt, 1997; Cicchetti & Toth, 1998).

A sense of others' perspectives pervades this quality of thinking. The underlying key to this behavior lies in the ability to appreciate that others can observe and describe themselves. Children consolidate various reflected perspectives into a generalized other. They can, at this point, cooperate in society with greater insight cognitively and morally (Selman, 1980).

Successive decentrations make it possible for children to take the points of view of others. Compensations for distortions caused by perceptual changes can be made. Children are able to relate physical and psychological meanings and to shift from a self-oriented to an other-oriented point of view (London, 1990; Wigg, 1993; Sabornie & deBettencourt, 1997).

Mutual-respect relationships, characterized by reciprocity of thought, gradually emerge at this time. These relationships are chosen with free will and shared values. Along with the ability to take the other's viewpoint, there is now personal commitment and obligation to the relationship. A system of conserved values forms in a similar way to logical reasoning, implying a logic of feeling (Wadsworth, 1997).

A sense of autonomous feelings in children is seen as a necessary prerequisite to the formation of mutual-respect relations with others. Mutual-respect relations are typically established after the emergence of autonomy. However, serious limitation exists since children at this stage can take the perspectives only of persons with whom they are actually interacting (Wadsworth, 1997, p. 10).

As young children develop, they center less and less on the actions of self and more on the actions of others in the course of social interactions. Decentration may be evidenced by increased abilities to understand verbal and nonverbal cues emitted by the other person, greater sensitivity to the needs of the other for clarifying statements during conversations, and increased responsiveness to ambiguity in messages from others. Decentration refers to the progression from egocentric thought to sociocentric thought. With this progression children become able to consider perspectives other than their own.

Thus, developing children come to consider the thoughts, feelings, motives, and needs of others (Pullis & Smith, 1981).

> . . . objectivity presupposes a decentering—i.e., a continual focusing of perspective. This ability to decenter—or adopt the point of view of another—may be extremely important for effective interpersonal functioning, in that it allows for optimal engagement in close relationships. It is almost certainly a prerequisite for true empathy. Decentration is not only a requirement for mutuality but also for maintaining a clear perspective of one's own as opposed to other's view of the world (that is, self-other differentiation). (Inhelder & Piaget, 1958, p. 345)

Conservation

The tendency to expand into reconstructed, higher level structures needs conservation as its base. Conservation leads to closure of a logical system within which mental operations can move in any direction and return to the starting point. It can be considered self-direction because it involves maintaining the self in balance with the environment (Furth, 1987).

Only when children are capable of objectifying their activities and symbols can they become aware of both the activity and symbols and of self as agent of them. Conservation is the capacity to grasp that despite certain changes in an object, there are particular properties that remain unchanged. Quantities do not change when their arrangements change. The power of conservation leads children to the realization that substantial changes may take place in a system without altering its fundamental characteristics. Conservation fosters a deeper sense of autonomy as well as peer cooperation. It is based on the capacity for fantasy (Inhelder & Piaget, 1964; Piaget, 1981).

With conservation firmly in place, children have reached a point where they can establish a set of attitudes that blend into a sense of self that is independent of what is occurring at any given point. This stable self abides over time and space. It is defined by the reality of the social situation and the inner stable independence. Children can be consciously aware of two realities and still feel a sense of stability (Greenspan, 1997).

Concrete operations ensure a harmony between assimilation and accommodation. Both assimilatory and accommodatory functions can now act on transformations as well as on states. This progressive self-regulation can be expressed in terms of centration and decentration. It is now possible for children to not only be aware of but to take into consideration the various logical methods of part/whole analysis. One remaining problem is that children have difficulty applying these logical abilities in nonconcrete situations (Inhelder & Piaget, 1964; Piaget, 1971).

With concrete operational meaning-making, children acquire the ability to conserve, decenter, reverse, and transform; they can conduct mental interactions between part-whole relationships. Conservation emerges from preoperational intelligence and continues throughout formal operational intelligence (Johnston & Johnston, 1984).

EVALUATION OF CONCRETE-OPERATIONAL PROCESSING

1. Does the child have any sense of separation of his or her transformations of part/whole relationship from him or herself?
2. Does the child have any recognition of others and their transformations of part/whole relationships? Does the child have any sense of separation from them?
3. Does the child have any sense of the transformations sharing a common psychological space?
4. How does the child select transformations from his or her repertoire?
5. How does he or she incorporate transformations received from others?
6. How does he or she use available transformations as means to achieve a goal?
7. How does he or she understand simultaneous arrangements between transformations located in his or her immediate psychological environment?
8. How does he or she understand simultaneous arrangements between transformations moving through a familiar psychological space?
9. Does he or she cause a reoccurrence of various simultaneous transformations and thus reveal his or her concept of the cause and interaction of these transformations?
10. Can he or she combine and recombine parts without distorting the parts or the whole?
11. Does he or she have a value hierarchy by which he or she can evaluate how his or her own activities play a role in situations?
12. Can he or she stay on topic, remain in a defined set, and clearly distinguish between what is "inside" and what is "outside" the system?
13. Can he or she take mental detours or alternative routes to the same goal?
14. In a two-person situation, can he or she think from the other's point of view?

MAKING MEANING WITH FORMAL-OPERATIONAL INTELLIGENCE

The stage-salient task of formal operational thinking, which usually occurs during adolescence, is the conquest of abstract thought. With higher level logic and the entire range of formal thinking, the adolescent can systematically generate all possible combinations of elements in a pattern or events in a situation. Meaning-making comes about through propositional logic, deductive thinking, and hypothetical reasoning. With mental action focused on transforming transformations, formal thought is possible. This assures that arguments get carried to logical conclusions on an abstract level, and that second order operations are mastered. Detailed memory and sophisticated cognitive routines are further indices of formal operational thinking (Sabornie & deBettencourt, 1997).

Logical regulations, the major landmark of formal thought, bring adolescents to the level of hypothetical thought that provides them with the criteria that can lead to rational objectivity. It enables them to generate alternative situations and courses of action, evaluate consequences of these alternatives, engage in perspective taking, and reason about probability and chance. The truth of a given solution can logically be discovered depending on the truth of the problem itself. Reasoning results in the ability to anticipate, predict, and evaluate how various combinations of actions might differentially affect personal life events.

With the capability of applying logical thought to all classes of problems—verbal, hypothetical, future, and emotional—adolescents are convinced simply by the power of the word. They are now able to discuss the perspectives of others in terms of scientific laws (Inhelder & Piaget, 1964).

> The first exploratory area considers four acquisitions of the formal operational period and their implications for psychological adaptation, dysfunction, and intervention. These may be categorized as the ability to: (1) use the combinatorial system, which allows the adolescent to generate alternative situations and courses of action, (2) evaluate consequences of these alternatives via propositional logic, (3) engage in perspective taking, and (4) reason about probability and chance. (Gordon, 1988, p. 55)

Formal operational thought allows for the classifying of all possible categories and leads to the ability to form an operation on other operations. This means true "reflection" in a cognitive sense since the adolescent can deal with whole patterns: the inversions, reciprocities, identities, and correlations. This reflective thinking leads to a fully mobile logic system and value system.

With more deliberation and more reflection, adolescents are more able to see more possible solutions to real or imagined problems. A capacity to compose hypothetical propositions exists. Adolescents can now cognitively handle a full range of possible variables with all the potential relations among them (Sabornie & deBettencourt, 1997; Cicchetti & Toth, 1998; Moshman, 1998).

Broader affective and conceptual perspectives can be taken and strategies can be adapted by attenuating negative content, amplifying positive aspects, stating reasons and justifications, and anticipating counterarguments. Reason about contrary-to-fact propositions is possible. Metaphor is now understood (Wigg, 1993; Greenspan, 1997).

On acquiring formal operational thought, adolescents are capable of composing hypothetical propositions whereby they can come up with a full range of possible variables and the potential relations among them. Adolescents who envision knowledge as a subjective construction show constructed identities. Those who view knowledge as simple and absolute show either foreclosed identities or lack of concern with identity formation (Moshman, 1998).

Formal operational thinkers can think about their own thoughts, consider alternative ways of interacting with people, construct ideals, and reason realistically about the future. The range of possibilities and interactions that might exist in their surroundings are available to the formal operational thinker (Cicchetti et al., 1988; Gordon, 1988; Sabornie & deBettencourt, 1997; Grobecker, 1998).

Going beyond the ability to generate alternatives, the formal thinker can evaluate these alternatives through the use of propositional logic, deductive thinking, and hypothetical reasoning.

> Formulating hypotheses about interpersonal interactions, systematically varying behavior, and logically evaluating the effect of actions can help adolescents make the first step toward developing theories about how past actions (of self and others) have influenced life events and how future actions might alter them. (Gordon, 1988, p. 58)

This kind of reasoning makes contact with people and objects available with all their affects and consequences. Knowing how current and past actions of self and others influence life situations, and anticipating how future actions may change these situations, can lead to the formulation of hypotheses about interpersonal interactions. Behavior can be systematically varied and the effect of actions can be logically evaluated. The world is more predictable and manageable and more appropriately planned actions are possible in an array of interpersonal situations (Gordon, 1988).

In addition, the growth of cognition to the formal operational thought allows adolescents to develop an interest in more elaborate, cooperative interactions. This level represents total involvement with peers. Outcomes of interactions are more important at this level, indicating an ability to function within a broad social structure. Not only must adolescents learn to cope with success or failure on a personal level, but they must also learn to cope with the constant interpersonal contact such interactions require (Harter, 1983).

Adolescents who have achieved formal operational thinking see themselves as being beyond a peer group and as part of a larger sociocultural reality. They can consolidate a wider array of past experiences and are far more synthetic and integrating in their social, historical, future-oriented, role-defined, and sexual realities. Social exchanges with others can now be viewed from the viewpoint of an impartial outsider. Personal social interactions and those of others are viewed in an abstract, objective, unbiased way. What is possible from the attainment of formal thought and beyond is a societal perspective-taking level during which youths can remove self from a personal interaction and take on the perspective of the larger society. Broader affective and conceptual perspectives can be taken. A strategy can be adapted by attenuating negative content, amplifying positive aspects, stating reasons and justifications, and anticipating counterarguments (Selman, 1980; London, 1990; Sabornie & deBettencourt, 1997).

Formal operational children gradually come to recognize the self as the agent of their own ideational system. Others are recognized as agents of their own ideational systems (Piaget, 1962, 1964, 1971).

These thinkers actively self-regulate their behavior by being able to construct possible scenarios, which in turn influence and motivate their behavior. Problems are solved and probable outcomes are estimated symbolically. This saves time from enacting all problems and learning by trial and error. The ability to estimate the probability of event happenings may render the world more predictable and manageable. It also allows for the planning of appropriate action in a variety of interpersonal situations. This is relevant for making adaptive life decisions, for experiencing true mutuality and empathy, for understanding feelings and interpersonal situations, and for adaptively altering affective and behavioral reactions through realistic appraisal of life events (Gordon, 1988).

Formal operational thought allows for greater appreciation of the unconscious self. They can now recognize that they have hidden thoughts, emotions, and motivations that can be reflected upon but that cannot be easily analyzed through introspection. Continuing this development, they can view self in more abstract psychological terms that include personal characteristics that are enduring over time.

For the development of a sense of identity, formal operational thinkers can make several defining selections of personal, career, sexual, and ideological charges. This derives from considering many potential selves as well as the consequences of commitment to particular ones.

Feelings are not simply retrieved from the past but are reconstructed to fit individual current interpersonal structures. Past events are reconstructed through a complex assimilative inferential process. As the underlying cognitive structures change, feelings evoked in past situations may be altered by new and different ways of understanding. Current situations are assimilated into situations experienced in the past, and past situations are assimilated into those currently being experienced. With the consistent ability to apply operations to operations and transformations to transformations, formal operational thinkers bind all experience together. Self becomes a complex composite of thoughts and feelings in a body (Sabornie & deBettencourt, 1997; Cicchetti & Toth, 1998; Moshman, 1998).

> Feeling, properly speaking, appears, disappears, and oscillates in intensity not because it sinks into or emerges from the unconscious but because it is created, then dissipates, then is recreated. In other words, it is constructed or reconstructed on each occasion. (Piaget, 1981, pp. 50–51)

According to Piaget (1950), disruptions in self-regulation occur when a state of tension or disturbance is experienced when the element of the field no longer fits the "reality" that had previously been constructed. This state of being provides a strong motivation for learning or change. Equilibration is reestablished when even a few elements, previously in disequilibration, strike a balance. The emergence of reversible operations ensures a harmony between assimilation and accommodation since both can now act on transformations as well as on states. Logical justification for conflicts can now be given. Formal operational thought signifies the optimum balance between assimilation and accommodation (Cicchetti et al., 1988; Gordon, 1988; Sabornie & deBettencourt, 1997; Grobecker, 1998).

EVALUATION OF FORMAL OPERATIONAL PROCESSING

1. Does the adolescent have any sense of separation of his or her thoughts from him/herself?
2. Does the adolescent have any recognition of others and their thoughts? Does the adolescent have any sense of separation from them?
3. Does the adolescent see thoughts as sharing a common psychological space?
4. How does the adolescent select thoughts from his or her repertoire?
5. How does he or she incorporate thoughts received from others?
6. How does he or she use available thoughts as means to achieve a goal?
7. How does he or she understand mental arrangements between thoughts located in his or her immediate psychology environment (thought system)?
8. How does he or she understand mental arrangements among thoughts moving through a familiar psychological space (comparison of thought systems)?
9. Does he or she cause a reoccurrence of various thought systems and thus reveal his or her concept of the cause and relationship of these thought systems?
10. Can he or she arrange elements in such a way as to systematically test all possible combinations?
11. Can he or she coordinate two thought systems rather than two variables?
12. In a two-person situation, can he or she distinguish each party's point of view from that of a third person, i.e., be an impartial spectator?
13. Can he or she think about his or her own thoughts?
14. Can he or she see him or herself in an infinite variety of possibilities?
15. Can he or she see him or herself as a balanced system?

Stage Salient Functioning

Stage	Conservation	Expansion
Sensorimotor stage	Logic of action	Object permanence
Preoperational stage	Symbolic formation	Social language
Concrete-operational stage	Logical consistency	Takes in viewpoints of others
Formal-operational stage	Prepositional thought	Takes in and compares value systems of other people (Furth, 1987)

Stage	Activity	Task to Accomplish
Sensorimotor	Logic of action	Object permanence (self/other awareness)
Preoperations	Symbolic formation	Social language (referential thinking)
Concrete operations	Logical consistency	Viewpoints of others (decentration)
Formal operations	Propositional thinking	Incorporation of other peoples thinking (comparison of hypotheses) (Furth, 1987)

Chapter 4

SELF-REGULATION

What is needed for adaptive behavior is the building
of some kind of self-referential, self-regulating,
self-knowing set of structures.
(Bronfenbrenner, Kessel, Kessen, & White, 1986, p. 1220).

Specifically and clearly, Piaget's genetic epistemology serves as a primary description of cognitive processes as conscious self-reflection. It addresses the issues of the nature of changes in consciousness as a function of age and experience. However, it rejects the concepts that consciousness is passively received or additively associated. Self-awareness of one's thinking processes is essential to normal cognitive development. As consciousness transcends repeatedly through a progression of hierarchical stage developments, a more widening perspective of self, other, and world is created with every advance. How children acquire knowledge and experience emotion at any particular stage is shaped by the form of the self-other relation at that stage. Any advance in the form of self-other relationships will shape how children make meaning of their experiences (Piaget 1970, 1976; Kegan, 1980, 1982; Chrzanowski, 1982; Rosen, 1985; Jarman, Vavrik, & Walton, 1995).

Existing boundaries between children and their overall environments are always in a state of elaborate interpretation or ecological balance. The development of the self is inseparable from the development of the construction of the environment. Children, rather than fixed entities, are an integral part of the environment, constantly struggling with the existential dilemma of retaining personal integrity and needing to change. Personal realities are generated or constructed with the self as the central referent and director of that reality. The physical world is interactive with human thought and affect. Matter and mind are seen as coexisting within the wholeness of an acting self. Contact, awareness, and dialogue are three underlying processes describing the basic way in which children engage in and disengage from the environment (Frew, 1986; Rhodes, 1988; Zinker, 1991).

The process of organismic self-regulation, as reflected in contacting and awareness, is itself involved in a developmental process: the development of one's uniquely human becoming. It is not enough to say that contact and awareness serve our biological and emotional needs. There appears to be a kind of onto-logical imperative, an urge toward growth, so that these processes operate at in-creasingly finer levels of complexity and abstraction from biology. Contact and awareness are not merely the processes that express the dynamic relation be-tween stasis and growth; they are themselves spiraling developmental processes, always emerging and transcending. The epitome of their development is lived through in the dialogic relation. (Jacobs, 1989, p. 63)

Piagetian epistemology provides a model for analyzing naturally occurring change. It explains not only how structures are acquired but also the functions, or dynamic mechanisms, behind their acquisition. Additionally, the descrip-tions of the dynamics of cognitive and affective acquisition provided by this model lead to understanding the link between cognitive dysfunction and adaptive difficulties (Gordon, 1988).

Piaget's explanation of cognitive and affective development is best pre-sented in constructivistic terms. It deals with the sequence of stages by a pro-cess of equilibration or self-regulation. The developmental stages define equi-librium as a continuous process of cognitive structurations. The structurations are formed in an orderly way so that when each new construction attains a state of relative equilibrium, it opens up new possibilities. Each step in the process is necessary for a subsequent one (Gallagher & Reid, 1981).

Piaget elaborated and detailed not only the self-organizational structures but also the self-regulatory mechanisms of human behavior. Indeed, he believes that only a hypothesis of progressive self-regulation can account for a theory of development. When read from a developmental perspective, there is a clear parallel between cognitive organization and self-regulation (Gallagher & Reid, 1981).

Self-regulation is a process of self-correction and a means to the reorgani-zation of behavior. It leads to a better understanding of the roles children play in their own development. It also results in a growth to responsibility. The extent that children are answerable for their behaviors is correlated with their degree of mobility, meaningful speech, personal relationships, and choices (Sigel, 1969; Piaget, 1971; Cocking, 1981; Morgan, 1986).

Children function according to the principle of homeostasis, that is, they pro-ceed through phases of self-monitoring, self-evaluation, and self-reinforcement. Homeostasis refers to the ways in which children maintain their equilibrium and thereby their health. The homeostatic process goes on all the time even while its equilibrium is being constantly challenged and constantly interrupted by its many needs.

Whether it is biological or cognitive, self-regulation consists of an open sys-tem with interdependent parts. A hierarchical integration of structures exists within higher order totalities. Each element within any given structure is able to interact with the external world. The cohesiveness of the totality and the differentiation of the figures within the structures are in an ever-changing balance (Smock, 1981).

There is every indication that from the moment of birth, if not before, all children have a need to become actively engaged with changing stimuli. As action, perception, cognition, and emotion are combined and recombined, there is structuring and transforming of self, objects, and events. How children process all of this, as well as how they perceive life generally and in specific situations, is crucial for understanding their behaviors relative to their cognitive and adaptive abilities (Cowan, 1978).

Adapting the self to the environment as well as adjusting the environment to meet the needs of the self, involve the whole organism. Consequently, a sense of union depends paradoxically on a heightened sense of separateness. It is this precise paradox that children constantly seek to resolve. Self-regulation synthesizes the need for union and for separateness. It is the lifeblood of growth and the very means for changing oneself and one's experience of the world. Self-regulatory functions involve the whole body with all its muscular activity, senses, feelings, spontaneity, and energy without constraint or suppression. These functions allow ideas, memories, images, and emotions to be experienced fully and sharply (Cowan, 1978).

In broad terms, self-regulation refers to the ongoing process of constructing a logical concept of elaborate, interrelated aspects of the physical and social worlds. As they construct more sophisticated self-other interactions, children are faced with the task of relating what they observe to what they have previously inferred. The innate, internal self-regulatory process governs the coordination of the relation between self and other, as well as between observation and inference (Hoemann, 1991).

Self-regulation, with its focus on self-direction and agency, is the norm. It remains the primary mode of development unless it is derailed. In school settings, such derailment is often caused by repeated experiences of failure causing children to subsume their own internal inclinations toward self-regulation to those external to them.

In addition, self-regulation looks at the way children engage in meaning-making in the context of personal experiences as well as at how they resolve the stage-salient developmental hurdles. The reorganization and incorporation of particular issues into biological, cognitive, affective, and social systems is a major concern of self-regulation (Cocking, 1981; Piaget, 1970b, 1985).

The construction of a coherent concept of complex, interrelated aspects of the physical or social world is ongoing. An innate, internal, regulatory process governs the coordination of the relation between a knowing child and the objects known to him or her. This dynamic process maintains a relative balance between environmental demands and a child's capacity to understand them.

> [It signifies] . . . the coordination that takes place when an individual assimilates some aspect of the environment and at the same time accommodates to its specific features. (Hoemann. 1991, p. 236)

This constant, adaptive process through which solutions to problems are found involves sequential states of equilibrium or closure. These equilibrated, closed states are defined in terms of compensations. Children are never just independent of their environments, nor are they ruled by physical laws of automatic self-regulation. They adjust to, and adjust, situations by deliberately acting to compensate for external disturbances. Children actively construct and generate their own structures that are always passing from a simpler to a more complex form in a never-ending process. This constant reconstruction organizes and integrates present awareness so as to facilitate its use in new situations and to bring into awareness what is unaware. A central aspect of cognitive development is the increasing capacity for anticipating events and mentally acting on them in advance of any physical action. The relationship between a knowing child and the objects known to him or her includes the mental acts of remembering, imagining, thinking, or any other meaningful internal self-object contact.

Children must construct more sophisticated concepts of self-object interactions and more advanced forms of behavior by relating any new awareness to what they have previously inferred. Through self-regulation, a lower state of balance evolves to both a higher state of balance and to a reorganization of behavior. There are two important aspects to this evolution: a conservative, self-maintenance and a self-directing closure. The former refers to children's participation in activities at their own individual levels of constructive ability. The latter refers to a sense of completeness that is brought to a relationship without changing its meaning. A tendency toward an entropic increase in closure within a given system coexists with an expansive tendency to open to possibilities. These tendencies are responsible for the generativity of intelligence. The two functions working together motivate children to maintain and develop self. The conservation drive aims at keeping children in balance with their environments. Coupled with logical structure, closure implies self-direction. These closed logical structures, in turn, allow mental operations to move in any direction, including a return to the starting point. Overall, this balancing function is a necessary base for the expansion drive, which aims at the formation of new structures at a still higher level of conservation. The two drives represent a developmental sequence that is valid for all areas and at all stages of development (Piaget, 1970a, 1985; Cocking, 1981; Furth, 1987; Chapman, 1992).

SELF-REGULATION AND LEARNING

Piaget's theory provides a vehicle for investigating the origins, structures, methods, and validity of knowledge. It focuses on the structures that guide the organization of behavior, that is, the ways in which children organize their perceptual experiences through acts of differentiation, selection, and construction; as well as the distinct aspects that exist in the monitoring process: evaluation, planning, and regulation. It also calls for the schematic and precise identification and examination of self-other relationships. Endorsing a dialectical position on knowledge acquisition, the model gives a balanced account of a child's role in the meaning-making process with an account of social construction (Paris & Myers, 1981; Wright, 1984; Chapman, 1992).

From birth, all children self-regulate their learning and development with varying degrees of appropriateness and success. There is a constant interaction among internal structures (the developmental ability to acquire knowledge), the content to be learned (the external environment), and the functions (the process of acquiring knowledge) (Schmid-Kitsikis, 1973).

Self-regulation seeks an increased number of possible choices, a growth in coherence, a coordinated system in which all parts of the biological, cognitive, and affective subsystems are interdependent. There are two general concepts influencing the self-regulatory approach to learning. First, children are inherently motivated to comprehend their surrounding environments and to give meaning to them in order to extend knowledge. Lack of this meaning-making results in a conflict with existing states of knowledge and provokes a search for new explanations. If these conflicts are addressed, then children can move to resolve them. True compensation of a conflict must result in reconstruction. Second, children's experiences in social situations are gradually internalized and effect the restructuring of cognitive development (Piaget, 1968; Schmid-Kitsikis, 1973; Swanson, 1987; Jacobs, 1992).

The adaptation in the person-environment interaction is a polar one that begins with an awareness of various combinations of sensory-motor perceptions. Perceptual/motor excitation serves as a figure that begins to integrate a relationship between a child and the environment. The excitations are sharply differentiated functional structures and are the motivating energy that allows a child to experience the environment as his or her own.

In addressing the self-regulatory behaviors of children, awareness and the construction of emerging functions are seen as the vehicles for changing self-experience. Knowledge is the flowing together of the motoric, affective, and cognitive elements in a learning situation. The development of body awareness, accurate sensory decoding and encoding, positive self-conceptualization, healthy interpersonal communication, rational thinking with adaptive decision making, and positive values clarification are the areas of focus (Brown, 1971, 1975; Kelly, 1972).

Studying self-regulations allows the evaluation of the degree of stability of the responses children make in any given situation. This study makes available an understanding of the ways in which children in a controlled situation discover new information, and how they attain new constructions. Focus is on the ideas that children use, the role of contradictions in their self-regulations, and the coherence of their gradual constructions (Schmid-Kitsikis, 1973).

> [Self-regulation] theory proposes that learning is subservient to development, i.e., what is learned depends on what the learner can take from the given by means of the cognitive structures available to him. What motivates learning are the questions or felt lacunas arising from attempts to apply a scheme to a "given" situation. (Smock, 1981, p. 59)

ASSIMILATION AND ACCOMMODATION

Children experience disequilibrium when their current models of organizing experience are tried and found insufficient to explain inconsistencies and contradictions in knowing or understanding objects, people, or events. In such states, children strive to resolve their conflicts, and to reach a state of self-regulation as well as reorganize their cognitive structures. Self-regulation then represents the coordination of assimilation and accommodation into progressively more encompassing levels of equilibrium. The resulting temporary dynamic rebalance exists simultaneously within each child and between that child and the environment (Pullis & Smith, 1981).

Each child is a unique self-regulatory system of needs that are always manifestations of disequilibrium. Nothing is constructed unless there is a felt need. All movement, all thought, or all emotion respond to a need. There is a need when something, either outside or within, changes. Behavior has to be adjusted as a function of this change (Piaget, 1968).

The functions of assimilation and accommodation are responsible for creating and using cognitive and affective structures. These functions are invariant and present at every stage of development. A relative balance between them is necessary for any and all developmental progress. Assimilation is defined as the method by which children interpret the environment through existing internal psychological structures; accommodation is contrasted as the method by which children modify these existing psychological structures because of environmental interference. Because cognition is thought of as an extension of biological adaptation, both nature and nurture leave their respective stamps on behaviors. Nature, the assimilative processes, directs mental capacities responsive to inner promptings. It prevents cognition from being a passive copy of reality. In contrast, nurture, the accommodative processes, directs the content of thought responsive to environmental encroachments. It prevents cognition from constructing a reality that does not correspond to the external environment. Reason is thinking characterized as a balance between assimilation and accommodation and is consequently autonomous of both inner and outer forces (Elkind, 1970; Gordon, 1988).

The self-regulatory processes explain human behavior with assimilation serving as a conservative process seeking to preserve, restore, and maintain life; and accommodation seeking growth and expansion (Schmid-Kitsikis, 1973).

Growth demands participation in both the assimilative, metaphorical process as well as the accommodative, inventive process. Conceptually it is possible for assimilation to become instances of accommodation, which in turn become departure points for further assimilation. Conservation lies behind every assimilation; indefinite openness of choice, behind every accommodation (Furth, 1987).

Assimilation, the constructing agent of the mind, is completely child-centered and includes those aspect of the environment that fulfill his/her needs. This need-fulfillment moves toward greater self-regulation. Need occurrences always indicate a disruption in self-regulation. Furthermore, it signifies that an adjustment has to be made either internally or externally. By assimilating new knowledge, as well as objects and people into the self boundaries; children increase their personal spaces, develop their cognitive faculties, and integrate their personalities. This remains so as long as opportunities to master self-regulation present themselves and as long as there are no insurmountable dangers (Anthony, 1956; Piaget, 1968).

At first, through inherent motivation and self-directed change, children attempt to extend self-knowledge and to understand the world. When meaning fails to occur, confusion results and new meanings are sought. Following this, restructuring of cognitive, affective, and psychomotor behaviors are affected through the gradual internalization of social interactions. Development progresses from a state of balance to a sense of contradiction; followed next by a search for closure, and finally to an adjustment to a different, higher state of equilibrium. Children respond to intrusion of balance by attempting to compensate for any sense of contradiction. This is compatible with the concept of an open system. Balance is best described as ". . . a stable state in an open system" (Piaget, 1968, p. 101).

Equilibrium can be both mobile and stable. An operational system is a system of actions, a series of essentially mobile operations which can remain stable in the sense that, once constituted, the structure which determines them will not become modified. (Piaget, 1968, p. 150)

When children are at rest, a state of conservation exists. Challenged by a disturbing factor, which may be internal or external, causes an expansion of personal reality and figure/background awareness. Answers to situations are sought to compensate for any disturbances. This decreases tension and leads to a reconstruction of cognitive structures and a return of organism balance, that is, conservation (Furth, 1987).

Assimilation predominates in the earliest stages of life. As children grow, the accommodation factor increases, until a stable rational balance is reached, normally, around age twelve. Assimilation and accommodation find different balance points within children's cognitive behaviors, varying with the levels of development and the problems to be solved (Anthony, 1956).

Coordination takes place when an assimilation of some aspect of the environment simultaneously occurs with an accommodation to that environment's specific features. Children arrive at knowledge when they recognize what something is, what something does, and what procedures need to be used to appropriately solve a problem. Learning implies a relation between knowing children and the objects that are known. This knowing relation also includes meaningful contact through such mental acts of remembering, imagining, and thinking; between specific environmental features and the children who know them. The structures or operations involved in this process are active. They can be modified as a result of new relations that make possible a new equilibrium between the content that children perceive and what they conceptualize about this content (Hoemann, 1991).

Errors do not arise when children inaccurately perceive empirical phenomena, but rather when they lack a suitable framework to incorporate or organize the perceived information. This lack of structure is a reflection of an incomplete evolution to adult thought and provides convincing evidence that children really do construct their own views of the world. In studying development, both specific stage attainment and the dynamic process of self-regulation with its temporary states and types of assimilation-accommodation balances must be taken into consideration (Schmid-Kitsikis, 1973; Cowan, 1978; Ditishein, 1974–75; Noam et al., 1984).

ADAPTATION

Adaptation occurs when children purposely modify their self-owned cognitions, affects, or actions in order to achieve a goodness of fit among individual needs, interests, and motives, on the one hand, and the demands of the environment on the other. Selecting a new behavior involves the rejection of a present environment and selecting a more consonant alternative, future environment. Children must be aware of problems with the present environment, identify a new environment without such problems, and be capable of effecting the selection (Piaget, 1971).

Cognitive and emotional adaptation demand not only assimilation of information but a systematic decentration process that is a necessary condition of objectivity itself. Three pertinent criteria for adaptation are: (1) bodily health, known by a definite standard; (2) the progress of children toward helping themselves; and (3) the elasticity of the self-environment formation.

There is a connection between self-regulation and development of the self. The levels of ego development have particular structural features as well as themes. Basic security is the initial process of self-regulation. It gives children a sense of confidence in the ability to remain calm, regulated, and interested in the environment. Lacking this, children may experience a sense of being overwhelmed or fragmented. The result may be rigidity and overmanipulation of selected experiences. Building and sustaining of close relationships cultivates a feeling of security with others and a sense of positive support. Lacking these, children may come to feel isolated and empty. They may come to doubt whether or not they have any impact on others. Interactions may seem chaotic, fragmented, or unpredictable. Preoccupation with inanimate objects and avoidance of intimate social contact become common behavior patterns. Children so involved may overreact to temporary losses and disappointment and feel a sense of undifferentiation. They often have a need for unconditional acceptance (Greenspan, 1997).

Self-regulation processing leads to the ability to define boundaries. Intentional motoric, cognitive, and affective communication help to construct more defined psychological states and contribute to the most fundamental sense of reality and mastery. A lack of clearly defined boundaries interferes with the ability to set self limits. Common problems that can arise are polarization of feeling states, self-absorption, and preoccupation with fragmented partial objects (Greenspan, 1997).

Self-regulation processes come together to help children form organized behavior patterns. These are used to negotiate needs dealing with such themes as dependency, assertiveness, curiosity, pleasure, and anger. Organized patterns lead to the creation of an elaborate, imaginative capacity and a rich, internal symbolic life. The imagination can embrace important themes that arise. Difficulties are evidenced in fears of separation and undue worry over danger. Children may hold back ideas and reflections and depend too much on action patterns.

Increased capacity to create and use symbols and words helps to expand the self. Thoughts become more flexible and logical. Exploration of past, present, and future is more imaginative. Awareness of what is already known is at deeper levels of the mind. Children can deal with basic issues as personal security, the depth, scope, and stability of relationships, and the formation of motivation and affect. They come to a sense of who they are, what they want, and how others will treat them (Greenspan, 1997).

The Organizational and Self-Regulating Aspects of Adaptation

All Children have an inveterate need to make meaning of themselves and their world. Self-organization and self-regulation abide in their very nature. The ability that they have to organize, structure, and restructure their experiences is the fundamental concern of the constructivist process. Normal development that encompasses organization and self-regulation is evidenced by (1) the presence of stage-appropriate structures, (2) proper balance of figural/operative functions, and (3) proper balance of self-regulatory functions.

The self-regulated learning process is defined in terms of any learner's ability to organize, structure, and restructure experience in accordance with existing cognitive structures. The structures, in turn, are modified and enriched in the course of interaction with the physical and social environments. As the organizational properties that underlie thought and behavior, structures provide the systemized frameworks that make experiences meaningful. Additionally, functions are the processes that account for development, refinement, and transformation of cognitive structures (Cocking, 1981; Smock, 1981).

Organization, balance of figural-operational function, and balance of assimilation and accommodation are critical to knowing. To understand the growth process, it is crucial to know how children receive and organize information as well as how these functions influence and determine further knowledge acquisition. Self-regulation emphasizes activity. Basically, cognitive structures develop through the personal discoveries children make about the interpersonal world. Such active discovery, with respect to assimilation and accommodation, promotes changes in how children think. It is generally thought that at all developmental stages, enhancing reasoning powers necessitates stimulating and mediating structural organization, balancing figural-operational balance, and improving self-regulation (Gordon, 1988).

Organization

It is through cognitive structures that children organize self and environment. They represent developing systems for meaning-making. They allow for action rather than being the action itself. Structures become coordinated when a new goal is sought that requires actions that have not been combined

before. As structures become more coordinated they also become more differentiated (Gordon & Cowan, 1983; Piaget & Garcia, 1991).

Structures are self-regulatory, transformational systems. Learning is sub-
servient to development since it depends on the laws of development an competence according to a cognitive level. What children can learn depends on
what they can take from the given data via the cognitive structures available to
them. Their activity is at the very center of the development of intelligence.

In order for the structures to evolve, there must exist a tension between the
conserving and transforming energy patterns of their activity. As structures extend and reorganize their form, disturbances emerge. If newly formed structures are stable enough, the disturbances will be faced and reality will be redefined. If sufficient stability and tension needed to sustain the process of change
is lacking, reality will not be transformed. Transformations lie in the interaction of the forces of the intrapersonal and interpersonal systems (Grobecker,
1998).

The dynamic action of the structure works toward internal consistency. The
content of the structure includes logic as well as the influence of the environment. Biology and society do not shape development but are boundary conditions that constrain it. Development is neither the exclusive product of the
interioration of actions and objects in the environment nor the internal coordination of internalized representations. Cognitive development consist of
many related internal activities along with the external resources to support
them (Oyama, 1999).

As children incorporate the stage-salient tasks of lower stages into more
advanced stages, they attain more flexibility and prowess to adapt. The accomplishment of more complex cognitive structures results in the appearance
of qualitatively different characteristics. The distinctiveness of these different
characteristics is referred to as a stage. Each stage has exclusive milestones that
must be overcome for its completion. Meaning-making is directed by the particular proficiency of each stage. For example, at the sensorimotor level, structures are related to actions that gradually become goal directed and eventually
lead to the formation of object permanence. Structures of the preoperational
level are related to the symbolic functions of play, imitation, imagery, and language. They are one-way functions and qualitative since they have no inverses.
As such they are semilogical. While they have a strong relation to the structures of actions, their great importance is that they are the necessary bases for
the logic of reversible and quantitative concrete operations. Structures at the
concrete operation level are related to the child's ability to transform information. Since they have reversibility and basic logic, they are two-way functions:
quantitative and conservative. They eventually lead to classification, seriation,
decentration, and conservation. Structures at the formal operational level are
related to the child's ability to categorize all possible classifications. They lead

to the ability to form an operation on other operations signifying true "reflection" in a cognitive sense.

ORGANIZATION

The meanings that children assign to experiences become the key processing underlying change. How these meanings are first constructed in infancy, how and why these meanings undergo change or remain impervious to change, and the role they play in a person's negotiations with ever-changing environments are major foci (Westman, 1990).

Sensorimotor
Stage-salient feature:

Sensorimotor logic:
Conquest of object permanence through meaning-making with movement, body sensations, and perceptions

Preoperational
Stage-salient feature:

Preoperational intelligence:
Conquest of symbolic functions through meaning-making with play, imitation, imagery, drawing, language; prelogical intelligence

Concrete Operational
Stage-salient feature:

Basic inductive and inductive thought:
Conquest of the understanding and manipulation of part-whole relations through meaning-making by the transformation of knowledge through classification, seriation, reversibility, conservation, and decentration

Formal Operational
Stage-salient feature:

Higher level logic:
Conquest of abstract thought through meaning-making through hypothetical and propositional thought

STAGE SALIENT FEATURES AND THEIR CORRESPONDING SOURCES OF ORIGIN

Object Permanence	Identity	Action is on objects
Symbolic Functions	Ability to see many scripts	Action is on states
Conservation	Ability to see part/whole relationships	Action is on transformations
Reflection	Ability to give logical justification for conflicts	Action is on transforming the transformations

Should children follow developmental paths incongruent with their chronological ages, they would experience delays, impasses, or fixations. Secondly, should children manifest imbalances in varying degrees of cognitive and affective disturbance, they would experience difficulties in adaption and the adapting processes.

Construction in the affective domain is similar to that in the cognitive domain. However, the close association between affect and cognition does not imply that one is the cause of the other. The association is marked by a constant and dialectic interaction transforming both to a higher organization of behavior. Both systems begin in primary biological drives. By pairing the affective system with the cognitive system, the child comes to understand the world. A stable value system emerges along with a stable logical system.

Self-concept and self-esteem develop in the same way and at the same time as the child's understanding about physical objects and other people. For example, in the sensorimotor stage the development of object permanence is the cognitive aspect of the development of motivating feelings. It leads to a sense of identity. In the preoperational stage the symbolic functions lead to the stabilization of both concepts and of feelings. Psychological life is fundamentally changed. Children now have evocative memory so they can recall past but absent situations. Feelings are allowed to acquire a stability and duration they have not yet had before. The simplest form of interpersonal feelings reside in liking and disliking others. In the concrete operational stage, the construction of classification hierarchies leads to a conservation of feelings and the beginning of a value system. During social interactions, children gradually center less on self-actions and more on the actions of other. This decentration leads to an increased understanding of the verbal and nonverbal cues of others, greater sensitivity to the needs of the other for clarification, and increased responsiveness to the ambiguity of others. Operations are fully reversible because actions in the system are arranged in inverse pairs (polarities).

In the formal operational stage, the reflective thinking leads to a fully mobile logic system and value system. Children actively self-regulate their behavior through thought by being able to construct possible scenarios and probable outcomes by considering all problem-solutions. Feelings are not simply retrieved from the past but are reconstructed to fit individual current interpersonal structures. Past events are reconstructed through a complex assimilative inferential process. As the underlying cognitive structures change, feelings evoked in past situations may be altered by new and different ways of understanding and interacting with other people (Piaget, 1981).

COGNITIVE STRUCTURES AND THEIR CORRESPONDING MOTIVATING FEELINGS

Sensorimotor	Object permanence	Feelings that motivate
Preoperational	Symbolic functions	Stabilization of feelings

Concrete Operational	Classification of hierarchies	Conservation of feelings and the beginning of a value system
Formal Operational	Reflective thinking	Fully mobile logic system and value system (Piaget, 1981)

A developmental, stage-salience frame of reference can be used to explain the behaviors of children with learning/behavior disorders and for planning interventions appropriate to their developmental levels. It reappraises learning/behavior disorders in terms of biologically based dynamic structures of mental activity, which are internally constructed and reorganized at higher levels as children make meaning of themselves and their environments.

Any clinical picture can be presented in terms of the present cognitive stage couched in appropriate relationship to the preceding and subsequent stages. This provides the necessary diagnostic label. A developmental approach places the present within the context of the past and the future. All disorder is a process that has extended through time and must be understood within its temporal context.

Many descriptions of cognitive stage disorders manifested by children with learning/behavior disorders have been given. These descriptions indicate that these children manifest structural disorders and show deficits in general sensorimotor acquisitions, coordination of action, object permanence, manipulation of objects, symbolic formation, fluid imagery, and conservation. Their disturbances in structural development often lead to misunderstandings and misinterpretations in their physical and social environments, and in the interaction between the two. Timing intervention measures and interventions accordingly may be as important, or more important, than their content (Anthony, 1956; Schmid-Kitsikis, 1973; Gelfand & Peterson, 1985; Keating, 1991).

Balance of Functions: Figural/Operational Dichotomy

Self-regulated learning is not a direct response to environmental factors but a response to internal conflict between figural and/or operational structures. It is achieved by several increasingly more complex processes. The self is a system that always strives to integrate perceptual-motor functions with its organic needs. Two mutually influencing factors underlie a self-regulating model: (1) the result of the immediate interpretation of the situational facts themselves, and (2) the inferences from those facts, whether subjective or logical. The former of these two general approaches to knowledge acquisition is basically mechanical; the latter, elaborative. The ability to understand and apply both functions brings about behavior change (Smock, 1981).

Thinking demands active participation as well as construction and reconstruction of knowledge whether it concerns figural or operational relationships. In normal growth the reconstructed knowledge, in turn, leads to the discovery of the physical and abstract properties of personal actions and eventually to reality (London, 1990).

> As a consequence, activity is critical to thinking and learning. To know something is not merely to be told about it; it is to see it, to modify it, to change it, to transform it, to act upon it. The thinking-learning transaction makes no distinction between, for example, the cognitive and affective, for indeed, feeling is an aspect of thought. (London, 1990, p. 84)

Behavior change can be brought about through these two different modes of experience that bring about the decoding, recoding, and encoding of data. The first process gives an assessment of the figural information, how objects or events are noted, plus the result of any manipulations on such objects and events. Figural activities merely refer to the routine recording of responses and represent reality as it appears. The physical experience of the figural functions allows children to discover and form representations of the qualities and properties of things. Any transformation of figural information depends on rhythmic, repetitive mechanisms involving space, perception, memory, and imagery. Their primary purpose is to decode and represent information gathered from these processes. Serving to maintain attention and accuracy, the mechanical aspects of these processes help children give more consistent and accurate performances.

The second process gives an evaluation of how relationships between the noticed figures and the resulting coordinations at each developmental level form. Such processing indicates the inductive generalizations and the elaborations of any new relationships that children make. Any transformation of these structural processes are governed by laws that are, in the strictest sense, operations. Operational functions are those activities that attempt to transform reality. They allow children to learn about the properties and relationships that belong to actions upon objects. They are characterized by the ability to form and manipulate symbols, to effectively use metacognitive skills, and to effectively use planning strategies. Their powers of elaboration can help children generate, recode, and encode new knowledge and thereby attain greater insight. They refer to a self-questioning approach during which children ask open-ended questions allowing for a wide possibility of responses, which can result in alternative problem solutions. Their transformations depend on the interplay of anticipation and corrective feedback.

The evaluation of the way in which children discover new figures and reach new coordinations is enhanced by the application of the self-regulating process. A complete picture of cognitive development cannot be obtained unless both the figural and operative aspects of cognitive functions are considered. By using a combination of the figural and operational processes, children both monitor and reflect on their performances (Piaget, 1971; Schmid-Kitsikis, 1973; Loper, 1982).

Children with learning/behavior disorders may have permanent or long-standing imbalances in figural and operational functions. In some cases, the figural functions may be well-developed, but the operational functions may be well below expected chronological age level. When figural functions progress much beyond the operational, a misleading picture of the child's level of cognitive functioning is given. Careful observation shows behavior that reflects rote rather than creative expression. Overt speech may not be impaired but deeper-meaning language usage may be lacking.

Conversely, other cases indicate a normal or above-average comprehension capacity coexisting with a serious inability to decode figural information. Here, careful observation shows behavior that reflects deductive, inferential, and creative expression. Overt speech represents language with deeply nuanced meaning. Impairment rests in the manipulation of figural representations (Morgan, 1986).

Balance of Functions: Assimilation and Accommodation

A balance must be established between the activity of a child on his environment and the activity of the environment on that child. Assimilation and accommodation serve as the dynamic mechanisms by which the structures are constructed and reconstructed. When contradiction, challenge, or confusion disrupt the assimilation (causing an appropriate accommodation in existing structures), a new assimilation on a higher, more efficient, more flexible level of functioning is established.

Normal development requires this proper balance. As existing structures incorporate new information, they themselves are being transformed. Through the process of accommodation, the assimilatory structures are modified and applied to a diversity of objects and events. This fosters a greater coordination between structures and extends cognitive flexibility and objectivity. Ultimately, structures and overt behaviors become altered and this allows a child to cope with new knowledge (Piaget, 1971, 1970a, 1976; Cowan, 1978).

Lack of self-regulatory processes are commonly recognized in children with learning/behavior disorders: they may process these skills to some degree, but they do not always access them. Functional imbalance can be defined as difficulties in distinguishing between inner and outer realities. Overassimilation occurs when the outside world is continually distorted to agree to internal, subjective experience. Overaccommodation occurs when the inner world is continually negated to agree to the outside world.

Analyses of functional difficulties characterize children with learning/behavior disorders as seriously failing in self/other differentiation. Such failures occur because the child is either continually shaping the outside world to internal structures (overassimilation), continually shaping internal structures into conformity to the outside world (overaccommodation), or erratically vacillating between the two (Cowan, 1978; Furth, 1983; Gordon & Cowan, 1983; Morgan, 1986).

Piaget pointed to three broad areas in which causes of structural and functional difficulties may be found, namely, (1) in the child, (2) in the physical and social environment, and (3) in the interaction between the two. In the first instance a malfunctioning within the child's own assimilation/accommodation balancing mechanism would necessarily interrupt normal development and cause distortion in structural formation. In the second, a nonresponding, faulty-responding, or overresponding environment may cause the failure of normal structures to develop. In these instances disequilibrium may be too lacking, too distorting, or too challenging for any child to strive for reequilibrium. In the third instance, a chronic mismatch between the child's structure/function makeup and the demands from the environment may cause a chronic state of disequilibration. Pathology, cognitive or affective, would then be defined as structural and/or functional disorders or in a child/environment mismatch (Gordon & Cowan, 1983; Stolorow & Lachmann, 1983).

Maladaptive Self-Regulation

Many developmental problems abide in the self-regulatory cycle. Common atypical behavioral patterns include such descriptors as (1) delays in the emergence of communication skills, (2) prevalence of thought disorders, and (3) inability to focus and maintain attention on relevant task demands. These children must be seen, first of all, ". . . as struggling to understand and organize their own experience—even their painful and anomalous experiences. . ." (Rogers & Kegan, 1991, p. 130).

As self-regulation processes guide children to an interest in being logical, organized, and reality-based, imagination becomes complex and components are tied together into coherent and logical patterns. Difficulties arise when themes become polarized rather than integrated. Preoccupations with order, control, or limitations of pleasure may be seen. Common difficulties that appear pertain to themes such as the need to be admired and respected. Concerns over shame, humiliation, loss of love, and fear of injury to self and other are prevalent (Greenspan, 1997).

Disruptions, disturbances, or delays in the ability to order experience consistently and coherently may eventuate disturbed, profound, and disruptive confusions to a sense of self-identity. Children may be prevented from advancing into more self-regulated, self-reflective, planful, socially acute individuals. Their appreciation for the needs of others and for group goals may be restricted (Cicchetti et al., 1988; Rogers & Kegan, 1991).

Discovery of the regulatory processes enables the evaluation of what degree of stability children's cognition has reached and the manner in which they discover new knowledge and form new coordinations. An account must be made of the coherence of gradual self-regulation (Schmid-Kitsikis, 1973).

Achieving a reliable signaling system and self-regulation requires that children become simultaneously interested in self and in the external environment. To be able to signal need states and to master self-regulation demand an increased capacity to attend to the environment. Neurological, biophysiological, and psychophysiological difficulties, often found in children with learning/ behavior disorders, may cause failure in self-regulation such as hyperactivity, hypoactivity, or dulled signaling of needs states (Cicchetti et al., 1988).

An inability to master self-regulation may also be expressed as a failure in the development of a reliable pattern of signaling and a decreased capacity to attend to the environment. These self-regulation difficulties may be manifested in excessive irritability or excessive passivity. Ability to be readily calmed or soothed may be restricted. Children may be unable to interact in an organized way with their animate and inanimate worlds (Cicchetti et al., 1988; Rogers & Kegan, 1991).

The mechanisms of assimilation and accommodation are believed to operate at all developmental levels. They create and modify structures. A predominance of either assimilation or accommodation resulting from individual differences or environmental circumstances may impede development. Any dysfunction of these mechanisms might therefore contribute to either a lack of attainment of the age-appropriate structures, or an asynchrony in their balance. Functional imbalance may occur because of a lack of opportunity to assimilation and accommodation either globally or within a specific area. Difficulties in coordinating reasoning across different areas of knowledge can cause a non-adaptive predominance of either assimilation over accommodation or accommodation over assimilation. Disturbances may arise because of a lack of opportunities to assimilate and accommodate either generally or within a specific domain (Anthony, 1956; Gordon, 1988).

Since all developmental stages involve promoting and balancing assimilation and accommodation across different domains of knowledge and emotions, the ability to coordinate judgments from all the different domains can facilitate the making of more adaptive life decisions.

Throughout the life span there are three symbolizing styles associated with maladaption. In the first, an inner cognitive orientational style due to a fixation on immediate meanings can prevent new symbols from being constructed.

In the second, an outer cognitive orientational style due to a fixation on the influences of others in constructing symbols can prevent any contribution from personal psychic reality. In the third style, excessive shifts between personal meanings and external influences prevent the two from being integrated (Furth, 1983; Gordon, 1988).

Overassimilation

Should children fall into an overassimilative pattern, they may become impervious to feedback from the social environment. With limited opportunities to encounter the perspectives of others, children consequently may have difficulty adapting personal perspectives when confronted with different views. There may be little occasion to apply attitudes or ideas to new knowledge domains, or conversely, new knowledge domains may not be applied to attitudes. Cognitive and affective development may be hindered.

Overassimilation can hinder adaptation to reality by impeding the development of psychological structures. Overassimilating children may insist on their own interpretations of interpersonal problems, may have a tendency to blame others, and may have difficulty considering different viewpoints. Such children foster accuracy of their own interpretations while having difficulties with modifying impressions of themselves or of others by considering different viewpoints. Limited opportunity to encounter the perspectives of others may leave children with difficulty to adapt personal perspectives when confronted with different views. There may be little occasion to apply attitudes or ideas to new knowledge domains. In both cases, cognitive development may be hindered (Furth, 1983; Gordon, 1988).

In an overassimilative frame of reference, children demand their differences and are unable to tolerate likenesses to others. They center on their own actions and their own viewpoints. There is a surrender to keeping distance and contact is resisted at any price. The result is a loss of the other. Such children are isolated and taken over by self in order to maintain separation. In overassimilation, the characteristics of the external object are not accounted for. To an extreme pathological degree behavior may even be considered autistic (Cowan, 1978; Swanson, 1988).

Perseverating on a stance to the point of overassimilation blocks adaptation to reality and hinders the development of psychological structures. This may be manifested in the child's elaboration of personal feelings without the consideration of any alternative perspectives. Children resist integrating particular experiences into a higher-order system. Earlier developed structures are used even though more developed structures exist. As a result, the products of these overassimilations become encapsulated in behavioral sequences.

These encapsulations are themselves dependent on the developmental level of the earlier structures to which they are associated. Each may take physical form based on magical thinking. Or, they may be focused on the body survival images experienced during previous physical separation situations. Additionally, the encapsulations may remain oriented on the self-view of a child who needs to act on and manipulate the world deceptively to get his or her needs met (Noam, 1988).

Rigidly closed boundaries are experienced as a safe refuge from invasion. Unable to tolerate any neediness, seen as weakness, an overassimilating child surrenders to an overvalued autonomy and self-sufficiency (Swanson, 1988).

Overaccommodation

In contrast to overassimilation, overaccommodation manifests itself either in a maladaptive conformity to the environment or a denial of personal interpretations of events. This maladaption prevents the creative modification of developing internal structures. One can observe withdrawing behavior, and refusal or inability to elaborate on both personal reactions and personal feelings to situations involving others. Creative modification of internal structures may be hindered by dependent conformity to an environment or a denial of personal interpretations of that same environment (Gordon, 1988).

Children in an overaccommodative frame of reference are driven to behave like others and therefore are unable to tolerate differences. There is a move toward likeness with the environment and a hanging on for contact at any price. The result is a loss of self. These children may allow themselves to be swallowed up and taken over by others in order to maintain a connection (Swanson, 1988).

An overaccommodative type of behavior pattern tends toward overconformity to the environment. Also, if there are limited opportunities to encounter other people's points of view, children may be hindered in the ability to modify their own personal viewpoints. Without such encounters, children may not have many occasions to apply and affirm their already formed ideas. As a result, in any of these situations, cognitive development as a whole may be hindered. Children consequently may have difficulty adapting personal perspectives when confronted with different views. Little occasion to apply attitudes and ideas to new knowledge is yet another source for this maladaption to occur (Noam, 1988).

Because children in such patterns suffer from a lack of opportunity to use their existing functional processes, they may develop serious structural deficits. Whether globally or within a specific knowledge domain, children must experience sufficient exposure to situations in which both assimilation and accommodation can occur (Noam, 1988).

Children change and grow by maintaining a difference between themselves and their environments by assimilating their environments to their personal differences. The selection and appropriateness of what can be assimilated and accommodated is made through contact with others. Maladaptive interruptions, inhibitions, or inappropriateness of interpersonal contacts may disturb the course of self-regulation. Children may withdraw or refuse to elaborate on personal reactions to situations involving others (Furth, 1983).

Serious Fluctuations

The self-regulatory processes of assimilation and accommodation require a degree of stability between the cognitive level reached and the manner in which new knowledge is discovered and coordinated. Contradiction, challenge, and confusion disrupt assimilation causing the need to make structural accommodations. Normally, this leads back to a new assimilation on a higher, more efficient, more flexible level of functioning.

When balance between assimilation and accommodation has not been restored, the task is not completed. Whereas completion brings new knowledge, what remains incomplete keeps children unaware, out of touch, and more and more incomplete. The self fails to be either maintained or optimized by the creation of something new. Maladaption occurs causing children to make repeated but unsuccessful attempts to satisfy needs (Schmid-Kitsikis, 1973).

A lack of self-integration and considerable fluctuations between more mature and less mature cognitive and affective states are clearly observable in children with learning/behavior disorders. Effective intervention for these children calls for the determination of the direction of the imbalance so that the nondominant function can evolve. Intervention should be used that is flexible enough to adopt either an assimilative or accommodative approach (Gordon, 1988; Noam, 1988).

Functional imbalances also may lead to avoidance of contradiction, refusal to disequilibrate, and/or unwillingness to use probabilistic cognitive terms. All may lead children to a state where experimenting with alternative problem-solving behaviors is avoided. Functional difficulties are noted by the manifestation of:

1. considerable fluctuation between advanced and less mature levels of thought;
2. dominance of static over fluid imagery;
3. difficulties in applying anticipatory imagery in sequential tasks;
4. egocentrism;
5. incomplete mastery of subcomponent skills resulting in their exerting more mental effort than would their chronological agemates;
6. difficulty using immediate feedback of the results of their efforts; and

7. experience maladaptive interactions with significant others in their environments. (adapted from Gordon & Cowan, 1983)

Overaccommodation	**Overassimilation**
Merging	Isolating
Noncontactful due to loss of boundary through: fluidity	Noncontactful due to loss of boundary through: rigidity
Permeability	Impermeability
Dissolving	Distancing
Loss of self	Loss of other
A hanging on for contact	Closing the boundaries for protection (adapted from Swanson, 1988)

Piagetian thought can provide enrichment to psychological and educational interventions. Its emphasis on structural organization and self-regulation leads to a better understanding of the children's play in their own development (Sigel, 1969).

> Piaget's system is one of changing gestalts or wholes that are reorganized and redefined in the course of growth. (Sigel, 1969, p. 468)

This paradigm has been considered a useful vehicle for ordering intervention strategies into a developmental hierarchy for normal achieving children and has been championed as applicable to the academic and affective problems of learning/behavioral disordered children. All children are viewed as having internal ego boundaries comprised of stimuli from their inner biological and psychic worlds, plus external ego boundaries constituted by stimuli from the physical world. Reality is constructed from a reciprocal interaction between the external and internal ego boundaries. Subsumed in this theory is the belief in a hierarchical level of development. At each succeeding level, children achieve a greater mobility, stability, permanence, and field of application.

Children with learning/behavior disorders, at any point in their development, may fail to reach adaptive solutions to stage-salient issues. With repeated adaptive attempts resulting in failure, they are likely to believe their difficulties are insurmountable. When viewed from a constructivist frame of reference, children with learning/behavior disorders show deficits in general sensorimotor acquisitions, coordination of action, object permanence, manipulation of objects, symbol formation, fluid imagery, conservation, and propositional thinking.

> . . . their spiral of mental structuring is not as expansive as that of their same age peers as it winds itself upward and outward through exercise of its form. Thus, the cognitive systems of these children are less complex, preventing them from acting on, and thus, transforming, material forms using age-related, higher-ordered relationships. (Grobecker, 1998, p. 219)

Table 4.1

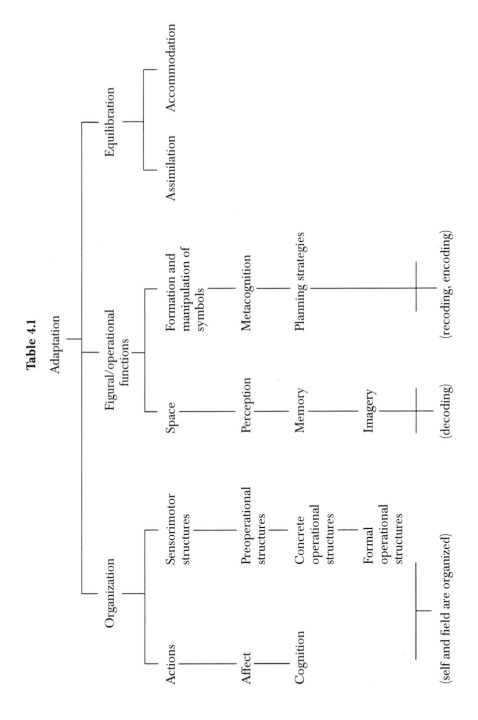

A description of children with learning/behavior disorders within the framework of a constructivistic model focuses on cognitive discordances, instability, and absence of certain concepts as well as on the problem of the developmental stage hierarchy. It strives to analyze not only sensorimotor and perceptual activities, but also the child's mental operations. This two-factor theory approach would look at the way a child handles and distinguishes the figural aspects from the operational aspects of symbols (Kimmel & McGinitie, 1984).

Learning/behavior disorders can result from a child/environmental mismatch, either because the environment does not meet the demands of the child's unfolding capabilities or because the environment fails to provide the child with a particular required responsiveness. Consequently, certain internalizations crucial for the structuralization of the representational world are interrupted (Gordon & Cowan, 1983; Stolorow & Lachmann, 1983).

Experiencing frustration and discouragement when attempting to make meaning may cause children to lose the desire to extend energy into the environment. Too much excitement may be experienced when structures are forming into a new higher order and there is little capability to sustain the tension. Children in such situations often return to lower levels of organization. The number of future interactions that can be allowed and coordinated into the system becomes limited. A system with rigid boundaries results, prohibiting normal assimilative/accommodative equilibration. Cognitive activity becomes minimized, motivation is decreased, and vital logic is stultified.

Learning/behavior disorders can be analyzed according to developmental criteria. The stage aspects, figural-operational functions, and self-regulatory functions can help professionals understand children with learning/behavior disorders by realizing that: (1) one child may move through one or more stages at a normal pace but be delayed in attaining others; (2) there may be distortions in the route that various children take to attain the same stages; and (3) a child may have stage abilities and cognitive functions (namely, assimilation and accommodation), but may not use them appropriately (Gallagher & Reid, 1981; Rogers & Kegan, 1991).

While differences in genetic endowment and culture play a crucial role in individual susceptibility or invulnerability to disorders, their cumulative effects can be mitigated by positive experiences throughout the life span. Subsequent appropriate experiences can do much to ameliorate earlier deprivations in, and disruptions of, normal development. There are two possible ways that deficits can be approached. The first is by looking at the effect deficits have on the nature and organization of knowledge. The second approach concerns itself with the effects the deficits have on the manifestations of a normally structured knowledge (Elkind, 1989; Rosen, 1991).

Chapter 5

CONTACT, AWARENESS, AND DIALOGUE

We must strive to lead the child to construct for himself
the tools that will transform him from the inside—that is, in
a real sense and not only on the surface.
(Piaget, 1974, p. 121)

The concept of organismic self-regulation is the true theoretical core of Piaget's theory. It reflects a field theory perspective and is accomplished by the self's functioning in the individual-environmental field. Self-regulation stresses the idea that a field is always in some sort of controlled tension. It encompasses the concepts of awareness, contact, and dialogue, which are deeply embedded in the theoretical basis of developmental epistemology (Piaget, 1968, 1972, 1973, 1976, 1981).

FIELD THEORY

Field theory is a basic tenet of a constructivistic psychology. Field, equivalent to life space, is best thought of as a sphere of influence. In a field theory context, behavior is considered from a framework of multiple interrelated forces and not caused by single, linear agents. Certain laws govern all fields. The first law is that a field is quantitatively and qualitatively different from the sum of its parts. Secondly, a field takes on the best possible form, one that is simple, regular, symmetrical, and closely packed. All elements in a field are subordinate to the whole and every modification of the elements refashions the entire assembly. Every element is considered an integral part of the total field. The meaning of any element in the field relies on the environmental context (Piaget, 1970a; Crocker, 1992).

Relative to people, field theory focuses on the relationship between the individual and the environment. From a field theory view, children are seen as striving to maintain an equilibrium with their environments by becoming aware of personal needs and personal striving for fulfillment. They self-regulate by attending to the moment-to-moment figures that come into awareness (Frew, 1997).

The particular backgrounds that children bring to relationship episodes are comprised of their cognitive functions, values, usual problem-solving strategies, and personal styles of contacting. All these parts are dynamically interrelated and each part can be understood only in relation to the other parts. Actual behaviors emerge from their structured backgrounds as children struggle with immediate situations.

Children interpret information from their individual worlds and construct personal meanings on previously acquired knowledge and experience. Reflections on personal physical and mental actions, as well as social interactions with others, lead children to build more knowledge. In adequately adapting children, the relation of figure-ground is a meaningful process of emerging and receding figures. All meaning is dependent on the background that serves as the context in which any element appears. Any element can emerge as a figure. The effect that the field exerts on the selection of a figure is of central importance. Field organization directly influences how an individual figure is processed and selected. Field effects are the observed immediate, simultaneous interactions among elements as they mutually relate. Any element that becomes the center of a motor, perceptual, or cognitive field is by its very centeredness overestimated. The noncentered elements, however, are diminished in relation to it. The overestimations or underestimations are proportional to the number of elements being considered (Piaget, 1970a; Rogers & Ridkin, 1981; Bereiter, 1985; Swanson & Alexander, 1997).

In every actual situation, children share in an irreducible unity with their physical and sociocultural fields. The relationships between children and their environmental fields are dynamic and circular in that children choose and modify their environments while being dependent on them. The integrity and coherence of these relationships are interpreted in light of their contexts.

Piaget's observations of children's thinking led to conclusions about how they experience their environmental fields. These observations also offered explanations of why children behave, cognitively and psychologically, as they do. Piaget distinguished two different modes of behavior-changing experience: the physical learning experience and the operational learning experience. The first concerns itself with the properties, characteristics, and relation of elements. The analytic quality of physical experience enables children to better differentiate among various features in their environment. It changes *what* is experienced. The second mode focuses on actions that children perform on these elements. The synthetic quality of operational learning helps children organize events into larger wholes. It changes *how* children experience. This distinction involves the actions of children on things and the reorganization of their fields. Children learn the laws of organization from their actions on the environment. Progressive mental growth does not alter the physical contents but radically alters the operational contents. Accordingly, children in learning situations are not unfolding according to nature, nor are they always being passively conditioned to respond in a given desired way. Rather, at each child's level of maturity and comprehension, differentiation and reconstruction occur in both self and environment (Elkind, 1970).

AWARENESS

In recent years, psychology and education have given much attention to the problem of characterizing the nature of cognitive awareness, knowledge acquisition, and self-regulation. They looked at how children acquired knowledge about their own (1) cognitive events, (2) patterns of cognitive strategy use, and (3) ability to consciously execute these events and patterns (Jarman, Vavrik, & Walton, 1995).

How children respond to their environments is greatly influenced by their unconscious cognitive processes. There are two general interpretations to the term unconscious:

> The first refers to a state of being unaware of . . . the stimuli that impinge upon receptors but fall outside the metaphorical spotlight of selective attention. The second interpretation refers to the lack or failure of introspection. Thusly, one is unaware of the occurrence, causes, or other attributes of attended objects, events, or actions when one cannot report those properties' validity. (Werner, 1982, p. 767)

The position taken here is that the unconscious is not simply dichotomous with all psychic content as either conscious or unconscious. Rather, children progressively transcend the unconscious with each advance constituting a widening perspective of self, other, and environment. Changes in reality result from an understanding of behavior that, in turn, must come from the conscious awareness of some sort of contradiction or conflict. Inner contradictions or conflicts are for the most part reliable in the sense that they can be trusted to be attempts at self-regulation. If they are brought into awareness, they can be incorporated with existing information for resolution. They need to be resolved, not dissolved (Rosen, 1991).

Knowledge acquisition requires a consciousness of the significance of something, a consciousness of the rules involved in relational structures, as well as a consciousness of the intention of an entire system of thought. The source of consciousness of systems of thought is awareness, defined as the capacity to organize, integrate, and reorder experiences. It is an active dual process. On the one hand, it makes the unconscious conscious. On the other hand, it structures and coordinates what is now in consciousness in such a way as to make it useful in other contexts. Awareness is but the process of reconstructing what is already known. The intent is to throw some light on the relation between consciousness and physiological mechanisms (Piaget, 1954, 1970b; Tenzer, 1983).

> Operations never develop separately but always in coordinated systems . . . We have attempted to trace developmental stages in terms of total operational structures. Such structures not only help explain changes in consciousness itself but are eventually isomorphic with corresponding neurological structures. (Piaget, 1954, p. 139)

Awareness is also the agent of growth. As the only basis of knowledge and communication, awareness is the very source of meaning-making systems. Changes in reality result from an understanding of behavior that, in turn, must come from the conscious awareness of thoughts, feelings, and conflicts. By grasping awareness, children search for and bring into conscious regulation, or new ways to understand and control their behaviors. Children in awareness use their full psychomotor, affective, cognitive, and motivational supports to remain attuned to their self-environment fields. As they approach rational consciousness, they arrive at an accurate awareness of their real natures as persons, their natural and social environments, and their connections to the outside world. Rationally conscious children are those whose perceptions are accurate and who have the abilities to act on their accurate understandings of reality (Perls, Hefferline, & Goodman, 1951; Piaget, 1954; Werner, 1982).

Insight is the goal of awareness. Even though on the surface insight may seem to be a sudden burst of awareness, it is often a gradual development to consciousness of a striving figure to reach clear formation. Its initial force is the physiological figures that emerge from a body background. Every awareness implies a period of reflection on a problem and that awareness is, in itself, the result of a preceding phase that may not be conscious at all. Understanding is nothing but a reconstruction, and the awareness is the resulting structure that is achieved when this work has been done (Piaget, 1981; Furth, 1987).

As a function of attention and concentration, awareness brings into the open all internal and disowned parts of the personality as well as external bodily senses and movements and the external environment itself. Awareness, especially of cognitive and affective contradictions, aids in differentiating the functions of the organism—body, emotion, and thinking—and in taking responsibility for their functioning.

Because it is developmental and not sudden, awareness consists of a constant reconstruction. The prerequisites that characterize the initial stage of awareness development require that children show some degree of affect, maturation, active involvement, and intentionality. Next, as children gain a greater degree of self-observation, behaviors reside halfway between an unconscious state and awareness of them. What already has been learned in previous stages is now generalized and incorporated into different aspects of behavior. As children attain greater reciprocity with their outside environments, they become more involved in exploring the implication of their behaviors. Finally, awareness becomes the very source of progress as well as the point for a reorganization of a great number of behaviors. It can be generalized, that is, what has been learned in previous stages is now incorporated into different aspects of behavior. The force of assimilation into existing structures is overcome so as to allow for accommodation. Achieving new patterns of behavior, children can see themselves differently. Children can now engage their thoughtfulness and curiosity in an active assumption of and responsibility for themselves (Tenzer, 1983; Furth, 1987).

Awareness results from self-regulation, which occurs in every behavioral event and always produces changes in cognitive structures. It emerges from a conflictual encounter of either cognitive structures and reality or of cognitive structures with each other.

Awareness also results as figures emerge from and brighten against their fields. The development of the powers of observation, communication, decision making, and rational consciousness leads children to an understanding of their own behavior and their connections with the outside world. Rationally conscious children have accurate perceptions as well as the ability to act knowingly on a self-understanding of reality.

Awareness is the process of being attuned to the most important elements in an individual-environment field with full psychomotor, affective, cognitive, and motivational support. It allows one to respond to a given situation in a fashion appropriate to one's needs and to the possibilities of that situation.

Awareness of cognitive processes is developmental and plays a significant role in attention, memory, language acquisition, reading and language arts, verbal encoding of information, oral comprehension, problem solving, and social cognition, as well as self-control and self-instruction. Children are motivated through a conscious awareness of their own processes and abilities to control these processes through planning, choosing, and monitoring (Werner, 1982).

Constructivist educators devote much of their work to the learner's process of awareness. Dysfunction may result from the loss of awareness of any current pattern of contact with others, along with the distortions that can arise from this.

Awareness and Emotions

There is an inextricable link between cognition and affect that governs the totality of behavior. Affect prescribes and assesses end-products and provides the needed energy to attain them. Cognition finds the means to these end products. Because of this link it would follow that cognitive disturbances must

Table 5.1 Development of Awareness

	Awareness of specific	Awareness of the manipulations of	Awareness of relationships among	Awareness of coordination of
SENSORIMOTOR	Awareness of specific sensations and movements	Awareness of the manipulations of sensations and movements	Awareness of relationships among sensations and movements	Awareness of coordination of sensations and movements and the cause and effect of sensations and movements in an interaction ———— **object permanence**
basic motor reflexes				
PREOPERATIONAL	Awareness of specific symbolic functions	Awareness of the manipulations of symbolic functions	Awareness of relationships among symbolic functions	Awareness of the coordination of symbolic functions and the cause and effect of symbolic functions in an interaction ———— **social language**
private meaning of symbols				
CONCRETE OPERATIONAL	Awareness of specific transformations	Awareness of the manipulations transformations	Awareness of relationships among transformations	Awareness of the coordination of transformations and the cause and effect of transformations in an interaction ———— **conservation (ability to objectify actions)**
part-whole relationships				
FORMAL OPERATIONAL	Awareness of specific ideas and reflections	Awareness of the manipulations of ideas and reflections	Awareness of relationships among ideas and reflections	Awareness of the coordination of ideas and reflections and the cause and effect of ideas and reflections in an interaction
hypothetical, propositional thought ———— **true reflection**				

have deep emotional components. Understanding children's behaviors relative to their cognitive abilities demands a knowledge of how they process emotions and how they envision their general life space as well as specific life situations. Action and emotion combine with perception and cognition into meaningful symbolic thought (Anthony, 1956; Cowan, 1978).

The emotions are not obstructions to, but means to, cognition. They provide information to children of the states of their organism/ environment fields. Emotions are the vehicles by which children become aware of the appropriateness of their concerns. Although they can at any given moment be fallible, they can develop into the more settled feelings that accompany deliberate orientation (Perls, Hefferline, & Goodman, 1951).

There is as much construction in the affective domain as there is in the cognitive. A structuralization of feelings coexist with the structures of intelligence. There are elementary feelings, such as interpersonal likes and dislikes, that are initially not conserved. Unimpeded they eventually evolve to the highest level of emotional functioning, that is, systematically developed autonomous moral thinking, which assures the stabilization and conservation of certain values. There is general acceptance that affective life is rhythmically structured. For example, excitation alternates with depression, joy with sadness. A structure with laws of organization exists for the simplest affective states and all affective phenomena occur in relation to a field. There is an affective relativity linked to figure/ground contrast (Piaget, 1981).

> We have assumed that affective decentering is a correlate of cognitive decentering, not because one determines the other, but because both occur as a result of a single integrative process (Piaget & Inhelder, 1969, p. 25). An organism is a self-contained law-abiding entity that generates its own laws. It is law-abiding in the sense that it is the source and development of its own laws. (Silverman, 1991, p. 31)

Emotions begin from a lack of differentiation between the self and the physical and human environment and develop toward the construction of a group of emotional investments that attach the differentiated self to other persons through interpersonal feelings. When the self remains undifferentiated, it is not conscious of itself. All emotion is centered on the child's own body and action. When the self can dissociate the other, decentration, whether affective or cognitive, becomes possible.

Children become used to the emotional states they are generally in. As they become aware of any change in those states, they become alert and may note additional changes in motor reactions, facial expressions, visceral reactions, and response possibilities. The change may also provide motivation for them to make cognitive interpretations (Piaget & Inhelder, 1969; Kagan, 1978).

Various behaviors combine to express habitual patterns. The habitual patterns are continually revised as they accommodate to and assimilate environmental opportunities. As they evolve throughout the life span, they provide psychological growth, adequate adaptations, and a sense of competence. However, in the process, it is the developmental principles that operationalize the particular behaviors that are given a meaning (Furth, 1983).

Self disorders are the adjustments made when a figure of consuming interest is incomplete and becomes the focus of interest. If an environment does not support contacting attempts, differentiation does not occur.

Very often children with learning/behavior disorders are unable to grasp the pathways leading to awareness of how to reconstruct their meaning-making structures. Inadequately adapting children do not fully experience each present moment but limit recognition of emerging events because they are not aware of, or are too occupied with, unfinished patterns. Blocked awareness prevents healthy interactions. There may be little or no involvement in mutual, intimate, give-and-take relationships. Should the environment become the all-powerful figure, the attainment of personal needs, even when in awareness, is difficult. To enable distressed and/or disturbed children to experience fuller contact with their environment, they must develop a systematic way to observe emerging patterns of awareness (Rogers & Ridkin, 1981; Tenzer, 1983; Mulgrew & Mulgrew, 1987; Rosen, 1991).

Emotions displayed at a very early age are at first dependent on general rhythmic activities of the organism, for example, alternations between states of tension and relaxation. A differentiation results from the attempts to search for agreeable stimuli and a tendency to avoid disagreeable stimuli.

The motor ability of children often advances beyond their ability to conceive of that activity. Consequently, they often cannot reflect on their own actions and therefore will remain unaware of their actions. And, if children can experience emotional ambivalence but do not conceive of it, they can be described as unaware of their ambivalent emotions. The concept of unawareness is neither motivated nor emotionally determined. That is, unaware emotions do not escape conscious scrutiny because of their primitiveness but because they are too complex for the existing conscious cognitive system to comprehend (Breslow, 1988).

The reason why some experiences do not reach awareness is that they receive no meaning from the child's initial psychic reality. They remain unnamed and out of awareness, yet operational. These particular experiences become incompatible with, or in conflict with, what is already in awareness. The conflict may cause them to be actively held in unawareness. However, if brought into awareness and repeatedly revised, the experiences facilitate psychological growth.

Before the self interacts with others, there is evidence of an elaboration of a whole system of interactions through imitation. Children then begin to react to other people in more and more specific manners. Following this, an awareness of causality coming from others is established.

CONTACT

The issues of the nature of changes in self-reflection as a function of age and experience are addressed by awareness of one's thinking processes as well as contact with internal and external pressures. Awareness and contact are essential to normal cognitive constructions. Self-regulation and autonomy will follow once they occur (Jarman, Vavrik, & Walton, 1995).

Adaptation involves self-modification of one's actions, cognitions, and emotions, with the goal of trying to achieve a desirable match between individual needs, interests, and motives on the one hand, and the environment on the other. As children identify with certain elements of their fields and separate from others, they come to realize themselves as actively regulating their own deliberate wants and interests within definite, but shifting, boundary changes (Piaget, 1981).

As integral parts of the physical and interpersonal worlds in which they exist, children are systems open to various forms of contact with their environments. As a result, existing boundaries between children and their overall environments are always in a state of elaborate interpretation or ecological balance. Contact leads to self-organization and stabilization of the systems. It also expands the possibilities for the generativity of intelligence (Chrzanowski, 1982; Chapman, 1992; Stone & Conca, 1993; Stone & Reid, 1994).

According to Piaget, children are driven by two tendencies: to conserve and to expand. The first tendency aims at keeping children in balance with their environments. Connected to the equilibrium or closure of a logical structure, it implies self-direction. Closed logical structures allow mental operations to move in any direction and return to the starting point. It is a necessary base for the second tendency, expansion, which aims at the formation of new structures at a higher level of conservation. The two tendencies represent a developmental sequence that is valid for all areas and at all stages of development. The sequence follows accordingly:

1. conservation
2. expansion
3. disturbance
4. compensation

5. reconstruction
6. conservation (Furth, 1987)

The life-span process of development tends toward integration and inclusion, separation and independence, and finally, intimacy and interdependence. It can be presented schematically in terms of stages. Stages represent a linear, hierarchical progression and also a series of horizontally balanced self-object relationships. In normal development, any disturbance in balance results in action toward a rebalance. The disturbances indicate to children that their existing forms of meaning-making are inadequate to resolving new conflicts. Rebalance widens the capability for conflict resolution and adaptation. It must be kept in mind that developing children are not equated to the stages, but to the very activities involved in their evolutionary processes that constructs the stages (Rosen, 1991).

The origins of the self lie in the innate sensorimotor structures of early life. As these structures emerge during the course of development, they can be distinguished as: (1) the self-as-agent (the "I will"); (2) the self-as-locus of experience (the "I want"); and (3) the self as object (the "me") (Westman, 1990).

> In the course of development, the first to emerge is the self-as-agent, or as a doer and knower (one month) and a knower (by four months). The second is self-as-locus (end of first year). Self-as-object (about two years) allows one to observe oneself in the form of how others react to oneself and then proceeding to integrate those cues with one's own acts through imitation. Finally the clear differentiation of one's will from other's will is seen as oppositional behavior through which one asserts oneself by saying "I won't do it." (Westman, 1990, p. 285)

Children interact with their environments with biological structures. Environmental data are assimilated in three possible ways: (1) biological contacts are established between children and their environments, (2) previously neutral environmental situations become psychological stimuli, (3) adaptive responses are made (Piaget, 1963).

Contact is ultimate reality. It is the central task of human life and serves the two major purposes of conserving knowledge (assimilation) and expanding knowledge (accommodation). Contact boundaries are the points where children either attempt to fit the environment to meet their internal structures or adapt their structures to environmental pressures. The functions of conserving and expanding knowledge strive to mobilize the self and to dissolve patterns of behavior that interfere with self-regulation. When children acknowledge, recognize, and cope with the "other" in their existence, they make contact. In the continuous, interacting flow of experiencing self and others at the contact boundaries, children recreate themselves and the other. Intellectual development results as they make changes in their contacting behaviors.

Contact makes growth possible. It serves as the vehicle children use to make adjustments to their environments. It is the medium through which the boundaries between self and other are frequently transformed as children grow into adulthood. Going beyond creating new boundaries and new relationships between self and other, contact creates entirely new constructions of the two. To sustain an undisrupted, balanced self-other process, children must identify with their normal flowing creative excitement as well as alienate what does not belong to them (Piaget & Inhelder, 1969; Latner, 1982; Cahalan, 1983; Breshgold, 1989; Rosen, 1991; Frew, 1992).

Growth involves

> more than a new relationship between self and other; it involves a new construction of self and other; it involves a redrawing of the lines where I stop and you begin, a redrawing that eventually consists in a qualitatively new guarantee to you of your distinctness from me (permitting at the same time a qualitatively "larger" you with which to be in relation). (Kegan, 1980, p. 131)

Contact is a special observation made to confirm or discover something unknown. In short, it facilitates meaning-making. Through contact children expand their capacity for accommodating new perspectives rather than assimilating them unchanged into preexisting modes of thought. Contact leads children to awareness. It brings out inconsistencies in perceptions, between what is experienced and what is known to be reality, between what is felt and what is thought, and between what is done and what is said about action. It can be used to counter any stumbling blocks children may be facing through inabilities to decentrate, to assimilate, or to accommodate adaptively (Piaget, 1981).

As each new developmental level is encountered there is continued renegotiation of the balance between being connected to others and being autonomous. Increased differentiation between self and others is a manifestation of increasing autonomy. Autonomy also springs from an emerging awareness of one's cognitive capabilities, goals, activities, feelings, and actions (Cicchetti et al., 1991).

Effective balance between assimilation and accommodation requires enough flexibility at the contact points to allow support to enter, and enough rigidity to maintain autonomy. Healthy adaptation is characterized by a rhythmic movement between engaging the environment and separating into self-awareness. This involves the ability to discriminate, to recognize, and to appreciate both similarities and differences. Children are thus enabled to differentiate between merging and keeping a separate identity (Gallagher & Reid, 1981; Swanson, 1988).

The evolving, spiraling, and developmental processes of contact show a certain transitory movement from a beginning point to closure. Its developmental resonance expresses a movement through time. A major forerunner to development and later integration of new knowledge is an ability to effectively confront discrepancies and contradictions. Any incongruity is the source from which progress emerges and energizes children to seek beyond their existing states for new solutions to problems (Piaget & Inhelder, 1969).

Contact begins as a multisensorial complex that can see, hear, touch, and so on, and from which the actions, thoughts, and emotions persists. More recent interpretations and extensions of Piaget's concept of self-other contact concern four core issues. First, individual intention is seen as equally important as truth testing (logic), that is, subjective interpretation is associated with objectivity. Second, procedural knowledge occurs developmentally before operational knowledge. Critical to cognitive and affective adaptation is the expansion of new structures of knowledge. Thirdly, the driving force in development and the rationale for an understanding of cognitive development as a constructive process is self-regulation. Fourth, social and cultural factors are vitally involved in the process of development. Contact advances self-regulation and autonomy (Piaget & Inhelder, 1969; Beilin & Pufall, 1992).

According to Piagetian thinking, the categories and processes of contact involve a self-other separation or each level of development. This is imperative for the achievement of self-regulation and the establishment of reality. Assimilation, the use of available knowledge, cognitive structures, or strategies, is the first effort at solving a particular problem. If these available resources work and the problem is solved, there will be no modification in the knowledge system. However, should the structures of assimilation prove inadequate, a contradiction arises and creates a state of disequilibrium.

Categories of Contact

The evolution of the categories of contact viewed from a Piagetian stance follows. At first, contact is not relational although there is a realization of personal wants and needs. This initial contact exercises already existing structures that, while indicating active involvement with the environment, do not lead to new knowledge. At this point, much activity that children perform in the environment is repetitive and pleasurable for its own sake.

At the next level of contact, children have gained the ability to bracket a figure off from the background and make repeated observations on it. They discover new properties of their situations and of the implications of their own behaviors. With an awareness of causality, children are carried to the discovery of new knowledge. Greater exchange with the external world leads children to perform activities within their environments that lead to new knowledge. However, this type of contact limits them to the properties and characteristics that their environmental objects possess. At this point, the contacts are mostly one-way affirmations of what is known. Children cannot grasp

polarities. However, the inner workings of the figure situation become apparent and children come to the awareness that there are many realities.

Next, contact takes on the characteristic of deliberate reasoning. Reflection
on their activities themselves allows children to discover, along with the characteristics and properties that elements do possess, those qualities that the elements do not have. Children now have object permanence, awareness of a
field, the grasp of polarities, the ability to declare what they do and do not want,
plus the capacity to analyze their own behaviors. As they attempt to integrate
new information by changing their structures, children extend the possibilities
for responding.

Process of Contact

There is also a Piagetian explanation of the process of contact. Initially, contact attempts are made to neutralize rather than integrate the contradiction. The
original strategy is changed as little as possible. For example, if the contradiction is not in awareness, the problem will be ignored. With a vague awareness
of the contradiction, only a minor modification of the assimilatory processes
will be made. If there is certainty that a contradiction exists, but uncertainty that
the new information fits into already established structures, another cognitive
classification will be formed consisting of just that contradiction. However, that
contradiction exists in an unintegrated and dissociated state.

The second method of making contact involves clear accommodation.
Rather than ignoring a problem or trying to cancel out the contradiction, attempts are made to integrate the new knowledge by adopting a new classification. The contradiction now becomes a variation of the integrating strategy.
Possibilities for responding are extended. The aim is not to cancel out the
contradiction but to modify the assimilatory structure itself in order to accommodate the new information. Knowledge of specific properties are replaced
with new information and nonproperties are understood. Polarities become
apparent.

The third method of contact does not involve any cancellation of a contradiction. Possible alternatives to integrating a variety of new information are
anticipated. Easy accommodations of the assimilation structures are achiev-
able (Piaget & Inhelder, 1969; Piaget, 1970b; Gallagher & Reid, 1981).

In sum, growth is provoked when children (1) come in contact with an
inconsistent situation; (2) realize an inconsistency exists between acquired
knowledge and behavior; (3) lose a significant object; (4) anticipate a threatening event; (5) have a goal blocked; (6) require nurturing; or (7) are released
from stressful situations (Inhelder, Sinclair, & Bovet, 1974; Kagan, 1978;
Rosen, 1991).

With the help of their ever-evolving cognitive structures, children create and recreate three different worlds:

1. a practical world of undifferentiated perceptual-motor consciousness;
2. a world of images and symbols extending space beyond the distant receptors and coordinated with the world of others;
3. a world of autonomy where thinking is governed by mobile, reversible operations and where social behavior is determined by objectivity and respect for the point of view of others. (Anthony, 1956)

Contact difficulties stem directly from experiential, cognitive, and communicative barriers. That is, children may lack experience per se, the understanding of experiences, or the ability to share experiences. To resolve these problems, a child must be helped to create and encounter missed experiences, undeveloped thinking skills, and nonexisting communication skills (Kamii, Clark, & Dominick, 1994).

Children with learning/behavior disorders can become overpowered when confronted by typical developmental tasks that impose new burdens on their cognitive-personality resources. Processes of awareness, contact, and self-regulation may not appear until later stages of development. In addition, environmental interferences with the needs and/or rights required by a particular stage of development can prevent certain crucial experiences from being brought into awareness (Piaget, 1973).

DIALOGUE

The core of psychological development is the constantly changing relationship between affect and cognition fostered within interactions with significant others. Of late, education has seen the role of social factors as a major influence in determining the substance and course of children's learning. This focus, directed to the importance of the interrelational quality of human existence, deals with how children's psychological processes arise within self-other contexts.

Piaget's developmental epistemology endorses the dialectical position on knowledge acquisition. His theory details a balanced account of a child's role in the meaning-making process with an account of social construction. Since meaning-making abides in complex and dynamic relationships, it cannot be reduced to simple causality. Acknowledging the role of social interaction, Piaget rejected transference-based relationship theories and focused on dialogic-based relationships. He considered experience and not explanation to be central to living. This position was based on the concept that a child lives in two dialogic worlds. The first arises from interactions with adults while the

Table 5.2 Development of Contact

SENSORIMOTOR	The child performs activities on objects in the environment that do not lead to a new awareness about objects	The child performs activities on objects in the environment that lead to a new awareness of the properties of the objects	The child performs activities on objects in the environment that lead, through reflection on the activities themselves, to a new awareness of the negations as well as the properties of objects
basic motor reflexes			— **object permanence**
PREOPERATIONAL	The child's use of symbols in interactions with the environment does not lead to new awareness about referents	The child's use of symbols in interactions with the environment leads to a new awareness of the properties of referents	The child's use of symbols in interactions with the environment that leads, through reflection on symbols themselves, to a new awareness of the negations the as well as properties of referents
private meaning of symbols			— **social language**
CONCRETE OPERATIONAL	The child's use of transformations of his knowledge does not lead to a new awareness of part-whole relationships	The child's use of transformations of his knowledge leads to a new awareness of the properties of part-whole relationships	The child's use of transformations of his/her knowledge leads to, through reflection on the transformations themselves, a new awareness of the negations as well as the properties of part-whole relationships
part-whole relationships			— **conservation (ability to objectify actions)**
FORMAL	The child's use of his hypothetical thought processes does not lead to a new awareness of his cognitive and moral systems	The child's use of his hypothetical thought processes leads to a new awareness of the properties of his cognitive and moral systems	The child's use of his/her hypothetical thought processes leads, through reflection on the processes themselves, to a new awareness of the negations as well as the properties of his cognitive and moral systems
hypothetical, propositional thought			— **true reflection**

second arises from interactions with peers. Children need both adults and peers to provide carefully controlled support in order to make any growth in their cognitive and affective lives as well as to gradually assume responsibility for their behaviors (Chapman, 1992).

Learning procedures developed from Piaget are based on following both the constructivist hypothesis relating to the activities of children as well as the interactionist tradition involving a dialogue between the child and another or a dialogue with an object (Kamii, Clark, & Dominick, 1994; O'Hara, 1998).

> . . . we must accept simultaneously that individual [children] are unique centers of consciousness and also heirs to, participants in, and cocreators of our social and psychological worlds. (O'Hara, 1998, p. 161)

Dialogue is a special form of contacting and is a very important aspect of any constructivist, self-regulating approach. Contacting in a dialogue context is the way in which a child nurtures self and directs the satisfaction of personal needs. Since it is considered grounded in the natural biological rhythms of all organisms, it is imperative that contact emerge organically from the dialogic process in such a manner as to reflect the next step in a child's becoming. The essence of any interaction consists of both verbal and nonverbal communication patterns in a goal-directed situation. Dialogue is a process of creating shared understanding. It is the manner by which self-knowledge is learned and understanding of others is gained. Dialogue demands self-awareness.

Children become unique only through relationships with others. In true dialogue there is a reality that encompasses both self and other. The most fulfilling self-knowledge comes only through an ongoing dialogue with one who is an equal in some important way. A child comes to the realization of separateness by participating in either "I-Thou" (between self and another person) or "I-It" (between self and an object) modes of contacting. Existence in both the "I-Thou" or "I-It" modes is an ". . . evolving, spiraling developmental process . . ." (Jacobs, 1989, p. 35). Finding the proper balance between the two signifies creative and healthy living.

The place of dialogue is the intersubjective field that holds the subjective and objective dimensions together. The highest form of contact is the "I-Thou" moment. Neither the self nor the other is lost. The boundary that separates a child and the environment is something that limits, contains, and protects that child, while at the same time touches the environment. Any serious interruption in true dialogue may result in cognitive and affective disorders (Jacobs, 1989).

There is a cycle of dialogic tension and resolution between the sender and the receiver of a message. To be successful in dialogue each participant must take into consideration what the receiver needs to understand in the messages being emitted. The receiver, when invited to share the sender's view of the situation, becomes part of the meaning-making. The tension created in the attempt at resolution engages each in a search for meaning.

> Adults can invite inferences on the part of the child, but it is the child's responsibility to make those inferences, and without them the child will not take over the adult's view of the task. (Stone & Reid, 1994, p. 77)

Process of Dialogue

From the beginning children are active partners in the learning process. As equal partners each individual child takes responsibility for evaluating and selecting strategies toward understanding issues brought up in the dialogue.

There is a development to the meanings learned from the dialogue. Children do not directly translate adult understanding into their own knowledge structures. Rather, they strive to integrate their own interpretations of new information onto what they already know.

Cognitive development builds on intersubjective disequilibration brought about by differences of opinions and interpretations. Children must generate, consider, and weigh reasons for and against opposing propositions. Contradictions are overcome through the construction of negations to balance every affirmation. Gaps in knowledge represent another cause of disequilibration. These gaps can make children aware that, when following a goal, they do possess the means necessary to achieve it. Reconstruction involves filling in the gap in question (Chapman, 1992).

Development emerges from interaction. Both emotional and cognitive growth depend on affective interactions.

> Affects stemming from interactions become the foundation for both ego growth and differentiation and, more broadly, for intelligence. The role of the psychologist or educator then is to be a collaborative constructor of experience. (Greenspan, 1997, p. 19)

Self-regulation begins from an emerging interest in the environment through the senses. Shared attention characterizes the first stage of development. This forms the basis on which infants build their ability to maintain a calm, alert, and focused state. It is the foundation from which organized thoughts and behavior derive. Secure regulation and control of the body play a very significant role in the way in which children use gestural communication. Engagement and shared attention arise from a "... type of rhythmic connectedness . . . evident in the way the infant and parent use their senses, motor systems, and affects to resonate with one another" (Greenspan, 1997, pp. 390–391). Confluence characterizes the first stage of development. There is no clear internal differentiation between self and other. Only what is similar will be foreground. Differences will be felt as threatening to any sense of unity (Westman, 1990; Youniss & Damon, 1992; Stone & Conca, 1993; Butler, 1998).

At very early ages, dialogue relies on how children interpret the actions and intentions of others. At first the communication involves rhythmic movements that imitate and copy exact movements of another. This allows practice of action patterns to better control. These interpretations are based on experiences rather than cognitive reflections (Stone & Conca, 1993; Butler, 1998).

As the infant/toddler increases skill in appropriately interpreting personal and other's gestural-motor behavior, the ability to communicate becomes more complicated, organized, and meaningful. Children understand that they and the other have different roles in the same activity but each participant plays only his or her own role.

Children enter the next stage of development when they have formed mental representations of their elaborate and shared motor meanings. They can call forth internal organized multisensory experiences. The representations are used to express thoughts, desires, ambitions, and anticipations. When the models of other people's actions become internalized, they become mental representations that can be voluntarily recalled. Children then know their own roles as well as those of others. In addition, they can now play the roles of others as well as their own roles. Actions are now incorporated and not merely mimicked. When words are connected to these action patterns, the language process serves the ends of both external communication and internal representation. Language enables children to talk about the possible and the imagined; about past, present, and future (Stone & Conca, 1993; Butler, 1998).

Logic and reason are apparent at the next level. By drawing associations between their own ideas, children categorize meanings and solves problems. The logic serves them in coping with cognitive conflict, seeking prosocial solutions, and differentiating fantasy from reality. The complexity of affect begins to be understood and appreciated at this level. Children begin to distinguish thoughts, events, and feelings that arise from within and those that are external. Self-representations emerge from this distinction.

For successful creations of relationships with boundaries, children must secure a number of highly refined capacities. For example, they must come to value others as the self and internalize them into their own psychic spaces. They must become aware of and incorporate the viewpoints of others into their own viewpoints. Distinctions have to be made concerning not only the ownership of all viewpoints, but how the self is viewed by others. A more advanced level of self-other separation is reached when children are able to form positions from points that belong to neither self nor other, that is, from a neutral third party position (Westman, 1990; Youniss & Damon, 1992; Stone & Conca, 1993; Butler, 1998).

Following developmentally based constructs, it is necessary to

> first determine the level of the patient's ego or personality development and the presence or absence of deficits or constrictions. For example, can the person regulate activity and sensations, relate to others, read nonverbal, affective symbols, represent experience, build bridges between representations, integrate emotional polarities, abstract feelings, and reflect on internal wishes and feelings? (Greenspan, 1997, p. 381)

Establishing a dialogue requires a shared definition and the making of effective moment-to-moment judgments about where the focus of the attention exists. Collaborative problem solving should not be one-sided but a more equal enterprise where children have a share in defining both the task and the strategies. Children must be guided to connect ideas and link them to prior knowledge at the same time they are engaging in interactions with peers and adults. At first it is important that they establish a shared definition and common context of communication. They next engage in collaborative problem solving to help shape their approaches to task demands. Children then need support for their abilities to interpret the adult's comments or questions in a dialogue fashion. Questions or comments should continue appropriately until an understanding of the features of the task demands are inferred (Stone & Conca, 1993; Butler, 1998).

> [Interaction should be] . . . bi-directional, so that in the communicative interchanges, inferencing, and regulation of cognitive processing flow more equally between children and adult . . . and . . . accounts for both individual and sociocultural influences on learning. (Butler, 1998, p. 383)

Children have two central tendencies: one that allows them to take on new experiences according to new abilities and maturational capacities, and one that satisfies their need for self-control or self-regulation. Children are constantly struggling to keep these two tendencies in balance in order to maintain equilibrium. Paramount in knowledge acquisition is support from interpersonal interactions. The two forms of support are agreement and disagreement, both to be looked at as cooperation. Agreement results in co-construction of new knowledge while disagreement results in conflict and opposition and an awareness of resistance to new knowledge. Each can foster collective reasoning toward higher cognitive processes and outcomes (Pontecorvo & Zucchermaglio, 1990; Greenspan, 1997).

Originating from an awareness of and commitment to the interpersonal interactions in the world, Piagetian theory holds that dialogue builds along two routes. One is of unilateral authority, the other of mutual cooperation. The first represents an early "heteronomous" stage in which the judgments of children are based on conformity and respect for authority. Children act as subordinates attending to the view of an authority figure. Tradition and rules are seen as the ultimate decisive factors. When in this stage, children lack the ability to take the perspective of another and operate on the assumption that rules are the same for everyone, regardless of situational factors and individual perspective.

In interactions of mutual cooperation, knowledge is co-constructed when children build on the ideas of peers while making explicit their own ideas. This later "autonomous" stage is characterized by a spirit of cooperation and mutual respect. Interaction with peers allows children easier access to the understanding of different perspectives. This eventually engenders a respect for all involved individuals rather than rules. To be autonomous, children have to take a stand on the mutual exchanges and objective discussions and know how to accommodate to them in order to gain respect. Autonomy is learning to understand others and be understood by them. It is based on a relationship of empathy.

Peer interactions are quite different from adult-child interactions in that they are marked by mutuality and cooperation rather than impositions and constraint. Presentation of the perspectives of the adult and/or peers may provoke disequilibrium and thus prompt children to reconceptualize the cues, dynamics, and expectations of the situation. Attempting to coordinate their views with the differing points of view of their peers results in some degree of disequilibrium and therefore facilitates cognitive progress. Children are able to take the role of their agemates and thereby expand their views of the world (Pullis & Smith, 1981; Youniss & Damon, 1992).

Dialogue and Learning

Learning is not merely the universal transfer of knowledge from one individual to another. It is, at the same time, a personal and an interpersonal construction. A dialectical force drives the interaction between the two.

> Once invented or discovered, knowledge can be transmitted from person to person or from one generation to another, but that knowledge first must be invented or discovered before it can be transmitted in this way. . . . Moreover, the act of communication presupposes that subjects already share knowledge of some semiotic system and whatever domains of experiences to which it refers. (Piaget, 1932, p. 52)

Children learn through the exchange of viewpoints with others, adults and peers alike. They construct their convictions and knowledge from the inside through these interchanges. As a result, the interchanges cause children to rethink their behaviors and to construct more acceptable ones. Intellectual autonomy derives from the ability to determine the relevancy of facts and ultimately to the construction of truth. As children repeatedly encounter the same experience, they build more complete and accurate understandings of that experience (Kamii, Clark, & Dominick, 1994; Mastropieri, Scruggs, & Whedon, 1997).

Dialogue is an open engagement and experience in others. Teachers and learners are equal partners in that they each take responsibility for evaluating and selecting problem-solving strategies on the basis of a mutual understanding of the issues brought up in interactions. They must be able to enjoy each others' actual presences, to make a commitment to be there for the other, and to welcome the self-revelations of others.

Dialogue is a vehicle that allows children to create meanings in a shared interpersonal interaction. It occurs when two people have the experience of mutual openness and respect for each other. Shared action and symbolic systems with others gradually enable children to create alternative plans of action and meaningful communications. New possibilities arise from reenacting different roles previously preformed by others, sharing action with others, and practicing of one's own existing skilled actions. Children come to realize the meanings of both their own actions and the actions of others.

Children must acquire the ability to interact with others in specific ways that are at the same time academically beneficial, personally beneficial, socially accepted or valued, and mutually beneficial. Academic and social skills require a set of behaviors capable of varying with particular situational demands that produce positive consequences for any individual child within the norms of societal acceptability and responsiveness to others (Bhavnagri & Samuels, 1996).

Children become more active in selecting what and how they learn if they are given more responsibility for self-directing their learning. Whether verbal or nonverbal, dialogue is the major vehicle by which children can assume responsibility (Stone & Conca, 1993; Stone, 1998; Butler, 1998).

Fluent, effective, coherent dialogue prompts the child to problem solve and to generate options. This comes about when the child practices

> (a) isolating salient dimensions of communicative tasks and contexts; (b) recognizing patterns formed by the isolated dimensions; and (c) formulating hypotheses about the significance of the patterns relative to the communicative task, context, and/or objective. He or she must make decisions by selecting and organizing a plan of action for communication from among the options generated. Last, but not least, the speaker must monitor, self-evaluate, and revise based on efficacy and outcome, among other considerations. (Wigg, 1993, p. 171)

Knowledge of language and understanding the rules of social interaction are requirements of good communication. Getting the attention of others, adjusting personal messages to situation demands, and monitoring reciprocal interactions are skills children must acquire (Paris & Lindauer, 1982).

For true dialogue to occur, communication must follow the underlying meanings or scripts. As dialogue moves toward a goal, it must respond to the learner's knowledge and personality needs as well as conceptual and affective perspectives (Wigg, 1993).

Learning occurs in an intersubjective space. Through dialogue the participants can focus on generating questions about the problem, summarize what is already known about the problem, and clarify anything that interferes with the understanding of the problem. Dialogue allows children to be active in constructing their knowledge base in an interactive setting. In an interactive setting, children are allowed to be active in constructing their knowledge bases. Following this, children learn to apply the new strategy in new settings (Palinscar et al., 1993).

Intervention

Great benefit derives from an intervention program that broadens its base to include a more explicit dialogical approach in its methodology. Such an approach demands a serious alteration of the manner in which intervention is carried out.

A self-regulated learning approach is characterized by a dialogic interchange between adults and children in which (1) the children become involved in a meaningful and culturally worthy activity significantly beyond their current understanding and control; (2) there is a gradual withdrawal of the adult's assistance; (3) a wide range of the types of support is provided by the adult; (4) transfer of responsibility from adult to children is fostered.

> Each time a need, wish, or intention and its corresponding potential for loss of control and self-defeating humiliation and embarrassment becomes part of a shared experience with an empathic soothing adult (who meets the person at his or her developmental level), there is a new experience of a "me and you" rather than a "me and my appetites and counterreactions." (Greenspan, 1997, p. 250)

The experience of a shared sense of "me and you" can lead children to a two-way internal dialogue. This forms the foundation for continued experiencing and observing the self and eventually leads to an interconnection among all representations, that is, ". . . a person's ability to self-observe is abstracted from the ability to observe oneself in the process of communicating with another person" (Greenspan, 1997, p. 268).

There must be a collaborative dialogue between teacher and learner characterized by the building of a mutual understanding in a clear, shared context. The shared context engenders an attitude of joint activity rather than one of "your activity performed for me." When the teacher lets go of a concern for skills, knowledge, experience, and preconceptions in order to be present for the child, a transpersonal relationship has been reached. The teacher and learner must discover together the background out of which any distortion may be emerging. It is necessary to understand the specific background of a distorted process in order to choose appropriate intervention (Clarkson, 1997; Tenzer, 1983).

The study and treatment of any academic or affective disorders demands a regard for ". . . complex patterns of communicational inference . . ." (Stone & Reid, 1994, p. 75).

In addition, the group can be a powerful vehicle in guiding learning. It can have more impact on each of its members than would be accorded to a single member. Members construct their socioemotional knowledge in group interactions. Dialogue, in dyadic or small group situations, may co-construct more advanced knowledge structures during problem solving by considering each other's statements, actions, and gestures. Success in a group intervention approach allows the members to be "consultants" in identifying problem sources and problem solutions. Group members generate target behaviors. With proper support and training in problem definition, the group members become engaged in a sense of personal control and responsibility (Henker, Whalen, & Hinshaw, 1980; Johnston & Johnston, 1984).

Support from others must be gradually withdrawn in order for the learner to internalize and take control of knowledge and knowledge acquisition processes. Learners are systematically brought to responsible self-direction needed to construct meaning of an ongoing activity. They eventually come to take on greater responsibility for transforming the understanding of their activities to new situations (Stone, 1998).

However, only when accurate feedback is provided does the opportunity to work with someone facilitate performance over working alone. Vague or confusing explanations do not bring about consistently correct performance. Social collaborative processes influence whether or not a new solution to a problem emerges, solidifies, and survives. For example, children who generate correct strategies may abandon them if other people do not respond positively. Recognition, reward, punishment, and forgiveness are involved in the assessment of whether a child's actions are responsible or irresponsible.

> To recognize, discuss, elicit, model, reward, or honor responsible behavior is more constructive than to deplore, punish, or forgive irresponsible behavior. (Pritchard, 1998, p. 50)

In guiding children to assume responsibility for their actions, the possibility of partial voluntary choice should be taken into account. Pure accidents, full voluntariness, and all stages in between have got to be considered. Serious consideration of this continuum changes the appropriateness of praise or blame.

The developing child does not have the physical, emotional, or cognitive capacities of the mature adult, which can mean that children do not deserve the same blame as an adult. (Pritchard, 1998, p. 40)

Taking responsibility involves shared expectations. All involved must understand what activities will take place and their roles in those activities. As children join in shared expectations, they benefit from others' responsible behavior and learn to make their own contributions. In so doing, they become part of the dialogue they are participating in.

Three overlapping dynamics reflect this process. As learners engage with a dialogic learning task, they jointly construct meaning. As they work collaboratively, they learn from and with others in the joint encounters. As personal interpretations are shared, self-expression is discovered (Pritchard, 1998).

The quality of adult-child interactions and child-child interactions in any intervention approach has considerable importance. Formal analyses of these interactions would focus on their structures, functions, and content. In order to define academic and social skills, it is necessary to determine how and by whom the value of a given skill is evaluated (Stone & Conca, 1993; Bhavnagri & Samuels, 1996).

> . . . the value and meaning of a particular skill actually may be assessed from a number of different perspectives including: 1) the effect of the overall functioning of a group from the point of view of an adult (e.g., the teacher's assessment of appropriate skills for the classroom); 2) the effect on the youth's social standing from the point of view of his or her peers; 3) the effect on the youth's own feelings of social competence and belonging. (Bhavnagri & Samuels, 1996, p. 221)

How children question, approach, and respond to adults and peers must be carefully attended to. Negotiating meaning with others allows continual reconstruction of a sense of self in that environment. Children learn what they are capable of, who they are, and who they may become. Diverse opinions must be appropriately invited and affirmed.

> The self does not simply reflect social forces; rather, it represents an intrinsic growth process whose tendency is toward integration of one's own experiences and actions with one's sense of relatedness to the selves of others. (Oldfather & Dahl, 1994, p. 150)

DIALOGIC PROBLEMS OF CHILDREN WITH LEARNING/BEHAVIOR DISORDERS

Intervention dialogues can point to the ways in which children regulate their responses and processing as well as form and elaborate relationships. They also indicate how children make intentional communications a part of their

Table 5.3 Development of Dialogue

Stage	Response	Conscious manipulation	Collaboration	Awareness
SENSORIMOTOR	Response to the specific movements of others	Conscious manipulation and/or imitation of the movements of others	Collaboration in the relationships among one's own movements and those of others	Awareness of the coordination among one's movements and the cause and effect of sensations and movement in an interaction
basic motor relfexes				**object permanence**
PREOPERATIONAL	Response to the specific symbolic functions of others	Conscious manipulation and/or imitation of the symbolic functions of others	Collaboration in the relationships among one's own symbolic functions and those of others	Awareness of the coordination among one's symbolic function and the cause and effect of symbols in an interaction
private meaning of symbols				**social language**
CONCRETE OPERATIONAL	Response to the specific part-whole transformations of others	Conscious manipulation and/or imitation of the part-whole transformations of others	Collaboration in the relationships among one's own part-whole transformations and those of others	Awareness of the coordination among one's transformations and the cause and effect of transformations in an interaction
part-whole relationships				**conservation (ability to objectify actions)**
FORMAL OPERATIONAL	Response to the specific ideas and reflections of others	Conscious manipulation and/or imitation of the ideas and reflections of others	Collaboration in the relationships among one's own ideas and reflections and those of others	Awareness of the coordination among one's ideas and reflections and the cause and effect of ideas in an interaction
hypothetical, propositional thought				**true reflection**

patterns of mental organization represent and elaborate their experiences, and differentiate their representations. Those dialogues that allow children to actively discover and actively construct knowledge in the context of their own experiences can promote self-sufficiency and assertiveness (Greenspan, 1997).

Learning and behavioral problems result if there are serious retreats from these intersubjective relationships. They can also arise from early interrupted dialogues. Disturbances may arise if children are unable to find and maintain the proper balance between self and other. A continuing confusion about this balance may cause interferences and interruptions of growth. A lack in a belief in their own self-regulation can cause defensive behaviors (Perls, 1980; Jacobs, 1989; Hycner, 1990).

> . . . many of these children experience significant limitations in language comprehension, memory, attention, pragmatics, and/or self-reflection and self-control that might interfere with the cognitive and communicational demands of scaffolded instruction. (Stone, 1998, p. 360)

Genuine dialogue has great value for children with learning/ behavior disorders. The quality of child-adult, as well as child-peer, interactions is of crucial importance in any intervention with such children (Stone & Conca, 1993; Stone, 1998; Butler, 1998).

Interactional teaching approaches have been designed to help children with learning/behavior disorders make integrated use of background knowledge in their meaning-making processes. These approaches are characterized by a focus on the importance of both graduated assistance and the role of adult-child dialogue. They have particular significance for instructional contingencies as these approaches consider communicational and interpersonal dynamics. Dialogue, collaboration, and interactive learning characterize all good strategy instruction (Stone, 1998).

Learning outcomes are mediated by classroom dynamics such as teacher attitude toward individual learners, teacher willingness to provide needed educational alternatives, learner's engaged time on academic tasks, and teacher-child-peer interactions. Effective interventions for children with learning/ behavior disorders demand neutralizing negative environmental attitudes, perceptions, and behaviors. Direct, positive feedback and task restructuring can increase constructing and constructive active time-on-task. Peer teaching and cooperative learning arrangements encourage healthy dialogue (Wood & Swan, 1978; Lago-DeLello, 1998).

Children with learning/behavior disorders will achieve success to the degree that they effectively interact with those in their environment. They respond best in situations in which they are allowed to observe skills that are modeled and mediated through an interaction of describing, elaborating, questioning, and prompting. The mediation is open-ended with questions that call for the child's opinions, recall, and reflection. Prompts are cues that gradually guide the child to more sophisticated, elaborate responses. Feedback must parallel the development and sophistication of the learner as well as the learner's background knowledge of the skills or concepts being learned. Directive feedback is needed for those learners who cannot self-regulate the learning process because of difficulty accessing background knowledge, short-term memory problems, and/or difficulty connecting and associating information. Not only does it provide help in the direct identification of the problem and recommendations for solutions, it also provides modeling and coaching in applying any solution as needed (Ellis, 1998).

Question-answer strategies must be seen in the total sphere of problem solving. In learning question-answer strategies the student must understand that questioning is a request for information and that, if the question is answerable, whether the source of information needed to answer the question resides in the self or in some external source (Gavelek & Raphael, 1982).

> Learners must become familiar with the various functional relationships that exist between questions and their responses. Learners must be aware of the following ideas: There are questions for which no answers exist. The response source for some questions resides in one's mind or is a part of one's background knowledge. The response source may sometimes consist of partial knowledge, which should be recognized as such. One must often search the external environment for appropriate information sources, and these sources may be another individual or an inanimate source, such as a reference book. One must often integrate information from a number of different information sources to adequately respond to a question. (Gavelek & Raphael, 1982, p. 76)

Prompts, cues, and questions that help a learner identify the problem and formulate a personal solution are effective if the learner is relatively able to gain insight and correct it or invent alternatives to addressing the problem. Improved performance will extend to willingness to take risks and confidence. If children have few opportunities to confront the views of others, they may be limited in adaptively modifying personal perspective. If these children also have few opportunities to use their personal perspectives in new realms of knowledge, cognitive development may be hindered (Gordon, 1988).

In addition, maladaptive social behaviors and the absence of satisfying interpersonal relationships are often characteristic of children with learning/behavior disorders. One possible cause of the unpopularity often experienced by children in the latter group may be their inability to understand the role of the other person in a social interaction.

Social competence is

> the ability to discriminate situations in terms of response requirements, as well as the ability to emit appropriate responses. This requires the ability to identify

and interpret social problem-solving variables that define social task parameters and influence task difficulty. Social problem-solving variables can be conceptualized as variables that help one determine how difficult it will be to produce an effective social response as well as which response might be most appropriate. (Larson & Gerber, 1987, p. 202)

Adaptive behaviors are the result of responses made, through biological competence, to environmental pressures. Sensory deficits or physical impairments may cause children to suffer from a disruption of physical experience. Disadvantaged environments may cause children to have severe problems with regard to social experience. Learning/behavior disordered children may experience mismatches between their abilities and the challenges made by society, or between their needs and the support provided by society. Many academic and affective problems have their roots in the absence of confirmation or even active disconfirmation. Defensible evidence indicate that often both parents and teachers adopt an interaction style that is less challenging to children with learning/behavior disorders than with average-achieving children of comparable age and general ability (Friedman, 1990; Stone & Conca, 1993).

Summary

The development of self emerges from the need to replace merging with the environment with self-other separation. Study of this developmental process identifies the points when children are capable of more and more contact. Children come to an increasingly deeper realization of how the self is different from the environment.

Self then, is developmentally apt figure formation . . . [it] is the system of present contacts and the agent of change. (Latner, 1984, p. 103)

The functions of contact, awareness, and dialogue can only be understood in light of individual-environment relationships. The kinds and processes of these functions are exhibited by children as they try to identify and make meaning of the various needs that figure in their life situations (Frew, 1986).

contacting and awareness . . . [are] . . . involved in a developmental process: the development of one's uniquely human becoming. It is not enough to say that contact and awareness serve our biological and emotional needs. There appears to be a kind of ontological imperative, an urge toward growth, so that these processes operate at increasingly finer levels of complexity and abstraction from biology. Contact and awareness are not merely the processes that express the dynamic relation between stasis and growth; they are themselves spiraling developmental processes, always emerging and transcending. The epitome of their development is lived through in the dialogic relation. (Jacobs, 1989, p. 63)

All contact and awareness occurs within a dialogical context. Following this, a learning model demands that the relational be placed at the center of the intervention work.

> . . . all dialogue is contact—not all contact is dialogue. There are innumerable ways of making contact, but it is a rare event to have a mutual and genuine dialogue with another. (Hycner, 1990, p. 44)

Awareness, contact, and dialogue are central mechanisms of growth and development. They are basic to human development. Even very young children regulate their behavior through these mechanisms. How children go about making discoveries, encounters, and exchanges indicates the level of understanding they have of their problems (Brown & Palincsar, 1982).

All intervention must be seen within the context of a general dialogical approach. It needs to be always grounded in the intersubjective field. All strategies must arise out of the context of the relationship between the child and others in his or her environment (Hycner, 1985).

CONSIDERATIONS FOR DIALOGUE FROM A PIAGETIAN VIEWPOINT

Stage	Stage-salient skills	Questions
Sensorimotor	Sensations, Movements, Sensory perceptions	Does the gestural system exist in complex form?
		Do the breadth and range of gestures express affect as well as cognitive themes?
		Are countergestures reoccurring in which others respond non-verbally to the child's initiatives, and vice versa?
		When the child experiences intense affect and stress, does the gestural system remain stable?
Preoperational	Pretend play, Imitation, Imagery, Graphic imagery, Language	Does the symbolic system exist in complex form?
		Do the breadth and range of symbols express affect as well as cognitive themes?
		Are countersymbols occurring in which others respond referentially to the child's initiatives and vice versa?

		When the child experiences intense affect and stress, does the symbolic system remain stable?
Concrete Operational	Classification, Seriation, Reversibility, Conservation, Decentration	Does the transformational system exist in complex form?
		Do the breadth and range of the transformations express affect as well as cognitive themes?
		Are countertransformations occurring in which others respond with logical part-whole analyses to the child's initiatives and vice versa?
		When the child experiences intense affect and stress, does the transformational system remain stable?
Formal Operational	Hypothetical, Propositional, and Proportional thinking	Does the ideational system exist in complex form?
		Do the breadth and range of the ideational system express affect as well as abstract cognitive themes?
		Are counterhypotheses occurring in which others respond with abstract thought to the child's initiatives, and vice versa?
		When the child experiences intense affect and stress, does the ideational system remain stable?

Chapter 6

CHILDREN WITH LEARNING/BEHAVIOR DISORDERS

The treatment of children with learning/behavior disorders is
now seen as originating from "the study of the origins and
course of individual patterns of behavior adaptation with
special attention accorded to maladjustment."
(Gelfand & Peterson, 1985, p. 81)

Throughout its history, special education has endeavored to increase its understanding of the effects of early school failure on the development of children's cognition, motivation, and knowledge bases. Developing methods of identification and intervention have been two fundamental concerns of the field since its inception. The very definitions of learning/behavior disorders as well as effective intervention have been under careful scrutiny for many decades.

A historic review of educational practices for cognitively and affectively different children finds that for many decades many psychologists and special educators have held much dissatisfaction with traditional assessment and intervention methods. Many believe that traditional, deficiency-based intervention may be contributing to cognitive and affective delays rather than remediating them. They are arbitrary and stigmatizing, often leading such children to a self-fulfilling prophecy of failure. Continual failure may lead to diminished cognitive and affective development, poor academic functioning, and weak self-concept.

Psychology and education have long supported the belief in the existence of critical periods that favor development. Perplexity has arisen as to whether the hindrance or upsetting of these developmental factors can lead to either an arrest in development at certain levels, or to possible irremediable delays. Recent research indicates that an acceleration of the rate of cognitive growth is possible, and that delays can be partially overcome (Henley, 1980).

Currently there are two emerging views that have made professionals reexamine appropriate intervention for special education children. Learning/

behavior disorders are now being interpreted in terms of difficulties in self-regulating and metacognitive processes with a recognition of their multivariate composition. These processes attend to the awareness children have of what they know, how they know, and the conditions under which they know. At the same time, intervention is being redefined in structuralistic and constructivist precepts. More recent conceptualizations include an exploration of the role of context in determining the severity of a learning/behavior problem. Diagnosis has become more than a labeling or categorization; it is a differentiated description of person-in-context (Meltzer, 1993).

Traditional approaches to academic and adjustment problems hold strictly to matters of cognitive ability deficits, or to discrepancies between expected ability and actual classroom achievement. In contrast to these, constructivistic, self-regulated learning approaches view difficulties as a set of barriers that are either experiential, cognitive, or communicative. That is, children may lack experiences per se, the understanding of their experiences, or the ability to share their experiences. Overcoming or ameliorating these difficulties calls for intervention that provides children with the experiences, thinking skills, and communication skills that are missing. It thus makes available to children opportunities for organizing their experiences into meaningful wholes (Pullis & Smith, 1981; Cicchetti & Toth, 1998).

In studying the attributes of children with learning/behavior disorders, it is useful to look at problem sources as well as problem solutions. The manner in which these children receive and process information is dependent on their antecedent attributional styles. Within the rich conceptual framework of self-regulated learning, the dimensions of these problems can be arrayed along a continuum from relatively unchangeable to relatively changeable (Henker, Whalen, & Hinshaw, 1980).

In addition, individual differences can be studied from a continuum ranging from adaptive to dysfunctional patterns. In fact, some learning difficulties have been associated with a degree of undetected psychiatric diagnoses. For example, some types of children and adolescents with academic disability may be at risk for particular emotional or behavioral disorders. Children in these subgroups may show symptoms that would warrant a diagnosis such as Attention Deficit Hyperactive Disorder (ADHD) or depression. However, intervention for these deficits have concentrated primarily on direct, educational intervention rather than on conjoint attempts with psychotherapy (Cowan, 1978; San Miguel, Forness, & Kavale, 1996).

> The need for collaborative efforts between professionals in mental health and learning disabilities may be the most important implications of a psychiatric comorbidity hypothesis. (San Miguel, Forness, & Kavale, 1996, p. 259)

A PIAGETIAN PERSPECTIVE

An explanation of all diagnostic and remedial possibilities of learning/ behavior disorders can be provided by Piaget's theory. It offers well-defined descriptions of developmental processes, transition periods, and dynamic adaptive systems. It holds as its center the meanings that children assign to the experiences they are undergoing. All the studies done on the development of cognition make very clear the role that the children's own activity plays in the elaboration of their knowledge acquisition (Anthony, 1956; Piaget, 1970a).

> Piaget's theory is qualitative and describes the characteristics of cognition. For Piaget the issue is not how smart or how slow an individual child is but how the child interprets experience. He is interested in the type of mental operations a child acquires as he or she matures and interacts with the environment. (Henley, 1980, p. 6)

Since many children with learning/behavior disorders have experienced developmental histories that have led to serious academic and social-emotional dysfunction, attempts have been made to provide descriptions of the cognitive stage disorders they manifest (Jones, 1992)

Inhelder (1968) was the first to investigate the possibility of adapting Piagetian research to mental diagnosis. Examining the possible variations of psychopathological difficulties that arise from deficient construction of cognitive structures, she concluded that Piaget's model of cognitive development is powerful ". . . as an instrument of analysis in the diagnosis of reasoning in retardates . . ." (p. 61). Her research is based on the belief that ". . . operational stages could furnish a model of development against which deficiencies could be seen as arrestations and abnormal fixations . . ." (p. 18). Since then, children manifesting all kinds and degrees of special needs have been exposed to both assessment and instructional methods reflecting Piaget's approach.

Studies show that the mental disorders displayed by children fall into two broad categories: (1) those that reflect simple fixations or arrestations at some earlier stage of development and (2) those that reflect poor coordination of stage level abilities and that may show functional discontinuity only under stressful conditions. These may be seen in the form of emotional overreactions, attention disorders, or instability.

Children who show lags in stage development follow the same evolution process as normal children but at a slower rate and often with immature fixations. They vary in the rates at which they pass through these stages and the ceiling they reach in any given stage. Achievement of final equilibrium is often problematic. When matched with normals of similar mental ages, these children perform at approximately similar levels of stage development. However, their reasoning shows incomplete operational construction. Those severely involved are not capable of operational thought but remain in a sensorimotor mode using either motor or perceptual data for problem solving. Those moderately involved are limited to preoperational, prelogical thought. Those who are mildly involved may be able to reach the level of concrete operations, but never attain the level of formal or hypotheticodeductive operations (Inhelder, 1968; McCormick et al., 1990).

Children have distinctly and qualitatively different structures from adults. A basic factor of a developmental intervention is an understanding of the meaning-making strategies children use in each cognitive stage. Each stage of development has distinctive mediating processes. The meaning-making strategies of each of the stages of cognitive development bind the quality of mental activity. New cognitive structures are organized through the processes of assimilation and accommodation. In spite of any slow rate or distortion of intellectual growth, continued conceptual development is possible through appropriate environmental stimulation (Henley, 1980).

From such a viewpoint, learning/behavior disorders would be defined and assessed in terms of developmental structures rather than deficits. Consequently they are seen as developmentally delayed rather than deficient.

> . . . the age at which different children reach the stages may vary. In some social environments the stages are accelerated, whereas in others they are more or less retarded. This differential development shows that stages are not purely a question of maturation of the nervous system but are dependent on interaction with the social environment and with experience in general. (Piaget, 1971, p. 7)

Some cognitive and affective problems of children with learning/behavior disorders can be directly related to a lack of normal progress through age-appropriate stages and periods of cognitive development. Cognitive structures are often fragmented and do not share an interconnectedness. Inadequacies in sensorimotor performance, object permanence, use of symbol functions, conservation, operational thinking, and use of language may cause wide peaks and valleys in the cognitive structures (Gordon & Cowan, 1983).

Resistance to the incorporation of actions, feelings, and/or thoughts into a higher-order structural self-system indicates some form of disorder. Even though some life events are interpreted in terms of the existing structures, they may not be revised at the end of the original experience as children advance to more sophisticated stages. The resistance to their being assimilated to the more advanced structure of the self-system takes the form of dissociations. The self-system has not been enabled to assimilate the dissociated content into a more mature structure. The dissociated experiences may simply remain fixated at an earlier stage or they may change with development but in some aberrant manner.

The application of Piagetian theory to these children has led to the conclusions that some of them (1) may move through one or more stages at a normal pace but may be delayed in attaining others, (2) show differences in the routes that are taken to attain the same stages, or (3) do have stage abilities but may not use them appropriately. Often the information-processing approaches they use do not appear to exhaust, or even tap, their intellectual capacities (Swanson, 1987; Henley, 1980).

Of equal importance, a diagnosis of learning/behavior disorders becomes more comprehensive when an analysis of self-regulation is included. This would enable the determination of the different types and degrees of the condition. That is, the study of learning/behavior disorders must come not only from the standpoint of delay of stage development but also in terms of deviations of intellectual self-regulation. What needs to be determined along with the actual level of thought is its equilibrium, its mobility, and its consolidation relative to experience. Precise structures as well as the gradual evolution of particular concepts of logic can be detected and used as norms against which to measure individual differences (Inhelder, 1968).

> Most fundamentally, a genetic approach is characterized by seeing all behavior as relative to a mode of elaboration, and consequently interpreting any reaction as a function of the constructive process from which it results. . . . (Inhelder, 1968, p. 306)

Additionally, all children are open, active, self-regulating systems. Their progressive changes in the processes of active adaptation characterize their mental development. Normally developing children rapidly go through several successive stages of progression that separates self from earlier forms of reasoning. This growth in self-regulation of operations marks greater mobility and stability of logic. Normal reasoning becomes more and more mobile and increasingly wider.

Normal development is evidenced by the presence of stage-appropriate structures and proper balance of self-regulating functions. Structures are organized patterns of physical and/or mental action and provide children with systemized frameworks to make experience meaningful. What is helpful about using a developmental approach is that it provides some insight into the processes and mechanisms that children have at their disposal to organize and assimilate knowledge (Gordon & Cowan, 1983; Reid, 1993).

Any structuring must be addressed by the functioning, and any functioning by the structuring. Therefore, it is important to keep in mind that learning/behavior disorders cannot be defined as a simple deficiency in a particular cognitive stage. They also represent a deficiency in the ability to make a smooth coordination of cognitive functioning. They are best characterized by poor coordination of several mental components and/or cognitive areas. It is critical to know what mental processes underlie learning performance and to determine how accurately and efficiently those processes are performed. Children with learning/behavior disorders:

> . . . show wide peaks and valleys in their cognitive structures, so that diagnosis is not a matter simply of labeling a child in a given stage, but providing a differential description of levels of functioning in different domains. (Gordon & Cowan, 1983, p. 21)

Children, at any point in their development, may fail to reach adaptive solutions to stage-salient issues. When a solution in a current stage-salient issue is reached, reorganization and reworking of past developmental weaknesses are possible. In addition, it is necessary to consider the effect of any individual child's attitudes, beliefs, expectancies, and attributes in order to understand and predict any atypical behavior patterns (Pullis & Smith, 1981; Cicchetti & Toth, 1998).

There are three aspects to a structural deficit. The first, constitutional and maturational aspects, are determined by observing visual-spatial processing, auditory-verbal processing, underactivity-overactivity, and motor planning and sequencing. The second, interactive aspects, are determined by observing relationships between child and caregivers. The third, dynamic fantasy aspects, are determined by observing how a child's pictures of the world take shape, that is, his or her personal narratives with the events and people in them. With this knowledge, psychologists and educators can eventually create in a child an ability for self-observation (Greenspan, 1997).

> If the foci on structural change were systematically approached as the content is approached, and if our theoretical model could focus on issues of structural development as well as it does on dynamic issues, we would have a more complete model of the therapeutic process. (p. 378)

Children with problems that are essentially social/emotional have structures that oftentimes (1) are fragmented, (2) resist modification, (3) lack specialization, (4) become extremely repetitive and result in anxiety, (5) are sensorimotor in nature, (6) have no or little use of verbal anticipation, or (7) assimilate objects in a manner that distorts them. Their cognitive structures tend to be more fragmented and uncoordinated when compared to their normal agemates (Gordon & Cowan, 1983).

They often develop belief systems that can have a negative effect on achievement-adaptation strategies. Usually unaware of their own failures to comprehend, they often lack self-monitoring skills that can be used to discern inconsistent information.

It is not unusual to find that many of these children retain some of the sensorimotor qualities such as the absence of symbolism, primitive notions of causality, and actions that produce circular results in their behaviors. For example, it is often difficult for these children to experiment with new means in order to obtain a desired goal.

In addition, symbolic play is crucial to the mastering of social/emotional conflict. Children with learning/behavior disorders commonly evidence an impoverishment of figural representation of external elements and an inability to internally imagine actions. Disturbances also are seen in structures of verbal anticipation. Structures about the self and about the other are often intermingled, making pretending meager and/or difficult (Gordon & Cowan, 1983).

From the toddler years throughout adulthood, there are three symbolizing styles associated with atypical growth. In the first, there is a fixation of existing meanings preventing new symbols from being constructed. An inner cognitive orientation exists. Overassimilation prevails. In the second style, there is a fixation on the cognition, on the attributes of others in constructing symbols. This prevents or dulls any contribution from personal psychic reality. An outer cognitive orientation develops. Overaccommodation prevails. In the third, excessive shifts between personal meaning and external attributes occur, preventing the two from being integrated. At this point the capacity to perform and/or imitate an action executed by another has been developed. However, the actions are not yet incorporated into a personal repertoire. For self-other separation, mental representations have to be encoded into long-term memory. A sense of psychological relationship between self and the person who performed the original action is essential. Disturbances arise because there is a lack of opportunity to assimilation and accommodation either generally or within a specific domain. There is a strong and nonadaptive predominance of either assimilation or accommodation, or there is difficulty coordinating reasoning across different knowledge domains (Furth, 1983).

Although children with learning/behavior disorders do self-regulate to some degree, lack of specific skills in self-regulatory processes are commonly recognized in them. In addition, they often develop belief systems that can have a negative effect on achievement-adaptation strategies. Proper remediation of cognitive thinking behavior would foster more successful social and academic experiences for these children (O'Leary, 1980; Meltzer, 1993; Stone & Conca, 1993; Swanson & Alexander, 1997).

Many developmentalists, following a Piagetian view, consider egocentrism and decentration vital concepts in the cause of social difficulties. Children with learning/behavior disorders may experience self-image disturbances, difficulty regulating self-esteem, and difficulty with self-assertion. These disturbances stem from difficulties in structural and functional development, in physical and social environments, and in the interaction between the two. On the one hand, rather than being open to change, structures are repetitive and unmodifiable in new situations. Behavior becomes perseverative, often resulting in anxiety.

Deficits result in general sensorimotor acquisitions, coordination of action, object permanence, manipulation of objects, symbol formation, fluid imagery, conservation, and assimilation/accommodation imbalance. On the other hand, the result of functional imbalance results in difficulties in distinguishing between inner and outer realities (Gordon & Cowan, 1983).

When these children do engage in meaning-making, mental reflections, and problem solving, they tend to use behaviors characteristic of younger children. In spite of sensory dysfunctions, physical disabilities, slow rates of intellectual growth, learning disabilities or emotional disorders, these children are capable of continued cognitive development (Pullis & Smith, 1981; Cicchetti & Toth, 1998).

The bases upon which children with learning/behavior disorders understand and organize their meaning-making demand full attention. They must be seen, first of all ". . . as struggling to understand and organize their own experience—even their painful and anomalous experiences . . ." (Rogers & Kegan, 1991, p. 130).

PROBLEMS WITH REGULATORY FUNCTIONS

A relationship exists between regulatory problems and learning and behavior difficulties. If functioning normally, it leads to an integrated affective core. In a healthy interaction, as children use the sensory pathways, the environment helps them organize their early experiences. Rather than overwhelm them, the nurturing environment provides children with individually fashioned, age-appropriate experiences so that they can develop early regulation and interest in it. Children are then able to form satisfactory attachments, reciprocal cause-effect interactions, and cohesive cognitive, behavioral, and affective patterns.

> In the optimal case, the environment ameliorates the early sensory decoding difficulty, strengthens sensory processing in other modes, and supports a representational interpretative system that can use higher level abstractions to make sense, even out of a "somatic underbelly," which tends to send up confusing sensations. (Greenspan, 1997, p. 123)

To understand an individual child's regulatory profile, the first step is to determine which sensory modalities and motor patterns will enable that child to be more easily attentive and which ones need extra practice. Most significant is to appropriately open and bring closure to exchanges of communication

> . . . first on a behavioral, gestural level, then on a symbolic level, then at an internal level where the person sustains his attention by asking himself rhetorical

questions. The key is for the individual to use purposeful activity and purpose-ful thought, and string together these thoughts and activities as a way of sustain-ing attention. Active problem-solving is better than passive listening for the regulatory-disordered child. (Greenspan, 1997, p. 96)

An intact visual-spatial modality helps children organize and compare what is being experienced in that modality and gradually learn to abstract the di-mensions of emotional intensity connected to them. It is a continuous modal-ity. An underlying biophysical-developmental vulnerability in visual-spatial processing can result in affective disorders. Intensity of emotion is compre-hended but often without meaning. The self can become fragmented in terms of affect proclivities (Greenspan, 1997).

Visual-spatial difficulties can result in such conditions as affect disorders, anxiety disorders, depression, and manic-depressive states. Children suffering from these conditions are often fragmented and displaced in time and space. They fail to reach the integrity of their representational systems because of their difficulties in creating visual, tactile, olfactory, auditory, and affective images in their own minds.

An intact auditory-vocal-verbal modality is used to describe, represent, and play out degrees of feelings. The auditory-verbal modality tends to be discreet and segmented. An underlying biophysical-developmental vulnerability in auditory-vocal-verbal processing can lead to thought disorders. While affec-tive meaning is available, the intensity of affect may not be. The self can be-come fragmented in terms of its levels of meaning. Difficulties in the auditory-vocal-verbal modality can cause a lack of emotional detail and specific affects. Children may cognitively know how they should feel but their feelings are lacking subtle sensitivity. They also tend to lack emotional intensity or sa-liency. They need help in identifying and taking possession of their feelings. To communicate gradations of feelings segmented, verbal meanings can be used in novel ways to help them describe, represent, and play out degrees of feelings.

Good communication can be used broadly and flexibly to convey all the cognitive and emotional themes. In any dialogue between adults and children, care must be taken to see that communication is reciprocal and not misinter-preted. Children must be able to decode and understand the rhythm of audi-tory stimuli, the meaning of visual cues, symbolic referents, linguistics, and communicate across time and space. Normal children have a wide range of abilities to convey cognitive and emotional interactions. Children who use a limited, ritualistic communication style are not making good contact with their environments. They may become constricted and limited in their incorpora-tion of cognitive or emotional themes (Greenspan, 1997).

Difficulty	Pathology	Result	Intervention
Visual-spatial	Anxiety disorders, depression, manic-depression	Fragmentation, loss of big picture	Help the child picture his feelings; create a mental, multisensory image
Auditory verbal	Lack of abundant sense of emotional detail	Sees the big picture, good at representing affects	Increase sensitivity to detail and specific people

In addition, many children who fail in school fall into two general types of regulatory patterns, overactivity and underactivity. Two characteristic patterns related to overactivity or hypersensitivity are the fearful and cautious type of child and the negativistic and defiant type. The former type, marked by excessive worries as well as shyness, is intensified by caregivers who use vacillating responses (overindulgent or overprotective on the one hand and punitive and intrusive on the other). Such children can develop flexibility and assertiveness by being gradually encouraged to explore new experiences within gentle but firm limits.

The defiant type, marked by stubborn, controlling behaviors, is intensified by caregivers who use excessively demanding, overstimulating, or punitive responses. These children need intervention that soothes and empathizes as it avoids power struggles and allows different representation of anger and annoyance.

Characteristic patterns connected with underreactivity include the withdrawn and the self-absorbed types. At first, children who withdraw may seem apathetic, easily exhausted, and may show a lack in motor exploration as well as in responsiveness to sensations and social advances. Rather than having this low-keyed behavior reinforced, it is important that such children experience intense interaction and emotional engagement with highly salient persons and objects in their lives.

Self-absorbed children, while being creative and imaginative, are more in tune with their own sensations, thoughts, and emotions rather than the communications of others. Preoccupied or confusing environmental communications increase self-absorbtion. It can be countered by communications that are clearly marked by their openness and closure as well as their balance between fantasy and reality. Self-absorbed children must experience a sense of collaboration and shared reality.

Highly active, impulsive, and aggressive behaviors are often the result of a combination of underreactivity to touch and sound with poor motor modulation and motor planning. Seeking contact and stimulation, such children appear to lack caution, which often leads to destructive behavior. Intensification of this pattern comes about through poor limit and boundary setting coupled with over-or understimulation. Intervention that offers firm structure and limits, opportunities for consistently warm engagement, and well-modulated activity is called for (Greenspan, 1997).

When environmental conditions impart difficulty rather than flexibility, faulty character formation results. For example:

1. Children who are overreactive to touch or sound and have stronger auditory processing abilities and relatively weak visual-spatial ones tend toward the hysterical, depressive, and anxiety disorders. Those who have difficulty with movement in space tend toward phobic disorders.
2. Children who are underreactive to sensations and have low motor tone tend toward more withdrawn behavior. They tend to escape into fantasy, and, in the extreme, evidence more schizoid and autistic patterns.
3. Children with hyperreactivity to sensations along with stimulus-craving patterns, coupled with high activity levels and organized gross motor patterns, tend toward risk taking, and, if there is emotional deprivation, antisocial patterns.
4. Children with relatively stronger visual-spatial processing and overreactivity to certain sensations tend toward patterns characterized by negativism, stubbornness, and compulsiveness. (adapted from Greenspan, 1997)

Children who manifest regulatory problems tend to have a more difficult time in their interactions with others. Their maturational deviations may contribute one or several of the following patterns:

1. Over- or underreactive to loud or high- or low-pitched noises.
2. Over- or underreactive to bright lights or new and striking visual images (e.g., colors, shapes, complex fields).
3. Tactile defensiveness (e.g., overreactive to changing clothes, bathing, stroking of the arms, legs, or trunk, avoids touching "messy" textures, etc.) and/or underreactive to touch or pain.
4. Under- or overreactive to movement in space (e.g., brisk horizontal or vertical movements such as tossing a child in the air, playing merry-go-round, jumping, etc.).
5. Under- or overreactive to odors.
6. Under- or overreactive to temperature.
7. Poor motor tone (gravitational or postural insecurity, oral-motor difficulties–avoids certain textures).
8. Less than age-appropriate motor planning skills (e.g., complex motor patterns such as alternating hand banging).
9. Less than age-appropriate ability to modulate motor activity (not secondary to anxiety or interactive difficulties).
10. Less than age-appropriate fine motor skills.
11. Less than age-appropriate auditory-verbal processing or articulation capacities.

12. Less than age-appropriate visual-spatial processing capacities.
13. Less than age-appropriate capacity to attend and focus without undue distractibility (not related to anxiety, interactive difficulties, or clear auditory-verbal or visual-spatial processing problems). (adapted from Greenspan, 1997)

In summary, effective assessment and treatment of these children can best be brought about by an in-depth study of their structure formation and modification. This would involve an examination of "structural level, intercoordination, differentiation, assimilation, and accommodation" (Gordon & Cowan, 1983, p. 3).

PROBLEMS WITH COGNITIVE FUNCTIONS

Deficits in the use of cognitive strategies are partly responsible for information-processing differences between children who manifest learning/behavior problems and those who do not. The former may inflexibly and inefficiently represent, process, and evaluate information in the content areas. They show differences in cognitive structures and in knowledge of relevant subject-matter areas when compared to the nondisordered. They may indeed have inadequate knowledge bases. Whether due to inadequate environmental opportunities or constitutional inadequacies, if a knowledge base is limited in a specific area, then ability to process elements in that area will be impaired. An increased knowledge base permits not only more advanced forms of knowledge but also greater flexibility to execute the performance elements (Kolligian & Sternberg, 1987).

As active but inefficient in the learning process, children with learning/behavior disorders are not always able to access the information-processing bases that they actually have. They often have difficulty in retaining information in memory while simultaneously processing the same or other information. With insufficient awareness of their own thoughts and behaviors, as well as incomplete mastery of underlying cognitive skills, they may evidence inefficient use of problem-solving strategies. They will continue to use poorly sequenced steps in problem solving or neglect essential problem-solving information. These children may also have difficulty using immediate feedback of the results of their efforts. As a result of these processing disorders, they have to exert more mental effort than would normal students (Masson, 1982; Short & Ryan, 1984).

Less able learners do not seem to have the self-regulatory skills that more able learners use to organize situational information. The poorer learners are usually unaware of personal failures to comprehend. They seem to (1) lack knowledge of the purpose of what they are learning, (2) lack sensitivity to the need to act strategically, (3) fail to evaluate the efficacy of the strategies they do use, (4) be unable to apply strategies spontaneously, and (5) rigidly apply the strategies they do use. In addition, they may be unmotivated to employ the strategies in which they are competent. They do not spontaneously use rehearsal or inference. Self-monitoring skills that can be used to discern inconsistent information are missing (Masson, 1982; Short & Ryan, 1984).

Characteristically, children with learning/behavior disorders do not engage in information-processing approaches that effectively use their intellectual potential. Learning/behavior disorders interrupt the coordination of self-regulatory mechanisms such as checking, monitoring, revising, and evaluating problem-solving efforts. Any disorder may limit the ability to cope with errors, to self-reinforce, to self-question, and to make predictions. This impairs the spontaneous use of previously learned strategies in new situations (Swanson, 1985; Swanson, H., 1987).

Although it may seem reasonable to suppose that learning/behavior disordered children do apply cognitive strategies, these strategies may be inefficient, ineffective, or inflexible, regardless of what behavior is observed. If they are inactive in cognitive responses, they may not necessarily lack ability but they may fail to spontaneously apply appropriate strategies in situations of uncertainty (Gerber, 1983).

Inadequate strategy use causes children to be unable to shift from one strategy to another, to abandon inappropriate strategies, and to process information with one strategy and then select another. Being able to consider several processing approaches in rapid succession in order to arrive at a solution to a problem is another serious struggle for these children. Attempting to assemble, adapt, alternate, assess, or abandon certain cognitive programs in the process of performing a task that is relatively simple to nondisordered children often leads learning/behavior disordered children to more failure.

> These include lack of awareness of their own limitations as problem solvers and of compensatory strategies to overcome such limitations, and a general lack of self-management techniques for monitoring and checking their own progress. (Brown & Palincsar, 1982, p. 3)

Children with learning/behavior disorders have difficulty with such elementary operations as identifying incoming information, deploying attention, and searching memory. They fail to show spontaneous cognitive strategies when needed and do not carefully plan out the strategies they do use. They lack use of various types of attentional strategies, have deficits in planning, monitoring, and checking their behaviors, and are slower to encode. They show these deficits, not because they cannot remember, but because they are often unaware of critical aspects of the task and of themselves as active participants. Even when they are capable of performing the strategies, they do not readily know how and when to use them (Brown & Palincsar, 1982; Glenn, Rueda, & Rutherford, 1934).

Consequently they may choose not to (1) adapt to an environment; (2) modify the environment to fit their needs, interests, and motives; or, (3) reject the present environment and select an alternative, more effective one. They may suffer from inaccurate information and knowledge of their own cognitive strategies, leaving them unable to efficiently transfer and refine their learning processes (Swanson, H., 1987).

Because they do not have sufficient awareness of their processes and/or their self-regulating mechanisms, children with learning/behavior disorders often have problems accessing and coordinating knowledge. They often have a reduced range of experience and therefore may suffer from a lack of familiarity with particular classes of tasks. Automatization becomes a slower and more gradual process. Difficulty with and aversion to novel information in the specific domain can be partially explained by (a) inefficient functioning of lower order (e.g., knowledge-acquisition) components, (b) deficient cognitive strategies, (c) inadequate knowledge base, or (d) specific automatization failure.

When a new task is initially confronted, or when an old task is confronted in a new situation, the task requires exercising one's ability to deal with novelty. If, either for reasons of inadequate environmental opportunities or for reasons of inadequacies in the functioning of knowledge-acquisition components, the knowledge base is limited in a specific domain, then processing in that domain will be impaired (Pullis & Smith, 1981; Swanson, H., 1993).

Because the mental activity of learning/behavior disordered children is not as expansive as their same age peers, there is a limit to the number of interactions that can enter its cognitive system. In addition, their ability to mentally reflect on personal interactions with the environment will vary in degree of complexity throughout their life spans. Any negative affect encountered when constructing meaning can decrease a desire to interact with the world. Rigid boundaries may be established to keep out the negativity (Brown & Palincsar, 1982).

A process approach focuses on activities that permit a search for underlying strategies that bear on behavior. It strives to create conscious meaning-making and meaning-following (Swanson, H., 1993).

In addition, a student must have a complete model of strategy use. Good strategy users have (a) a variety of strategies to accomplish a task, (b) specific strategies that can be integrated into high-order sequences that accomplish complex cognitive tasks, (c) metacognitive processes to regulate competent performance, (d) appropriate beliefs about the payoffs in the strategies they use, and (e) an adequate knowledge base. (Swanson, H., 1993, pp. 64–65)

PROBLEMS WITH SOCIAL FUNCTIONING

Parents and professionals have long been concerned about the association of social characteristics and behaviors of children with learning difficulties. Open to debate are question such as:

1. whether or not children with academic disabilities are predisposed to other disorders;
2. whether or not children with other disorders suffer coexisting academic disabilities; or
3. whether or not children have a common risk factor for a comorbid condition (adapted from San Miguel, Forness, & Kavale, 1996)

Since the mid-1980s developmental psychologists have demonstrated a growing attention in the social competence in children. Social competence refers to the capacity to comprehend and effectively cope with interpersonal events and objects. It is being viewed as dependent on relationships and its definition should not arise from the characteristics displayed by individual children or particular types of environments. It is best defined from the mismatches between what is wanted by any individual child and what is asked of him or her by the environment. Also involved in this definition is what that individual child is willing to display (Glenn, Rueda, & Rutherford, 1984).

Theories evolving from a constructivist, self-regulated learning basis propose that the beliefs children acquire about their skills and efforts impact on their achievement. Children who believe that their efforts are useful persist when faced with difficulty and achieve more academically then do learners of comparable ability without this belief. A corollary to this is that if children attribute their difficulties to controllable factors, they will persist under challenge.

> Adaptive behavior may involve a wide range of interpersonal, social-perceptual, attentional, organizational, or "practical" behaviors that help disabled students achieve a better fit with their academic context. In the contextual subtheory, adaptive behavior is vitally important to the intelligent functioning of learning disabled students; it is an integral part of the ultimate expression of learning disabilities in the classroom. (Kolligian & Sternberg, 1987, p. 16)

Positive affect, whether self-induced or externally induced, can influence the social problem solving of these children. It also stimulates the recall of positive material stored in the brain and results in more effective use of cognitive material. It may also influence self-regulation and self-determination (Bryan, Sullivan-Burstein, & Mathur, 1998).

Self-regulated learning basically concerns the personal awareness of one's systematic use of efficient strategies for adaptation as well as learning. It entails and integrates several aspects of personality development such as fear of failure, need for achievement, internal versus external locus of control, and levels of aspiration (Wiens, 1983).

Children who come from environments with dysfunctional patterns of child rearing may not learn to access their internal feeling states. For example, young children may not develop an initial sense of autonomy or separateness if their environments hold back support when any attempt at individuation is made. Or stress caused by an environment expecting too much too soon while providing insufficient emotional support may impair the ability to develop mutual trust and take responsibility in relationships. In like manner, adolescence represents another separation period. The adolescent must not only separate from parents but must test out the new identity in many relationships. Problems of acceptance and rejection may arise (Jones, 1992).

The overt and unmistakable deficits in social skills evidenced by children with learning/behavior disorders are attributed to difficulties with interpretation of social cues, inappropriate responses to social cues, as well as inability to discriminate social situations to fit into a group. These difficulties can put such children in jeopardy of school failure, serious mental issues, delinquency, or substance abuse (Scruggs, Mastropieri, & Sullivan, 1994).

Parents, psychologists, and school personnel are challenged by the tenuous self-esteem of children with learning/behavior disorders. Any difficulties in the psychological lives of these children may not receive attention until they experience school failure. By the time such children are seen for school assessment they may already have encountered much confusion, discouragement, confrontation, and anger. Yet, conscientious assessment will often reveal extreme mood swings, high anxiety, and depression (Solomon, 1997).

Structural abilities of the ego demand observation. Children with learning/behavior disorders may fail to see how they operate and form patterns of behavior. They may lack sufficient intrapsychic structures necessary to understand their own cognitions and emotions and those of others. Along with self awareness, learning to form and make better use of more advanced cognitive structures leads to ultimate flexibility (Greenspan, 1997).

Analyses of functional difficulties characterize these children as seriously failing in self/other differentiation. States of a relative lack of differentiation between self and other evolve to states characterized by a polarity. This polarity allows children to consistently order experience according to stable categories of internal and external, subjective and objective, self and other, imaginary and real. Constructing and maintaining social and personal realities are made possible by these categories. They allow for increasing self-regulation, self-reflection, planfulness, social acumen, and deeper appreciation of the goals of other people. Any disturbances may lead to profound disruptions to a sense of self-identity. Such disruptions occur when children either continually shape the outside world to internal structures (overassimilation), continually shape internal structures into conformity to the outside world (overaccommodation), or erratically vacillate between the two (Cowan, 1978; Rogers & Kegan, 1991; Gordon & Cowan, 1983).

Considerable evidence indicates that children with learning/behavior disorder are rated more disruptive, more hyperactive, spend less time in on-task behavior, emit more competitive and fewer reinforcing statements, are inaccurate in their comprehension of nonverbal communication, and make fewer and less effective social contact attempts. These are related, not only to the specific situation demands and contingencies, but also to the ability to understand, structure, and restructure social input in accordance with specific levels of cognitive development. How these children come to think about and understand the dynamics of interpersonal interactions is crucial to diagnosis. It is the children's developmental level of social cognition that mediates their interpretations of social objects and events as well as their social actions (Pullis & Smith, 1981).

Because they often do not experience normal expectations, children with learning/behavior disorders encounter unique difficulties with significant others in their lives that deeply impact on their cognition. There is clear evidence that mental health problems are linked to poor academic performance, school alienation, and delinquency. Pervasive effects on academic performance can be the result of the feelings held about the self as a learner. To avoid contributing to any lack of motivation and mental health problems, schools have the responsibility to facilitate self-regulating growth as children progress through school (Brown & Palincsar, 1982; Cicchetti & Toth, 1998).

With repeated adaptive attempts resulting in failure, learning/behavior disordered children are likely to believe their difficulties are insurmountable. Consequently, they may avoid becoming engaged in the adaptive, achievement-oriented behaviors that potentially could mitigate the severity of the disabilities (Kolligian & Sternberg, 1987).

Research strongly suggests that motivational problems experienced by children with learning/behavior disorders arise primarily from their early learning struggles. Serious self-doubts and negative belief systems can occur because of the repeated failures these children often live through. In addition, any experienced success is often attributed to external controls so that the buildup of positive belief systems is diminished. Overcoming difficulties is not perceived as within their capabilities. This external locus of control belief and lowered expectancy of success affects academic achievement and interferes with adaptive oriented behaviors. Diminished effort leads to performance levels below the actual capabilities of the students (Licht, 1983).

Repeated failure has often been cited as an underlying cause for motivational problems such as inattention and off-task behavior. Negative beliefs about the ability to achieve may ensue and if overgeneralized, little effort to problem solve may put forth. Doubts in intellectual ability arise. Consequently, they may develop negative beliefs about their ability to achieve and put forth little effort because they overgeneralize them. Many children with learning/behavior disorders are prone to see their failures in light of low ability rather than insufficient effort. They also tend not to take credit for their successes. Even if their participation in the learning process is active, it may be inefficient (Gordon & Cowan, 1983; Glenn, Rueda, & Rutherford, 1984; Licht, 1993; Meltzer, 1993; Wigg, 1993).

The drop-out rate for children who are labeled learning/behavior disordered has caused great concern. There are many unanswered questions about the motivational factors underlying school drop-out problems. For example, having knowledge of task demands and of appropriate learning strategies positively affects student motivation. On the other hand, a mismatch between children and the school environment has been theorized as possible cause for loss of motivation. Adolescents with problems often report that they drop out of school not only because of poor grades, but also because they experience the school setting as fruitless, humiliating, and anxiety-provoking (Fulk, Brigham, & Lohman, 1998).

As many as twenty-five percent of American children under the age of eighteen are at risk emotionally. The troublesome behaviors of these children cause conflicts with family, school, and community, which drive them further from needed positive social bonding and make them resistant to traditional counseling strategies. Courts and mental health agencies are overwhelmed by the increasing numbers of alienated youths. The crises they cause in school and community are real but are only exacerbated by punishment and expulsion (Long, Fescer, & Brendtro, 1998).

Social competence is related to developmental levels and moral judgment. Children with serious emotional disturbances have problems with clearing up developmental confusions. Their disturbed behaviors are so interwoven with normal functioning that clear differentiation is difficult. Their knowledge of themselves, their lack of confidence in themselves, as well as their willingness to risk themselves in new situations are wanting (Long, Fescer, & Brendtro, 1998).

Children with learning/behavior disorders are not always skillful in the quantity and quality of the resolution of their social problems. For example, they often set unsophisticated goals and are inflexible in taking perspective. In addition, they often have a poor ability in understanding nonverbal social cues and a tendency to insert irrelevant information in forming conclusions. Consciously acting out specific covert and cognitive behaviors that produce positive outcomes and positive judgments of social competence when interacting with others helps to condition positive social skills. Positive social skills involve attending to appropriate cues, meaningful understanding of the cues, searching for possible responses, choosing appropriate responses, evaluating the consequences of various responses, estimating the probability of favorable outcomes, monitoring the effects on the environment, and regulating behavior accordingly (Bryan, Sullivan-Burstein, & Mathur, 1998).

The most common childhood problem referred to mental health professionals is oppositional behavior. There are two major groups of children who manifest oppositional behaviors. In the first group are children who internalize behaviors. They show symptoms of anxiety, phobia, depression, and somatization. In the second group are children who externalize behaviors. They exhibit conduct disorders, overt defiance, substance abuse, promiscuity, and various antisocial patterns.

The alarmingly poor overall academic performance and serious emotional struggles of these children may lead to a very high rate of dropout, absenteeism, and suspension. Because of an inability to keep focused on task demands, they do not spend as much time on academic assignments as their nondisordered peers.

Analysis of the dynamics of school crises have led to some cogent observations. School crises arise from many causes. Feelings of disappointment, shame, sadness, and/or overexcitability can interrupt normal development. Children who grow up in very stressful environments may have their attempts to become independent, win group acceptance, develop moral values, and seek close relationships frustrated. In addition, children can misinterpret interpersonal communications, be the brunt of teasing or cruelty, or be frustrated by assignments. Misfits exist between these children and the dynamics of the school. Another cause of school crises entails enduring psychological problems such as unresolved feelings of abandonment or abuse. Children suffering such problems have difficulty separating the emotional experiences at home from those they have in school. Notwithstanding, it is of great importance to see a crisis as unique time to help a child cope with important problems (Long, Fescer, & Brendtro, 1998).

In summarizing the research, the following hypotheses have been generated to explain these conditions:

1. social skills are posited to be a consequence of the neurological dysfunction presumed to underlie academic skills deficits;
2. the academic and learning problems of children with learning/behavior disorders may result in poor self-concept, rejection or isolation from peers, or other obstacles to the development of social skills;
3. these children may fail to acquire or perform social skills because of limited environmental opportunities to learn such skills and to be reinforced for them;

4. social skills deficits of these children are related to their familial social support system whose effectiveness is reduced by the stress of dealing with or adapting to their special needs;
5. differences in social skills deficits may occur because of the comorbidity of certain diagnoses such as attention deficit hyperactive disorder and depression. (adapted from San Miguel, Forness, & Kavale, 1996)

Problem Solution

Adaptation involves modifying thought, emotions, or actions while trying to achieve a desirable match between the needs of these children on the one hand, and the needs of their environments on the other. Children must be aware of their problems with the present environment, identify new environments without such problems, and be capable of selecting an appropriate one. The selection involves the rejection of the present environment and selecting a more consonant alternative environment (Henker, Whalen, & Hinshaw, 1980; Kolligian & Sternberg, 1987).

The process of self-regulation intrinsically involves the necessity to construct and to go beyond. It is hoped that by creating new experimental situations where nonequilibrated structures are put into conflict, children will arrive at the construction of a new solution, situated on a higher level of self-regulation than the previous one (Bovet, 1981).

Learning develops through procedures and knowledge bases. The procedures operate and develop through the knowledge bases. Learning is appropriate self-regulating control of the learning strategies. Difficulties may arise due to (a) inadequate procedures or knowledge bases or (b) an inappropriate system of self-regulating control (Masson, 1982).

The most effective way to help children with learning/behavior disorders is to create developmental and behavioral intervention derived from an understanding of the evolution of self-concept and stage-related tasks as well as understanding the issues and concerns of family and school (Solomon, 1997).

Considerations for intervention might consist of activities that encourage these children to discover relationships between parts of situations and the respective whole, between structures and objects on which these structures operate, and between themselves and other persons (Gordon & Cowan, 1983).

The main thrust of intervention would be to provide:

> . . . learning experiences and opportunities that will enhance the continued growth of their reasoning abilities. . . . A cognitive developmental model is concerned with fostering the underlying psychological processes that enable delayed children to learn about themselves and the world about them. (Henley, 1980, p. 10)

SELF-REGULATED LEARNING AND SPECIAL
EDUCATION CHILDREN

In terms of self-regulated learning, children with learning/behavior disorders:

- do process metacognitive knowledge to some degree, but do not always access the metacognitive bases they have;
- are likely to have experienced faulty resolution of stage-salient issues;
- often do not have sufficient awareness of their own thoughts and behaviors;
- often develop belief systems that can have a negative effect on achievement-adaptation strategies;
- often lack specific skills in self-regulatory processes;
- often have problems accessing and coordinating this knowledge because they do not have sufficient awareness of their processes and/or their self-regulating mechanisms;
- evidence inefficient strategy use because they may:

  (1) have incomplete mastery of underlying skills resulting in their exerting more mental effort than would normal students;
  (2) have difficulty using immediate feedback of the results of their efforts;
  (3) experience maladaptive interactions with significant others in their environments;

- can be described as having unused ability;
- are by definition not achieving what would be expected of them from indices of their general intellectual potential;
- are active but inefficient in the learning process;
- are not as expansive in mental activity as their agemates, so there is a limited number of interactions that can enter their cognitive systems.

Less successful learners seem to:

1. lack knowledge of the purpose of what they are learning;
2. lack sensitivity to the need to act strategically;
3. fail to evaluate the efficacy of the strategies they do use;
4. be unable to apply strategies spontaneously;
5. rigidly apply the strategies they do use;
6. be unmotivated to employ the strategies in which they are competent;
7. be unable to spontaneously use rehearsal or inference;
8. have experienced faulty resolution of stage issues;
9. lack the expansiveness of their chronological agemates;
10. have a limited number of interactions that can enter their cognitive systems;
11. have unused ability;
12. be active but inefficient in the learning process;
13. have problems accessing and coordinating knowledge because they do not have sufficient awareness of their processes and/or their self-regulating mechanisms;

14. have developed belief systems that can have a negative effect on achievement-adaptation strategies.

From a constructivist, self-regulated learning position they manifest:

1. impasses at some earlier stage of development;
2. absence of certain cognitive concepts;
3. poor coordination of stage-level abilities;
4. functional discontinuity manifested in the form of emotional overreactions, attention disorders, or instability;
5. cognitive discordances;
6. cognitive instability;
7. incomplete mastery of subcomponent skills resulting in their exerting more mental effort than would their chronological agemates;
8. difficulty using immediate feedback of the results of their efforts;
9. maladaptive interactions with significant others in their environments;
10. permanent or long-standing imbalances in decoding and encoding functions;
11. a lack of techniques for monitoring and checking their own progress such as:
    a. awareness of their own limitations as problem solvers,
    b. use of compensatory strategies to overcome such limitations, and
    c. self-management.

Children struggling with academic and/or affective disorders need learning experiences and opportunities that will enhance the continued growth of their reasoning abilities. The fostering of the underlying psychological processes would enable these children to learn about themselves and the world about them. A developmentally based approach can best serve their needs.

Chapter 7

SELF-REGULATED LEARNING

The major task of self-regulated learning is to help learners
overcome barriers to personal growth.
(Fuhr, 1998, p. 4)

The last few decades have seen a worldwide movement to reform many aspects of mental health and education. Evolving from countless research in cognitive psychology, infant development, and special education, new models challenge linear thinking and stress ways of enhancing awareness and engaging individuals in personal ways. Derived from humanistic values and positive conceptions of mental health, these models are based on the beliefs that affect and cognition, feelings and intellect, and emotions and behavior blend into an affirmative framework. They include the existential notions of human freedom, personal choice, and self-actualization, that is, commitment and fulfillment (Skolnik, 1987; Rosen, 1991; Nevis, 1997).

As a result, there have been redefinitions of children, their environments, and the nature of the interactions between them. Ways in which children progressively revise their thinking and feeling as they grow and learn more about themselves and their outside worlds hold prominence. A number of psycho-educational models have emerged that are concerned with facilitating social effectiveness, personal development, and competence within educational curricula and deal with values, morality, and emotional development (Van der Kooij & Vrijhof, 1981; Goldberg et al., 1983; Bronfenbrenner et al., 1986).

Concentration has been shifted to wellness and transformational learning, which make learners, aware of how they are learning. Their aim is to bring into education ". . . the connected, intersubjective, collective, and fundamentally co-constructive dimensions of consciousness . . ." (O'Hara, 1998, p. 163). Learners are taught to examine the contextual influences and assumptions behind their actions. They come to master the narratives that drive their behaviors and as a result increasingly gain more complex levels of mind. Growth, then, is a transformational movement that allows learners to become freer agents with higher levels of awareness, more complex epistemologies, and keener abilities to understand relationships. As learners dialogue with multiple contexts and develop new and multiple sources of identity, they become ". . . more fluid, emergent, contextual, and relational. . ." (O'Hara, 1998, p. 163).

There is a growing emphasis on teaching children how to regulate their own learning activities. In classrooms today children are expected to define, plan, and direct their own learning projects. More respect is being given to the active role children play in making sense of their worlds and in constructing individualized knowledge structures shaped by their personal unique experiences and idiosyncratic interpretations of new information. Learning ways of thinking is considered as important as learning content area skills (O'Leary, 1980).

In this light, self-regulated teaching/learning emphasizes an integration of mind, body, and spirit. It sees teacher and learner as inescapably related to each other with meaning-making a basically collaborative undertaking. It maintains respect for individual rights as it combines this with respect and responsibility for others, singly and collectively. Mutual respect for the dependency that humans have on each other is fostered. Its sphere of concerns is defined in terms of actual problems that the teacher and learner face. Learners are encouraged to continually invent and transform their development in their actual worlds. Teachers and learners are invited to open dialogue with others who have different worldviews and who face different life challenges. They are urged to look jointly for new ways to approach problems. It is an educational approach that supports awareness, challenges tradition, and extends empowerment to learners while at the same time keeping a pragmatic focus on usable results (O'Hara, 1998).

How children deliberately and efficiently process information has received much attention in the psychological and educational research. Piaget's theory has been found to be of great importance because of its value in explaining human behavior and its intensive study of self-science. The complex aspects of the human organism/environment field are its primary concerns. It serves as the basic property of physical and mental growth. It offers an explanation of a self-controlled system of cognitive strategies and operations for learning. The processes it describes have been considered basic to the cognitive growth of children. The acquisition of cognitive strategies and awareness of cognitive functioning it identifies are deemed necessary for cognitive development. The level of any child's development is reflected by the degree of flexibility and systematic use of acquired strategies (Paris & Lindauer, 1982; Cicchetti et al., 1991).

Logical and affective structures are not a simple product of physical experience alone but emerge from children's actions of these actions. This implies an autoregulation. Children coordinate actions on all levels of development in ways that involve some properties of order, inclusion, and correspondence (Piaget, 1971).

Human systems are always open and mobile, never closed and static. As a new level of equilibrium is stabilized they become preparation for a new disequilibrium. Each new level of cognition establishes a new equilibrium but also opens the systems to new forms of information and new possibilities for transformations. The general process begins with the activation of an initial assimilatory structure. If the activation is interrupted by external disturbances, attempts to reconstruct internal structures are made. Awareness, intention, and significance are important principles in the self-regulating process. Intention and significance refer to transformation and self-direction, respectively (Elkind, in Piaget, 1968, 1970a; Palinscar et al., 1993).

Piaget (1971) maintained that the important considerations in cognitive development are the biological presuppositions from which it emerges and the epistemological consequences in which it ends. Relative to nature-nurture interaction, he awarded a primary directive role to nature in the case of mental capacities, and a primary directive role to nurture with respect to the content of thought. Because cognition is conceived of as an extension of biological adaptation, both nature and nurture leave their respective stamps on behaviors. Children inherit the assimilative processes responsive to inner promptings and the accommodative processes responsive to environmental encroachments. Assimilation prevents cognition from being a passive copy of reality whereas accommodation prevents it from constructing a reality that does not correspond to the external environment (Elkind, 1970).

The purpose of any behavior—psychomotor, cognitive, or affective—is adaptation. There must first be an awareness and formation of successive differentiations of self from others. Following this there is an intellectual adaptation that occurs from information acquired through experience as well as from the progressive internal coordination of this information. Finally, cognitive relations are established through a set of structures that are progressively constructed by children continuously interacting with their external worlds.

The propelling force in Piaget's theory is the tendencies toward organization and equilibration or self-regulation. It holds that the incentive for adaptation requires a balance between intrinsic factors and experiential factors. The natural organizational, dynamic, self-regulating powers transform data as well as the process of growth through the functions of equilibration and disequilibration. These processes come into play at all levels of thinking including the simplest forms of perception. Conflicts, contradictions, and dissonance characterize disequilibration and reequilibration and hold the greatest potential for learning. When cognitive challenges cannot be accommodated by existing structural systems, a push toward the creation of new structures, coordinations, and operations comes about (Martin, 1998).

The adaptations children make to their environments through interactions with others and their self-regulating processes characterize their growth.

Growth can be measured in terms of the quantitative and qualitative successive differentiations children make between self and others. It is equally dependent on progressive internal coordinations and on information acquired through experience. Growth is established by a set of structures progressively constructed by continuous interactions between children and their environments. Knowledge is neither a simple copy of the external environment nor a mere unfolding of internal structures. If children are to know what is in their environments, they must be allowed to act on what they discover. To transform the environment they must displace connect, combine, take apart, and reassemble what they find there. Of serious consideration are the manners in which children discover, evaluate, generate solutions, and decide on an action in favor of one of a number of alternative solutions (Piaget, 1971).

Piaget looked at the way children reason about a problem and at the actions they create themselves when trying to regulate an environment that resists regulation. Self-regulating change comes about through the children's observation of transformations. Contradictions bring about transformations. They arise when children see a discrepancy between expecting a successful understanding of information and the realization that they had not attained it. In order to get children to transform their thinking, their existing expectations have to be confronted, challenged, or contradicted. The magnitude of any contrast must be such that children themselves realize that a change is needed (Moses, 1981).

Transformation refers to the ways in which children perfect and use their cognitive abilities and the ways they cope with problems.

> Transference means a fundamental revision of the structures of thinking; social, ethical, and aesthetic attitudes; self-concepts; and worldviews. (Fuhr, Sreckovic, & Grennler-Fuhr, 2000)

Knowledge acquisition is connected to transformation, that is, actions or operations. All actions contain a fusion of self and other. In order to become aware of their own actions, children must be exposed to objective information. However, they need the internal cognitive structures that ultimately are refined, through this exposure, to become instruments of analysis and coordination. They then are enabled to know what belongs to self, what belongs to the other, and what belongs to the action itself. They can envision the transformations of the actions from their original to their final states. Interactions imply two kinds of activities. Children either coordinate the actions themselves or become aware of the interrelation of objects (Piaget, 1971).

Structure, function, and content form the core of Piaget's theory. Structures are the existing underlying logical abilities by which children organize and reconstruct experiences. Function, in the form of assimilation and accommodation, represents the self-regulating characteristics of mental activity that leads children to an understanding of their abilities to generalize. These functions account for the development, refinement, and transformation of cognitive structures. Content represents substantive knowledge of the world. In the course of their interaction with the physical and social environments, children modify and enrich their very structures, functions, and content (Cocking, 1981; Sigel, Brodzinsky, & Golinkoff, 1981).

The construction of knowledge through transformation and self-regulation demands that children come to understand:

1. the relationship between their personal characteristics and objective reality;
2. the quality of their thinking;
3. the value in their learning strategies;
4. their own learning characteristics and methods enabling them to control, monitor, and evaluate self-direction;
5. strategies needed to do a task efficiently;
6. real-world knowledge;
7. motivation to use this knowledge effectively.

Piaget's model provides a framework that considers how both the processes and innate capacity interact during intervention. Envisioning this approach on a continuum, we see at one end the strategies of children being provoked through active modeling and interrogation on the part of the psychologist or teacher. At the opposite end of the continuum, after children have internalized self-regulated controls, they automatically and effortlessly deploy strategies (Swanson, 1993).

The position hold that:

a. the integration of information is for the purpose of making meaning of the self and its environment;
b. active meaning-making adaptation is built on a sequential unfolding of emerging capacities;
c. children are active processors of their own experiential data and relationships;
d. different levels of information processing exist in each domain throughout development; and
e. the characteristics of cognition can be described through the intraindividual changes that occur as children interact with their environments.

SELF-REGULATED LEARNING

As they looked to cognitive and developmental psychology for direction for designing teaching methodology, educators found that the concepts of self-regulation offers an optimistic view regarding psychoeducational intervention. It brings to clear attention the skills used by learners of different chronological ages and abilities. Explanations of problem-solving processes, that is, how specific and general problem-solving skills are acquired developmentally, were sought. Questions arose as to how problem-solving children perform in handling specified tasks. Answers were sought as to how changes in the conditions of children alter problem-solving behaviors as well as how changes in the conditions of the confronting task alter problem-solving behaviors. What resulted was a general framework for understanding differences in problem-solving performance understood in terms of the developmental capacities learners bring to situations. Different levels of cognitive structures underlie the structures for solving complex problems. The structures reflect the level of cognitive organization underlying the performance and summarize information about specific events and their relationships. Findings revealed that there are three types of variables that children must accomplish: (1) structure, the organization and activation of knowledge at appropriate moments; (2) strategies, the recall and effective use of cognitive strategies; and (3) metacognition, the awareness and control of components that impact on learning. Successful problem solvers are able to select reasonable goals and can generate suitable means to accomplish them. They can regulate and follow their chosen plans as well as monitor the effectiveness of these plans (Paris, Cross, & Lipson, 1984).

Self-regulated learning principles can be summed up as follows:

(a) Learning is the construction of meaning, (b) the child is self-regulating and self-preserving, (c) the best predictor of what will be learned is what is already known, (d) error plays an important role in learning, (e) feeling affects learning, (f) learning is enhanced when the child trusts those they are learning from, and (g) the belief that learning is a primary human function—it does not require coercion. (Reid, 1993, p. 13)

The dynamics of change are the central focus of self-regulated learning. Elements in a learning pattern are relativized with respect to each other, that is, each element is defined through its relation to all others. All elements are then reordered according to some universal principle, generalization, law, or function. Prior knowledge provides a framework to which new knowledge can be related, thus permitting a basis for the generation of inference and the evaluation of the accuracy and importance of text content. Being aware of one's own cognitive processes and products plays an important role in self-regulated learning. Procedures that enhance awareness positively influence comprehension (Cocking, 1981; Rogers & Kegan, 1991; Swanson & Alexander, 1997).

From infancy to adulthood there are basic changes in relational processes as well as in individual consistency in relationships. Individual differences in self-referent beliefs are likely to change with the emergence of new conceptual and representational abilities. These abilities contribute to a more refined self-system and self-regulation. The nature of interactions necessarily changes with its development (Thompson, 1991).

The meaning that children assign to experiences becomes a key process underlying change. How these meanings are first constructed in infancy, how and why these meanings undergo change or remain impervious to change, and the role such meanings play in personal negotiations with ever-changing environments are major foci.

Self-regulated learning leads to increased self-correction and agency. It creates a climate that encourages children toward successful meaning-making. It is not to be presumed that children's knowledge and awareness simply begin to occur. They are to be facilitated, collaborated with, and mentored through experiments that provide opportunities for self-regulation. Knowledge and awareness must be fueled by "contextual learning experiences" (Swicegood & Linehan, 1995, p. 341).

Self-regulated learning aims at techniques that result in deeper comprehension of what is expected to complete a task successfully. It involves attention to the process of change in comprehension as well as the end product. The conceptualization of and the correct sequence of steps in achieving the task become the goals. Indeed, it is necessary to establish comprehension before production. Crucial to helping any child toward this awareness is an interaction in which "an adult provides carefully calibrated assistance at the child's leading edge of competence" (Stone, 1998, p. 345). The provision comes in the form of enlisting that child's interest, holding that child's orientation toward the goal, accentuating that child's motor, perceptual, cognitive, and affective aspects, controlling that child's frustration, and demonstrating idealized solutions.

Because the self-systems of children are profoundly affected by the way they view their own competency, value their own actions, and expect their own success, they need to consciously reflect on their own cognitive activities and abilities as they attempt to problem solve. They must learn ways of thinking about their thinking as they learn other skills. Therefore, self-regulated learning is concerned with the ways in which children discover, evaluate, generate solutions, and decide on an action to a problem (Stone & Conca, 1993). It provides a model of self-functions designed:

> to ask about what the self does as it moves through this complex process, . . . to raise the question as to what fundamental types of abilities or powers it has. Stated succinctly . . . [it] involves looking at the self's actions, and then reasoning backwards to the self's functions which these actions exemplify and which make the actions themselves possible. (Crocker, 1988, p. 100)

Self-regulated learning focuses on the knowledge that children have about themselves. It includes affective components with traditional subject-matter content.

It encompasses the components, the experience, and the context of learning situations, as well as assesses intelligence in terms of the internal and external worlds of children. At a global level, cognitive processing consists of stages and components. Since it is held that the flow of information occurs in a sequence of stages, cognitive processing is conceptualized as a study of how sensory input is transformed, reduced, elaborated, stored, retrieved, and used. General concepts underlying processing theory are: (1) a structural component that defines the field within which information can be processed at a particular stage; (2) a strategy component that describes the operations of the various stages; and (3) an executive process by which learners' activities are monitored (Cicchetti et al., 1991).

While cognitive developmental theories give models of growth, they do not give detailed guidelines for skills development. Self-regulated learning provides a possible solution to how children develop functional control of their cognitive skills. This control is shaped by their social interactions with others, motivation and awareness of their personal skills, and motivation and awareness of task demands (Van der Kooij & Vrijhof, 1981; Goldberg et al., 1983).

Learning is a case of knowing how one event is a variation on some better known event. More than knowing which responses to select, learning is a case of knowing why certain responses should be observed, but remain insufficient by themselves to help the observer make a valid conclusion. Learning involves knowing what procedures change the unfamiliar into the familiar. It is related to the activities of children as well as their capacity for curiosity and spontaneous investigation. Knowing how to change events is more important that learning the static configurations of stimuli (Forman & Hill, 1981).

Cognitive processes, knowing the skills in problem solving, may be automatic and subconscious while self-regulative processes, knowing whether one was correct or incorrect in problem solving, demand conscious monitoring. The difference between the cognitive and metacognitive processes demands attention. It is a difference of self-awareness and control. Self-regulation and self-control are critical for future success. Both the knowledge base (cognition) and control (self-regulation) are developmental and interact with task demands (Bondy, 1984; Slife, Weiss, & Bell, 1985).

Metacognition

Cognition is different from self-regulation. Cognition infers knowing the skills in problem solving. Self-regulation infers knowing whether one was correct or incorrect in problem solving. Cognitive processes may be automatic and subconscious while self-regulative processes demand conscious regulation and monitoring. The difference between the two is a difference of self-awareness and control.

The knower, the process of knowing, and knowledge itself are specifically defined from a self-regulated learning point of view. The knower is a biological system consisting of gradually developing internal structures that form the architecture for decoding and encoding information. It is within this system that awareness of language, memory, and cognitive processes exist. A knowing child is an open system accessible to structural change regardless of any degree or level of development.

The processing of knowing strives to enlarge the knowledge base in the biological system. It involves changes in the basic structural nature of the cognitive processes that determine functioning. The process selects the information to be processed based on how relevant and meaningful that information is in the present moment. It is the active use of available self-regulation, awareness, and cognitive organization. If learners regard their strategies as useful means to their goals, they see them as reasonable plans for solving problems (Paris, Cross, & Lipson, 1984; Paris & Jacobs, 1984; Skolnik, 1987; Rosen, 1991; Meltzer, 1993).

Successful strategy use increases the strength of metacognitive processes. A strategy is a tool:

> . . . that can be used by learners to facilitate their analysis of the demands of a given problem or setting, to help them make decisions regarding the best way(s) to address the problem, and to guide their completion of the task while carefully monitoring the effectiveness of the process along the way. (Putnam, Deshler, & Schumaker, 1993, pp. 327–328)

Several kinds of knowledge inform the degree to which students understand reasoning skills. There are three kinds of knowledge: declarative, procedural, and conditional. The first refers to static kinds of knowledge that provide information about a specific topic. It is often called "knowing that." In contrast, procedural knowledge, "knowing how," refers to the dynamic knowledge of action. The third type of knowledge refers to the particular conditions under which learners use relevant declarative and procedural knowledge, that is, knowing "when, where, or to what degree."

There are three levels of metacognitive objectives. The first would entail the training of the subordinate processes of (1) rehearsal skills, (2) elaboration of existing skills, and (3) organized memory search skills (assimilation). The second level would entail training in the superordinate skills of coordinating, monitoring, and modifying the subordinate processes (accommodation). The third level lies in training how, when, where, why, and with whom to use the subordinate and superordinate skills. The concept of metacognition provides a clear connection between the intellectual and affective (Borkowski & Konarski, 1981).

This thinking offers an understanding of how children take in and organize information and respond to all the changes that affect them. It forms the basis for the creation of methods for encouraging new growth (Paris, Cross, & Lipson, 1984; Paris & Jacobs, 1984; Skolnik, 1987; Rosen, 1991; Meltzer, 1993).

Self-regulated learning involves both an awareness of the variables that impact on learning and an ability to take control of one's learning activities. In order to be self-regulated learners, children must have knowledge of strategies needed to do tasks efficiently. Metacognitive knowledge of personal learning characteristics enables children to choose, use, monitor, and evaluate not only their strategies but their specific knowledge bases as well as the motivations behind their knowledge (Palinscar et al., 1993).

If learning is the construction of knowledge through transformation and self-regulation, its goals should be problem solving, meaning-making, and adaptation. In addition, if learning is the process of changing and adapting, it must focus on how children are thinking rather on whether or not they understand. Children must not be provided with knowledge alone but also with opportunities to gather their own information. Their environments must be individualized so that they change their perceptions of themselves, thereby fostering their academic learning and personal insight. Their present environments are directed in a way to cause the development of more appropriate behavior in spite of past and present circumstances that cannot be changed (Nichols, 1986; Cicchetti et al., 1991; Anderson, 1996).

Self-regulated learners, when confronted with a problem, begin by drawing on their personal knowledge and experiences to interpret what is required to solve it. Personal interpretation of a task is a crucial step in self-regulation because it specifies the goal-set that influences the strategies used for the execution of the solution. As learners actively self-regulate, they construct their own knowledge and understandings. If allowed to actively participate in responding to task variants or obstacles, they learn to abstract principles from their experiences and come to construct general, decontextualized understandings that can be transferred across situations. The result is that they build domain-specific understandings as well as understandings about tasks, strategies, and self.

Self-regulated teaching/learning approaches involve children in interactive dialogues about strategies across contexts. By using strategies in context and in interactive dialogue with teachers and peers, children learn why, where, and how strategies might be useful. It requires that the teacher calibrate assistance to the difficulties encountered by learners as they engage in a task. Support must be matched to the unique strengths and weaknesses of learners with each of the processes of self-regulation. The support must be flexibly calibrated, increased or decreased as needed, through engagement in collaborative problem solving by means of interactive dialogue. As learners are supported to actively focus on and construct understandings about their cognitive activities, they gain experience adapting strategies across different contexts. The calibrated support received from others during the dialogue is provided and faded according to the needs of the learners. Responsibility for strategy implementation is systematically transferred to the learners (Butler, 1998; Palinscar, 1998; Reid, 1998; Stone, 1998).

> Meaningful learning that significantly affects the child's future thoughts and actions takes serious time and innumerable experiences. Even once the child has grasped the basic ideas, there will still be many additions, revisions, and refinements in the child's conceptions. (Pritchard, 1998, p. 36)

Effective intervention consists of confronting the child's discrepancies and contradictions wisely and accurately and in a timely fashion. Progress is made when disequilibrium incites learners to go beyond their present state in search of new solutions. The real challenge of intervention is to study the structural properties of a given pattern, discover the relationships of subsidiary patterns, and determine the boundaries of the system that is being studied (Inhelder, Sinclair, & Bovet, 1974).

SELF-REGULATED LEARNING AND CHILDREN WITH LEARNING/BEHAVIOR DISORDERS

Development of "normal" intelligence consists of an unveiling of the underlying cognitive structural mechanisms. The notions of developmental epistemology is being strongly endorsed by many educators as being effective for planning interventions appropriate to the developmental levels of children with learning/behavior disorders (Giordano, 1981; Gelfand & Peterson, 1985; Poplin, 1988a; Heshusius, 1989; Skolnik, 1990).

Researchers have sought an understanding of how the various ontogenetic domains are organized, especially in atypical cases. For example, various forms of learning/behavior disorders are manifested by such common indicators as communication skill delays and thought disorders as well as attention and concentration difficulties (Cicchetti et al., 1991).

Knowledge of how to process information and of self-regulation are necessary for academic success and affective adaptation. Lack of academic success and affective adaptation are due to insufficient strategies of learning and adaptation. The assumptions of Piaget reflect the self-regulated learning perspective, especially in the concepts of assimilation and accommodation, that is, equilibration. So, one possible way of reconstructing a learning/behavior disorder would be in terms of adaptation and the adapting processes (Rogers & Kegan, 1991).

The derivation of treatment guidelines from a cognitive-developmental perspective demands the consideration of the potential reasons behind the seeming inability of some children to make use of their structural development and functional skills. With regard to lack of structural development, further consideration must be given to the possibilities of global nonattainment of the necessary stage level structures, that is, the points where children do not yet seem ready to reason according to age-appropriate stage development in both interpersonal and noninterpersonal aspects. Should global nonattainment of specific stage-relevant reasoning exist, educators must create experiments that challenge cognitive structures in interpersonal as well as noninterpersonal areas (Gordon, 1988).

This approach looks at not only the differentiated elements of a system that may have been disrupted but also at the very integrating process of the system. Any threat or disruption to either may affect the entire structure. The study of cognition or learning/behavior disorders as developmental phenomena demands an understanding of how any behavior expresses a meaningful response, maladaptive or otherwise. The responses must be interpreted with reference to both earlier and later developmental responses (Rogers & Kegan, 1991).

Since children with learning/behavior disorders do indeed engage in problem solving, the concept of self-regulated learning cannot support the view that they are passive learners. Children who may not have experienced early cognitive and affective promise are not necessarily doomed to remain with negative consequences of being so. This is due in part to the flexibility of self-regulating system. Cognitive and psychosocial dysfunctions can be changed appreciably through intervention that is designed as a means to help these children reconstruct their existing knowledge base and become self-regulatory. If attention is directed to the purposes of their behaviors, the quality of their meaning-making and mental reflections as they are actually solving problems, intervention provides more security as well as new opportunities for the development of relational harmony (Thompson, 1991; Butler, 1998; Palinscar, 1998; Reid, 1998; Stone, 1998).

There is no intervention model that devotes sufficient attention to the systematic application of developmental epistemology to the problems of children with learning/behavior disorders. Although some experts provide theoretical and practical direction for this, there is a paucity of both models and research findings supporting any but the psychodynamic intervention approach (Achenbach, 1974; Swap, 1974; Piaget, 1975; Cowan, 1978).

Of late, special educators have been advocating self-regulated learning as viable intervention for children with learning/behavior disorders. Alternative approaches are being devised particularly for those children who do not learn effectively in traditional situations. Teaching methodology is being redesigned to enable children to learn how to learn. Following a more holistic perspective, it allows for elaboration of approaches that provide support and sufficient flexibility to accommodate individual differences among children. At the same time it assists children to increasingly take responsibility for their own behaviors (Butler, 1998; Palinscar, 1998; Reid, 1998; Stone, 1998).

> . . . it is important to recognize that all children self-regulate their learning and development from birth. They are born self-regulators. Self-regulation is the norm and it remains the primary mode or regulation unless it is derailed. In school, the derailment is often caused by repeated failure. After repeated bouts of failure, children subsume their own internal inclinations toward self-regulation to those external to them, [such as] the teacher, until they drop out. (Wadsworth, 1996, p. 174)

Piaget's theory can be used in two ways. First, it can be used along with commonly accepted intervention practices by providing a cognitive developmental component. Secondly, specific concepts of the theory can be used to generate new ideas concerned with assessing developmental disorders and with promoting development toward optimal functioning. Intervention from this perspective can allow children with learning/behavior disorders to restore the phase levels at which their development has been delayed, disrupted, or deficient. This would cause the construction of those necessary life forces and conditions that may not have developed, and the revitalization of those whose development may have begun but was abruptly ended. It can provide a vehicle by which learning/behavior disorders can be interpreted from a cognitive developmental perspective. It can lead to new hypotheses about the ways by which developmental disorders can be diagnosed as well as ways by which development can be promoted toward more optimal functioning. Placing emphasis on the meanings that children place on their internal and external events as well as their ability to understand and manipulate self and others, intervention matches developing internal structures of cognitive transformations while considering affective/social elements. A medium of expression and communication becomes available (Gordon & Cowan, 1983; Stolorow & Lachmann, 1983; Clarkson, 1997; Biemiller & Meichenbaum, 1998).

Children with learning difficulties or disabilities must be taught to do what normally achieving children often do for themselves, namely, learn how to learn. Very often children who are less able are not presented with academic tasks that are within their cognitive mastery nor are they given learning opportunities that allow them to execute self-direction in their attempts to make meaning of their environments and themselves. They rarely are given chances to apply any new skills they learn in new situations. These children must acquire skills and relevant task-directive language and must be placed in situations requiring increasing responsibility to apply what they learn. They need to be encouraged to take responsibility for much of their learning. Leadership roles are often denied them. Despite the recent focus on constructivist approaches to teaching special education students, very little attention has been directed to their sociocultural bases (Moses, 1981; Biemiller & Meichenbaum, 1998; Wong, 1998).

Five possible reasons why children with learning/behavior disorders may show a slow or different course of processing information are:

1. inability or unwillingness to construct or operate on specific forms of mental representations;
2. inability or unwillingness to recode certain kinds of information into higher order units that then make possible storage of greater amounts of information per mental chunk;
3. aversion to certain kinds of mental content (i.e., math);
4. lack of motivation for a specific subject matter;
5. specific neurological deficits. (adapted from Sternberg & Wagner, 1982)

SOCIAL ISSUES AND SELF-REGULATED LEARNING

In studying the development of meaning-making activities, self-regulated learning is as interested in the emotions as in cognition and does not reduce one to the other. It goes beyond the homeostasis seeking explanation of human motivation and includes an adaptive oriented motive of equal dignity (Westman, 1990). Its aim is to see how children perceive a contradiction and how they get out of a conflict:

1. by finding compromising solutions;
2. by reducing problems to ones that can be solved by the schemes children already know;
3. by overcoming the difficulties thanks to a greater effort of integration.

During the past few years there has been considerable research focusing on motivation and self-concept. Being able to successfully apply self-regulated learning strategies is inherently connected with feelings. Chronic school failure and persistent struggle with behavioral problems shape self-concept (Nannis, 1988). Debates about the place of social education in the school abound. They divide school and community, deplete resources, and impact on teacher training. They center around issues of:

"[v]iolence; drug abuse; irresponsible sexual activity; unwanted pregnancy; racial, ethnic, and religious prejudice and hatred; and lack of respect, either for oneself or for others." (Pritchard, 1998, p. 9)

At present, research confirming the validity of this social-cognitive problem-solving view of social adjustment has been encouraging when compared to training programs designed to modify children's problem-solving strategies. However, many times school settings are very busy providing environments in which children acquire the academic skills. They often do not feel that they have the manpower or methodology to deal directly with childrens' emotional problems. Indeed, it is not uncommon for some schools to keep opportunities for emotional responses at a minimum (Kneedler, 1980; Spivack & Swift, 1976; Urbain & Kendall, 1980; Nichols, 1986).

The school's association with children is modified by its specific social purpose. Its interest in appropriate behavior must be connected to its educational goals. Educators need to address what social lessons should take place as a part of education, rather than life in general. Social education is a legitimate part of teaching and should be an integral part of the ordinary activity of teaching and learning. Social and academic goals are consistent with each other and mutually reinforcing (Pritchard, 1998).

How educators speak with children about feelings lies in how they understand the source of emotional difficulties or concerns and how they focus their intervention. It is useful for these professionals to consider emotional understanding from a cognitive-developmental point of view. There are intervention implications arising from the assumption that there are differences in levels of children's emotional understanding relative to their cognitive development. They involve understanding the source of children's emotional difficulties as well as their linguistic levels and forms. In emotional disturbances children often subjugate one domain for the other. For example, more advanced cognitive structures may be either undermined or obscured by highly charged emotional issues. A cognitive-developmental conceptualization can be an effective guide in intervention (Nannis, 1988).

Children are constantly faced with the challenge of coordinating all their internal forces while engaging in external reality. Self-regulated learning offers opportunities for children to see their lives as personal creations. It strives to stimulate experiential learning and advance the evolution of new self-concepts. Attempts are made to complete unfinished situations and overcome blockages in the awareness-contact-dialogue cycle. Conflicts are integrated by associating cognitive understandings with the motoric and affective discoveries. Other important goals include helping children bring polarities into awareness, dislodge introjects, and to realign misplaced feelings, ideas, and actions. Accomplishing these, children "can feel and act stronger, more competent, more self-supported, more explorative, and actively responsible for himself" (Zinker, 1991, p. 74).

Since self-regulated learning provides a clear connection between the intellectual and affective, it is of particular benefit for children who have become marginalized in the school system. It has strong potential for children who abuse self, others, alcoholism, or drugs. It begins with the self as the referent center to help children realize the possibilities of their own choices in life. A vivid awareness of being a center of action helps children to become acting selves in using their cognitive and affective abilities constructively. Being active constructors of their own realities fosters and strengthens a vivid awareness in their own positive skills (Rhodes, 1988).

There are specific social issues prominent for every academic subject area. The developing cognitive capacities provide the foundation for psychological and social comprehension. The progress of children is fostered when they receive messages that convey an understanding of their abilities and well-being. These messages must also make apparent expectations that are clear and consistent, recognition and acknowledgment of the need for autonomy, and independent action. As children become more self-reliant and responsible, guidance should gradually diminish.

Autonomy, in the Piagetian sense, is self-regulation that is seen in all aspects of development—cognitive, affective, social, and moral. In the cognitive domain, autonomy involves making decisions for oneself and becoming aware of how to make choices that carry out one's own construction of knowledge and one's own problem solving. In the affective domain it involves making decisions with awareness of one's own feelings, hunches, interests, and motivations. In the social domain it involves making decisions according to one's own values as to what is right or wrong. All of this is necessary for social behavior based on true cooperation (Wadsworth, 1997).

Learning goes beyond the efficient manipulation of objects to arrive at a predetermined product to the orientation of interpersonal behavior. Children cannot be expected to understand their habits and attitudes until they own them. If they are to be infused with appropriate emotional attachment to appropriate behaviors, they must be allowed to consider aspects of a problem, imagine different alternates to its solution, choose what to do, and evaluate the outcome. The more actively involved they are, the more improved is their learning effectiveness (Pritchard, 1998).

Learning in the academic subjects requires understanding how to make certain kinds of moral judgments. Those judgments concern both how people pursue the goals of discipline and the application of knowledge derived from that discipline to human life. By learning how to make those judgments, students develop the ability not only to understand the world, but to do things in it. (Pritchard, 1998, p. 136)

The problem-solving behavior of children with learning/behavior disorders is greatly influenced by their needs. To relieve the internal stress created by the needs and thereby arrive at solutions to problems requires a reorganization of one's cognitions. The orientation of intervention is to closely align cognition and emotional responses. It demands an alertness and sensitivity to verbal and nonverbal cues, blocked emotions, unfinished conflicts, and fixations. Situations are reexperienced so as to reclaim each part and belonging to self. It is not just a matter of providing a safe place for children to vent their feelings. It is a matter of moving children toward a motor/cognitive/affective integration that is more differentiated and adaptive. Significant, long-term changes in the behavior can be facilitated if attention is paid to the emotions and developmental patterns associated with academic and behavior problems. As a framework for building new concepts and developing a more positive, integrated, and individuated sense of self, feelings need to be clarified and understood (Clark, 1982; Gordon & Cowan, 1983; Sherrill, 1986; Jones, 1992).

Their gradual coordination of the relationships between changes in self and changes in the environment bring children to the realization that static states are momentary positions in space and time. This helps them organize discrete events into useful, functional strategies. They attain internal loci of control leading them to construct an autonomous self. The course of an activity is dependent on one's own input and capacity. As a child comes to this realization, he or she learns to control personal actions and the outcomes of them (Piaget, 1971).

The rapidly growing interest in the nature of affect-cognition has taken the focus off chronological age and placed it on the level of development. Consideration is directed to how mistreatment impacts on various aspects of development as well as how a predisposition toward learning/behavior disorders impacts the role of mistreatment (Cicchetti, Toth et al., 1988).

The very concept of special education must be reformulated within a developmental framework. With structurally deficient and developmentally delayed children it is necessary to determine the ways in which any disorder works to restore or maintain inadequately integrated self and other representations. A crucial concern for intervention is the need to clearly distinguish between mental activity that is primarily hindering the solutions of mental conflicts, and the mental activity that is more accurately characterized by a developmentally determined inability (Stolorow & Lachmann, 1983).

Children with learning and behavior problems are not as apt to be in learning settings that focus on both skill acquisition as well as on the construction of and transfer of tasks to new situations. They need remediation that is designed to ameliorate such cognitive problems as metacognitive deficits, inadequate means-ends alternative solutions thinking, inability to consider consequences, and lack of spontaneous use of executive planning functions (Putnam, Deshler, & Schumaker, 1993).

Intervention must be guided by the cognitive levels displayed by children at different stages of development, that is, the level of meaning-making. It must assist children in gaining a repertoire of experiences and actions that they can reflect on and from which eventually arise new cognitive structures (London, 1990).

> To enable children to work with their own ordered structures and generate the possibilities necessary for meaning to evolve, it is necessary for us to begin to make contact with children's assimilative bases and to trust their intrinsic need to understand. (Grobecker, 1998, p. 220)

Self-regulatory instruction begins with assessing a child's present approach to a specific problem. It then moves to getting that child to identify any new alternatives in a supportive setting. The child is encouraged to model and practice the new alternatives under guided practice with feedback that directs and supports complexity, length, and difficulty. Instruction must inform the child as to the name, purpose, and sequential steps of a strategy; show the child how to apply the strategy; and teach the child when and where the strategy would be appropriately used (Palinscar et al., 1993).

To be authentic, children must be aware of their own needs and desires, and the environment must be aware of opportunities and obstacles to satisfy these needs and desires. It is to know what actualities and potentialities are available. A climate that permits children to experience the excitement of their growth and allows them to take risks improves self-functions and social interactions (Crocker, 1983).

> Promoting good education is a difficult task. Education's purpose is to pass along whatever wisdom and guidance our society has to offer about how we ought to live. Human life can be troublesome, painful, and demanding. It can also be fun, meaningful, and glorious. Its patterns are subtle, intricate, and powerful. It is filled with unpredictability, due to fate and human choices. What can we offer young people to help them overcome life's obstacles, enjoy its fruits, and make their mark on the world? (Pritchard, 1998, p. 248)

School personnel should constantly strive to create school environments that allow children to become aware of their passions and their concerns as well as their personal involvement in creating their learning agenda. They must be encouraged to associate what they learn in school with who they are. Their goals must be envisioned as being embedded in the experiential aspects of learning. The creation of such environments depends on socially constructed beliefs about the constitution of learning as the significance of the participation of teacher and learner, appropriate roles and relationships among members of the learning environment, and a view that learning is a motivating and worthwhile undertaking (Oldfather & Dahl, 1994).

The purpose of self-regulated learning is to provide a method of growth not of correction, that is, to bring children to the discovery of their uniqueness and difference from others. Arcane interpretations that children have of their history must be replace with the aliveness of the immediate experience. This concerns more than flashes of intellectual, rewiring behavioral circuits, or the mere release of strong emotion. Children must learn to take care of their own needs by being able to articulate them and to take steps toward effectively meeting them. This is as true for children with learning/behavior disorders as it is for nondisordered children (Swanson, 1988; Miller, 1989).

Self-regulated learning can be particularly effective when applied to the study of developmental diversity. The timing of treatment strategies may be as important or even more important than their content (Keating, 1991). In any given situation, children, at their personal levels of maturity and comprehension, differentiate and restructure themselves and their environment, thereby gaining or changing insight (Sadler & Whimbey, 1985).

Chapter 8

INTERVENTION

A true dedication to growth involves a commitment to helping
every child find his own abilities in his own way and in his
own time.
(Elkind, 1970, p. 103)

It was not until the mid-1970s that Piaget's constructs were beginning to be applied routinely to children with learning/behavior disorders. As attention was given to how each developmental area requires its own form of support and intervention, questions were asked as to whether disturbances of early experiences and biological disposition change in their effect and meaning throughout life. Attempts were made to clarify whether different stages of development bring out new academic patterns and maladaptive behaviors. Questions were also raised as to whether or not new resolutions were possible because of an advancement to a higher development stage (Noam et al., 1984).

The increased study of the relationship between the cognitive and affective processes has led education to redesigned intervention techniques for children with learning/behavior disorders. The variables of intervention have become the process of development and the related aspects of competence or incompetence. The attention of intervention strategies has been directed toward (1) the biological and psychological characteristics of children and their significant others; (2) the contexts in which children are developing; and (3) the transactional processes through which development is occurring. Systematic study has documented the deleterious effect of inappropriate intervention in every developmental domain. It has also articulated inappropriate intervention as a predisposing cause of future difficulties (Cicchetti et al., 1988).

A diversity of techniques and methods range across many systems of psychological and educational intervention. They are classified as affective, cognitive, or behavioral. Although a pluralistic approach is operationally defendable, cognitive reorganization accounts theoretically for any substantial and lasting change. Revision and reintegration of knowledge structures produce significant long-range gains. Given the cathartic powers of an affective technique or the rewards of a behavioral strategy, unless the knowledge structures are modified, little enduring improvement takes place.

The research models used by cognitive psychologists hold to the following common beliefs. First, focus on mental events themselves can lead to the investigation and description of the general strategies actually used by the learner to solve problems. Second, knowledge, thinking, and actions are interrelated and cannot be discussed independently relative to the learner's mediation of information. Third, the internal structures that summarize information about specific events and their relationships organize and store knowledge in the minds of the learner. Fourth, metacognition, the learner's knowledge of his or her own specific thought processes and how he or she uses them, can facilitate learning. Fifth, thought processes and actions undergo qualitative changes with the acquisition of more complex, interrelated, and accessible structures (Saarni, 1973; Eisenhart & Borko, 1993).

With many avenues effecting a cognitive reorganization, Piaget's assimilation/accommodation principles underscore all effective psychoeducational intervention, regardless of surface diversity (Breslin, 1988). Growing awareness of these concepts

> resulted in increasing acceptance of the importance of developmental changes for the learning process and greater recognition that children are active learners. There has also been a shift from a focus on the importance of materials and tasks toward an emphasis on the roles of learners and their specific activities. As part of this changing zeitgeist, the cognitive-developmental approach to learning and instruction has been more widely accepted (Reid, 1988), with its emphasis on the interaction between the child's developmental status and the cognitive and metacognitive components of educational performance. (Meltzer, 1993, p. 125)

Piaget's theory is the one that most challenged the way of looking at learning from a self-regulated learning framework. His developmental epistemology can be conceived as using "corrective cognitive experiments" toward the purpose of preparing the psyche to assimilate an incident and actively structure a new idea, motor pattern, feeling, and so on. It can be used to plan and construct intervention that is carefully tuned to the precise developmental demands made on any child. Serving as the media for psychomotor, intellectual, and emotional integration, the actual application of this intervention evokes a self-expressing, self-correcting experience. Corrective self-expression means giving vent to constructive forms of one's movements, feelings, and thoughts at one's own level of meaning-making. Best results come from the successful resolution of the most salient tasks issuing from a given developmental period (Gordon, 1988; Cicchetti et al., 1991).

A primary assumption of Piaget's concepts is that knowledge arises from an interaction of self-other unity. The expansion of knowledge depends on how children coordinate their inner structures of experiences and how they project these structures into the outside world. In order for children to be able to work through problem solutions, they must achieve a necessary degree of consolidation of self and other representations. Intervention exercises following this thinking must meet two criteria. First, they must introduce learning strategies in the context of existing organizations. This would require that the exercises be meaningful and that they motivate children to incorporate their learning strategies into existing organizational patterns. Second, the structure and substance of the exercises must be sensitive to individual organizational eccentricities by permitting a wide range of responses (Smock, 1981).

Piagetian principles direct the understanding of how children progress through their qualitatively different intellectual levels. Children make meaning of their existence as they examine particular situations and consider further courses of action with increasingly more complex thinking. As children are building cognitive structures, they are also creating an internal sense of morality, learning how to adapt themselves to others, and to see things from someone's else perspective (Johnston & Johnston, 1984).

There are different levels of cognitive processing in the psychomotor, cognitive, and affective domains throughout the life span. Important foci are:

1. how developmental delays affect the domains of information processing;
2. how children with learning/behavior disorders can be helped to integrate their different levels of processing into the construction of adaptive experiences;
3. how positive change in one domain can bring about positive change in another. (Goldberg, Sprafkin, Gershaw, & Klien, 1983)

To measure the level of meaning-making at any given time the following aspects need to be examined: the nature of the existing cognitive operations, the elements upon which they operate, the form taken by the organization of the operations, and the scope and power of resulting thought. All children should go through the pattern of stage progress. The rate of the progress varies according to individual situations (Neimark, 1980).

Children need to be provided with opportunities to model and practice potentially troublesome situations successfully by using the skills being taught. They need assistance in organizing concepts operative in figure-ground relationships. They should have opportunities to model and practice the skills being taught for situations that might actually occur in real-life circumstances. Children need opportunities that allow them to appropriately transfer and use their skills in new and novel situations. What is required is a wide variety of strategies to bring about transfer of training into real-life situations. Performance feedback, in the form of personal reactions, approval, praise, and/or appropriate criticism, from teachers and peers serve as ongoing positive reinforcements. Included with this should be a program of self-reinforcement (Van der Kooij & Vrijhof, 1981; Goldberg et al., 1983).

Self-regulated learning instruction is slowly gaining prominence in special education and remedial settings and results show that children with learn-ing/behavior disorders do respond well to it. Its procedures as mechanisms for promoting active task involvement are viable approaches. It holds that there is (1) a transactional relationship among cognition, affect, and behavior; (2) an active participation of children in the learning process; (3) a critical need to design intervention in terms of the developmental progressions among cognitive, affective, and behavioral dimensions; and (4) a critical need to consider the situational, cultural, and ecological variables of an individual child. Its stress on cognitive training offers the greatest possibility for transfer of training, enabling children to deal effectively with a variety of problems in a variety of situations. The overall objective of this instructional approach is the development of self-regulated learners (Keogh & Glover, 1980; Graham & Harris, 1993; Palinscar et al., 1993).

Intervention approaches that are developmentally based have the capacity for exploring the depths of the psychological processes in a way that remains close to clinical observations. Four important generic principles underlie a developmentally focused intervention approach: (1) harnessing core processes, (2) meeting a child at his or her development levels, (3) renegotiating bypassed levels, and (4) promoting a child's self-sufficiency. The first principle is that a child's natural inclinations and interests are build on so that connections of a number of core developmental processes are made.

> These core processes have to do with self-regulation, forming intimate relation-ships, engaging in simple boundary-defining gestures, and complex preverbal, self-defining communication. (Greenspan, 1997, p. 8)

Core developmental processes can be either deficient or constricted. If they are deficient, it means that processes naturally mastered at a particular stage were not mastered. Constriction refers to a partial mastery of the processes. When a child has not mastered a certain level, a connection must be made at the levels that have been mastered or constricted. Then a child must become engaged in experiences that will facilitate the emergence of new levels. Developmental processes are reworked.

Observations of a child's internal inclinations, spontaneous communications, affects, behaviors, and words will indicate the degree to which a developmental level can organize specific information. Helping a child negotiate unmastered or partially mastered developmental processes effects change. Following and dealing with a child's spontaneous verbal and nonverbal communications and inclinations facilitate a full range of thinking and feeling at that child's existing level and move him or her up to the next level.

Promoting a child's self-sufficiency and assertiveness should always be of prime importance. This is realized when a child's active construction of personal experiences leads to his or her own active discovery in the context of an intervention dialogue (Greenspan, 1997).

Effective intervention tries to get as much from the context of the actual situation as possible. Concentration on the context of the actual situation can lead to the dissolution of maladaptive elements. The structure of the situation is the internal coherence of its form and content. Concentration on this coherence will eventually reveal a child's ongoing self-regulation.

> The human being treated—no matter how graciously—as a manipulable object is in a different relation from the human being being responded to as a unique self; and he will in turn know himself differently (Schoen, 1989).

Effective self-awareness is likely to result if motivational and instructional interventions are integrated and occur in the context of the academic subject-matter areas. Intervention must include cognitive, affective, motivational, behavioral, and social factors of learning as well as their impact on the acquisition of knowledge. Efficient interaction includes clarifications of the content, affective nuances, and functions of the self/object configurations that a child is attempting to revive or maintain (Licht, 1983; Stolorow & Lachmann, 1983).

STRUCTURAL DEFICIENCIES

Substantial and durable change is accounted for by cognitive modification and reorganization. It is the revision and reintegration of knowledge structures that produces significant long-range gain. Changing the basic structural nature of the cognitive processes determines functioning. Unless knowledge structures are modified, there is no enduring improvement (Breslow, 1988).

> The source of the progress is to be sought in the disequilibrium which incites the subject to go beyond his present state in search of new solutions. (Inhelder, Sinclair, & Bovet, 1974, p. 264)

A structure is a routinely used process that responds to a child's underlying concepts, goals, or perspectives. Implied in this is the fact that efficient structural use follows intrinsic plans, moves toward a goal, and responds to the knowledge and personality needs of another person (Wigg, 1993).

The goal of intervention is to change the basic structural nature of the cognitive processes that determine functioning. It must see children as open systems accessible to structural change regardless of the cause, degree, or level of development of the learning/behavior disorder. Deeper comprehension of normal and abnormal development will result from focusing on stage-salient developmental tasks that require children to coordinate cognition, affect, and psychomotor behavior. Assessment would include the integration and differentiation of social-emotional, cognitive, and linguistic developments in concert with biological growth (Cicchetti et al., 1991; Meltzer, 1993).

Professionals are now seeking an understanding of how the various ontogenetic domains are organized, especially in atypical cases. They seek approaches that can be useful in the diagnosis, intervention, and prevention of certain clinical conditions that often occur in children who suffer deprivation of and/or disruption in their normal growth processes. For example, various forms of psychopathology are manifested by such common indicators as communication skill delays, thought disorders, and attention and concentration difficulties (Cicchetti et al., 1991).

Classical "definition of pathology" approaches, while useful, have not been able to provide a suitable framework to guide the intervention of structurally deficient, learning/behavior disordered children because cognitive structures can be overshadowed or undermined by highly charged emotional issues (Gordon, 1988; Nannis, 1988).

> . . . focus on cognitive development to the exclusion of socioemotional factors is likely to result in only partial improvement. (Cichetti et al., 1991, p. 90)

Consideration must be given to possible reasons why children are not using the cognitive skills available to them. Regarding cognitive structural development, two considerations must be borne in mind. First, the possibility that global attainment of interpersonal and noninterpersonal domains in a particular stage has not been reached. In such instances intervention must provide experiences that challenge structural development at that stage. Second, there may be irregular intervals of a particular stage's structural development resulting in use only in specific domains. With such asynchrony, intervention calls for the specific application of the particular stage reasoning to affective and interpersonal areas via discussion involving peers, teachers, and family members (Gordon, 1988; Nannis, 1988).

Intervention for children with learning/behavior disorders must strive for the maturation of the undeveloped structure that is missing or deficient as a result of some developmental mishap. These children must be allowed to revive those phases at which their development have been disrupted or have remained unevolved. Before any intervention can be decided on, it is necessary to distinguish between academic and affective problems that are the products of psychological conflicts and those problems that are the remnants of developmental voids, deficits, and arrests. What needs to be considered is whether growth has been prevented because of defensive behavior or because of a lack of the prerequisite cognitive structures for adapting to it. That is, a distinction needs to be made between children who are coping with events for which they are developmentally not ready and children who are defending against the perception of a particular event that would evoke anxiety. Assumptions that all children have accomplished all necessary steps in a particular stage cannot be made. If the necessary cognitive structures have not yet evolved, there may be developmental inability to affirm an event. Thus, developmental arrest may result from:

1. an unfavorable match between the environment and a developing child;
2. the environment not meeting a child's unfolding potentialities;
3. the environment failing to provide the particular empathic responsiveness a child requires. (Stolorow & Lachmann, 1983)

ASYNCHRONY OF FUNCTIONAL SKILLS

With regard to an asynchrony of functional skills where children seem able to reason age-appropriately only in specified domains, intervention requires specific application of the age-appropriate reasoning to the lacking area. Important to this process is disequilibrium caused by contradiction and conflict. When new observations and information are contradictory to a child's conceptualizations of the world, puzzlement occurs. Manipulation of the new information to construct a new understanding provokes movement through the developmental stages of cognition. The goal of intervention, then, would be to change any ineffective ways in which children approach thinking/behavioral tasks. They must be made aware of the factors influencing thinking such as knowledge base, attributions, expectations, goals, intentions, motivation, personal belief systems, attitudes, and feelings. What needs to be brought into awareness are the processes involved in successful thinking. These would include children coming to understand the relationship between their personality characteristics such as persistence, flexibility, and reflectivity, and the quality of their thinking, the value in any strategy used, and methods of controlling and monitoring self-direction (Jacobs, 1984; Gaskins & Baron, 1985; Meltzer, 1993).

If learning necessarily involves a self-regulated attempt to make sense of the world, then logically, the importance of cognitive conflict must be accepted. Researchers who use Piaget's theory to highlight the interplay between states of equilibrium and disequilibrium deliberately try to induce contradiction in learners. This leads learners to eventually reconstruct entire approaches to tasks and draws them into awareness (Forman & Hill, 1981).

Repeated experiences of the contradiction creates a sense of familiarity with the parts. Awareness among the parts of a contradiction evokes a clear recognition and expression of polarities and begins to lead to integration. With the experience of polarities comes the experience of organization and some control over one's behavior. What is suggested to help guide children to an integrated learning experience is the exacting use of activities that stress different aspects in a situation and those activities that stress the similar aspects that change. These strategies can lead children to an awareness of how different parts and feeling states are connected. They guide children to experience themselves in different states of feeling, action, and thought. They allow children to deal with basic contradictions without excessive threat of fragmentation as they bring attention to continuity in change. When an inner image of both self and other is maintained regardless of change, object constancy is obtained. Contradiction is an incomplete compensation, that is, an incomplete balance between what is known and thought to be obvious and what has to be constructed. The resolution of a conflict necessitates constructive activity. The construction is between what the child knows and what is gained from the data (Bauer & Modarressi, 1977; Gallagher & Quandt, 1981).

To move ahead in knowledge, it is necessary for children to deal with the voids and puzzles that are part of everyday life. Puzzlement and voids lead to going beyond the observable. The overall method for doing this is to set up situations in which the learner realizes a temporary sense of "I don't know that" or "How can that be?" The resolution necessitates constructive activity. A void becomes a spur to seek out answers. Therefore, the procedures must be designed in such a way that they bring children to a sense of positive disequilibrium. The cognitive structures must be met so that optimal contradiction is created that can then be overcome by augmentative equilibrium (Cicchetti et al., 1991).

In addition, the ability to adopt another's point of view may be of extreme importance for effective interpersonal functioning because it allows for optimal involvement in close relationships. Doubtless, it is a prerequisite for accurate learning and true empathy. It is needed not only for maintaining a clear self-other differentiation but also for mutuality (Gordon, 1988).

Egocentrism, a lack of differentiation in some sphere of self-other interaction, is the inability to view events and experiences from any other point of view but one's own. Egocentrism means to be clearly the center of one's own representational world. Egocentric children view situations and experiences only from their own personal perspectives. These perspectives become the standard by which they measure their representational world. Egocentrism continues to be of interest because of its relation to the aspects of childhood thought and behavior. Because it is closely related to every aspect of behavior, egocentrism is conceived as the connection between investigation of cognitive structure on the one hand and the exploration of personality dynamics on the other (Sabornie & deBettencourt, 1997).

Decentration, on the other hand, is the ability to separate and differentiate self from the rest of the environment. When children get beyond the application of their subjective perspectives of events and people present in their lives, they are able to comprehend the viewpoints of others and, eventually, society. If children have little opportunity to confront the views of others, they may be limited in adaptively modifying personal perspectives. If these children also have little opportunity to use their personal perspectives in new realms of knowledge, their cognitive development may be hindered. They have to learn to connect their internal dispositions toward the self-other relationships that gave rise to them. The goal is for them to gain greater strength "not by means of integrating separate structures but by means of enhancing the relationship of the self to itself" (Gordon, 1988; Rogers & Kegan, 1991, p. 139).

Two basic ongoing processes are necessary for decentration: (1) the principle of contradiction holding that children must experience situations as dilemmas not readily solved with their present structures; and (2) the principle of near-match, holding that growth to the next stage of development is advanced by their being challenged by solutions slightly more advanced than their existing ones. These principles of contradiction and near-match can be incorporated into an intervention that accounts for the active, self-constructed nature of cognitive processing. For example, contradictory situations that allow children to experience indecision and then provide the kinds of social feedback can expose them to slightly more adequate reasoning. They can give children circumstances in which they can consider issues and learn how others respond to them. Following this is the use of role-playing where children take positions and are encouraged to move from position to position as their opinions are changed by how they are swayed. The purpose is to get children to focus more on the interpersonal aspects of situations they are discussing, to get them to include more comments about how they are feeling as well as on what is happening, and to increase group interaction and interdependence (Cooney, 1977).

When children are given problems to solve, they should also be given full opportunities to manipulate the situations. Their attempts to acquire the new knowledge entailed in the problem can be stratified in a genetic series, passing from "transductions" and intuitions through the logic of action to prelogical manipulation of symbols to the logical understanding of relations and classes, seriations, analogues, and to the final stages of hypothetico-deductive reasoning with the employment of combination systems of propositional logic (Cicchetti et al., 1991).

A self-regulated learning definition of knowledge acquisition sees cognition as an active process of awareness and thinking. Learners select relevant, meaningful information from the environment and process it according to their available, efficient cognitive organizers.

Intervention must provide experiences and experiments from which children can build meaning (Jacobs, 1984).

Important principles include:

1. newly acquired information is related to the knowledge base learners already have;
2. learners are actively involved and responsible for what they learn;
3. organization and integration of new information is critical to learning and memory;
4. learning is holistic; focus should be on understanding part-whole relationships;
5. the self-regulatory functions are biological factors;
6. the process of equilibration, i.e., the balance achieved when new information is integrated into the internal structures of the individual plus the modification of the structures to accommodate environmental demands;
7. contradiction and conflict are important factors in problem solving;
8. contradictory observations and information will cause children to puzzle over, manipulate new information, and construct new understandings and movements through the developmental stages of cognition;
9. the adult provides the carefully controlled support children need in order to take a task beyond their present abilities and help them gradually assume responsibility for the task.

Classrooms can become supportive environments in which children can have safe immediate encounters with whatever is interfering with good contact. Support begins with creating the mood by defining the roles and setting the stage. Initially themes are elicited and lessons are constructed to allow these themes to be played out. Children are then allowed to work through problems by actually acting out the themes. Feedback and encouragement through discussion and renegotiation with the teacher and classmates lead to realignment and encouragement of change. Finally good contact leads children to evaluate and reevaluate their behaviors (Shub, 1981).

All children are to be taught ways of thinking as well as decoding skills. Especially with children who have learning/behavior disorders would the proper teaching or remediation of cognitive thinking behavior foster more successful academic and social experiences. Inappropriate motivational and/or environmental factors may be important influences on the academic or social deficits of children with learning/behavior disorders (Meichenbaum, 1980; O'Leary, 1980).

In addition to limitations in reasoning, problem solving, and decision making, strategy inefficiencies of children with learning/behavior disorders are related to at least three factors: (1) insufficient content knowledge, (2) ineffective processing, and (3) inadequate mastery of available processing resources. A self-regulated learning intervention would consider the prerequisite areas of content knowledge, pattern recognition, organization of behavior, and automatization of strategy use. Its strategy training would establish a goodness of fit with a child's knowledge base, and give equal attention to content and process.

Because any actual situation is always an example of a child's entire reality, it contains that child, his or her environment, and an ongoing need. The major task of self-regulated learning intervention is to pose a problem that the child is not adequately solving. By helping him or her to identify, rework, and assimilate any obstacles to the satisfying of problem solutions, more viable habits will then be created. The task is to provide a situation in which a child's customary, unfinished solutions are no longer leading to inadequate possible solutions.

Potentially, instruction can help decrease childrens' failure experiences and help them realize the significance of considering alternate behavior strategies. Several modes of intervention have been designed to teach children to believe that their efforts will be fruitful. They will respond more adaptively when taught to see their failures as due to insufficient strategy use then to insufficient ability (Licht, 1993).

Effective self-regulated strategy instruction usually requires learners to (1) become aware of their own strategies, (2) pose questions to themselves, (3) practice strategies, and (4) check and self-monitor. This demands that they develop a sense that they personally own the information they read and write. The relevance for intervention is that instruction must be developmentally appropriate to the children's skills and interests. Intervention must teach children to recognize the structure of tasks by giving them a meaningful context for learning. It must promote collaboration and sharing of effective strategies among peers and teachers. Finally, control must be transferred to children so they can gradually take responsibility for their own learning (Meltzer, 1993).

Metacognition

A large body of research supports the fact that children with learning/behavior disorders show deficiencies across several learning tasks. Since, in the Piagetian light, it is believed that children with learning/behavior disorders learn in the same way as do normal ones, they may become more active learners by being taught a system of learning strategies. The aim of these strategies is to provide such children with knowledge of their metacognitive skills. Children are motivated when they have awareness that their ability to control their own thinking connects with the pleasure in this control (Wiens, 1983).

Metacognitive performance and performance on Piagetian tasks are similar in that they both reflect logical executive processing abilities. For example, good and poor learners differ in their abilities to use efficient learning strategies, a phenomenon that could also be explained by their differences in operativity. Operativity is related to a child's ability (1) to use transitive relations for the purpose of ordering sets of elements, (2) to classify elements into groups according to membership, (3) to process components sequentially, (4) to engage in reversible thought, and (5) to use information to generate and assess hypotheses. Operative capabilities determine the efficiency with which children use contextual information sources (Inhelder & Piaget, 1964; Piaget, 1952; Byrd & Gholson, 1985).

Whereas Piaget's cognitive development theory gives constructs of growth, metacognition provides detailed guidelines for skills development. Together they provide a solution as to how children's acquired strategies are shaped by their social interactions with others, their motivation, and their awareness of their personal skills and task demands, as well as how they develop functional control of their cognitive skills (Paris & Lindauer, 1982).

Metacognition is a powerful starting point for designing instructional methods for learning/behavior disordered children who often have a serious lack of awareness of problem-solving strategies available to them. Increasing awareness of personal cognitive processes provides a stable base for future storing and retrieving of new information. However, teaching children self-monitoring techniques before they are cognitively ready to embrace them does not always result in self-awareness. Exposure to the use of a particular strategy does not guarantee its efficient use. Since there are clear developmental patterns of thinking, effective intervention must reach a goodness of fit with the level of understanding any child brings to a learning task.

> Developmental trends that occur in an understanding of task variables center around another developmental construct–the emergence of the child from an essentially egocentric individual who views the world in rather concrete terms into an individual who is aware of the relativity of his or her surroundings and the importance of personal intentionality. (Piaget, 1929, as quoted in Loper, 1980, p. 2)

Operating on the assumption that cognitive activity progresses in an orderly series of stages, it is possible to conceptualize learning or adaptation as a problem or deficit at one of these stages. It is under the jurisdiction of metacognitive processes that comprehension operates as a variety of interacting cognitive skills or procedures. Metacognition is a control structure or executive system that coordinates, interprets, and evaluates the results of procedures involved in comprehending. To begin with, learners must be capable of integrating new information with what they already know. For learners to comprehend, they must have the ability to integrate new information with prior knowledge and new ideas with each other at different points in a learning situation. They also need to be able to control the activation of relevant strategies and to detect inconsistent and contradictory information in a situation (Masson, 1982).

Metacognitive sophistication comes with maturity and experience. Learning develops through the acquisition of learning strategies, through the acquisition of knowledge bases on which these strategies operate, as well as through the learning of appropriate metacognitive control of the strategies. Difficulties may arise due to either inadequate strategies or knowledge bases or an inappropriate system of metacognitive control. There is little awareness and control of the cognitive requirements of a task in children who lack ability in a particular learning strategy. Considerable research evidence shows that the nonstrategic approach to learning tasks of children with learning/behavior disorders is similar to that of younger children (Baker, 1982; Masson, 1982).

A metacognitive experience is any conscious or affective response that accompanies and pertains to any intellectual undertaking, for example, a sudden realization that there is a lack of understanding of information immediately presented. The goal variables refer to how the intellectual undertaking should best be managed. The strategies are those actions that are apt to be successful in achieving the goals. Situations that stimulate a more careful, highly conscious thinking are most likely to result in metacognitive experiences (Flavell, 1979).

There are two general training approaches, namely, the mechanical and the elaborative (see Chapter Two). The former, mechanical training, refers to the routine recording of responses. It serves to maintain attention and accuracy. The latter, elaborative training, refers to a self-questioning approach that allows for a wide possibility of responses and can result in alternative problem solutions. Use of a combination of the mechanical and elaborative approaches allows children to learn how to both monitor and reflect on their performances. The mechanical can help them become more consistent and accurate in their performances while the elaborative can help them generate new knowledge and thereby gain greater insight (Loper, 1982).

The following activities are necessary for effective learning: (1) understanding the purpose of learning, (2) modifying learning strategies for different purposes, (3) identifying the important information in a learning situation, (4) recognizing the logical structure inherent in a learning situation, (5) considering how new information relates to what is already known, (6) attending to perceptual, symbolic, and semantic constraints, (7) evaluating the learning situation for clarity, completeness, and consistency, (8) dealing with failures to understand what was learned, and (9) deciding how well the information has been understood. Children monitor their learning better when they are given opportunities to evaluate their comprehension or to take appropriate means to handle failures to understand (Baker, 1982).

A vast array of intellectual undertakings are held in order by the interaction of metaknowledge, metaexperience, goals, and strategies. Metaknowledge is the awareness of the variables in any situation and how they act, react, and/or interact.

In a self-regulated learning model children are evaluated in terms of limitations and distortions in their awareness of reality. Increasing strategic awareness of and access to task performance is a necessary requirement of any explanation of adaptation. It follows therefore that components of information must be brought into working awareness before such information can be applied to a particular problem. Four basic factors that must be considered when exploring a learning situation:

1. the nature of the material to be learned;
2. a learner's current skills and knowledge;
3. the activities learners do when presented with "tests," used to evaluate the degree of learning;
4. the interacting factors influence learning, understanding, and remembering. (Bondy, 1984)

Systematic and planful self-monitoring along with reflective thinking are necessary for effortful performance in learning and social situations. They deal with the ability to describe and justify the strategies used and eventually facilitate the ability to "think about thinking." There are three major types of variables that could possibly affect performance: person, task, and strategy. What children come to believe about themselves and other individuals constitute the person variables. Person variables refer to the traits of a child such as structural aspects, familiarity of knowledge content, and perception of personal control. Task variables refer to the parameters and limitations of the generalizability of a task. Information available to children during cognitive enterprises constitutes the task variables. This includes awareness of ways in which the enterprise should best be managed and how successful children see themselves in achieving their goals. Cognitive actions that a child must take to guarantee comprehension and future retrieval constitute the strategy variables. Strategy variables refer to awareness of what actions would be most effective in bringing about the goals. All play a significant role in attention, memory, language acquisition, reading and language arts, verbal encoding of information, oral comprehension, problem solving, and social cognition, as well as self-control and self-instruction (Flavell, 1979; Bos & Filip, 1982; Meltzer, 1993).

The ability to monitor one's level of understanding is a major component of comprehension. Some awareness of goals and strategies must exist. The distinct aspects exist in this monitoring process: evaluation, planning, and regulation. Evaluation concerns checking one's present knowledge condition. Recruiting and selecting corrective strategies if confronted with lack of understanding constitutes the planning component. Implementation of the decided on plan represents the regulation component of the monitoring process. Flexibility must exist in this monitoring process for it to allow alternative plans. Poor learners may not have the abilities to evaluate and regulate their comprehension accurately. By concentrating too much on decoding skills, they seem to lack the ability to construct meaning from what they know. Comprehension can be improved by helping learners to attend to: the initial event, their internal responses, their attempts at solution, the consequences of their attempt, and their reactions (Paris & Myers, 1981).

Hypothesis testing has long been considered a crucial process of comprehension. Children must generate hypotheses about the outcomes of information they are learning in order to obtain its meaning. Accordingly, a basis comprehension process would be to evaluate the acceptance or rejection of these hypotheses in terms of their goodness of fit with the details of a situation. The generation of hypotheses comes about through either a top-down (deductive) or a bottom-up (inductive) technique. A deductive style presents the main idea with qualifiers whereas an inductive style presents related components leading up to a main idea (Kimmel & McGinitie, 1984).

There is some indication that some children with learning/behavior disorders are overly dependent or overuse one or the other of these knowledge acquisition methods. Those prone to overemphasize a top-down approach spend too much time on lower level cognitive processing skills and consequently sacrifice meaning. They are more often apt to concentrate on specific detail and not on inferential thinking. On the other hand, top-down processors may be restricted by their rigid adherence to original hypotheses showing a resistance to formulate new ones when presented with new information. A self-regulated learning approach emphasizes the belief that both top-down and bottom-up approaches are needed for comprehensive proficiency (Kimmel & McGinitie, 1984).

All too often children with learning/behavior disorders rely heavily on only a few modalities in an effort to preserve self. Repeated exposure to sharper awareness of movements, sensations, feelings, and thoughts is called for. These children are also deficit in problem-solving abilities. To ameliorate these problems such cognitive components as defining the problem, stating goals, delaying impulsivity, generating alternatives, considering consequences, implementing strategies, and evaluating results need to be included in intervention. Research results also indicate that a worthwhile approach with children with serious academic/social problems includes self-verbalization, rehearsal, modeling, role-playing, group discussion situations to problem solving, and identifying and interpreting emotions in self and others (Kneedler, 1980).

What we are looking for is a model that explains adaptations to a changing environment over the life span of the individual and the evolution of the species. Such a model can be useful in the diagnosis, intervention, and preven-

tion of certain clinical conditions that often occur in children who suffer deprivation of and/or disruption in their normal growth processes. Ideal intervention must contain rehearsal in the use of task-appropriate strategies, knowledge
about the significance of these strategies, and instruction about how to monitor
and control the strategies. For a particular child, the intervention as to which
specific and general skills to focus on will vary as a function of that child's ability and the difficult level of the strategies to be learned (Brown & Palincsar,
1982; Reid, 1993).

> Analyses of children's skills adaptation also requires consideration of the envi-
> ronmental/opportunities and individual differences in cognitive development,
> both healthy additions to traditional descriptions of universal, internal changes
> in cognitive functioning. (Paris & Lindauer, 1982, p. 346)

Summary

The construction of many basic cognitive capacities are the result of affective
interactions that bring together biology and experience. From the earlier levels, which have not been fully constructed, an interaction between a child and
the significant others in his or her life must be established. Through this, the
child can work up his or her own developmental ladder. Genetic, biological, or
environmental influences do not govern behavior directly, but influence the interaction between children and their caregivers. This eventually leads to adaptive or maladaptive organizations at each developmental level (Greenspan,
1997).

> Human beings adjust themselves in a creative way in every situation to the chal-
> lenges of the environment field according to their potentials, and simultaneously,
> they constantly search for an answer from the environment and for the creative
> possibilities of adjustment of the social environment to their individual condi-
> tions. Diagnostic statements therefore always refer to these creative adjustments
> of persons and their environment field, which they have developed within their
> physical, emotional, cognitive and spiritual possibilities, even though these ad-
> justments may be inappropriate and dysfunctional in the present situation. (Fruh
> et al., 2000, pp. 240-241)

The following principles have received consistent endorsement from experienced clinicians and are infused with a developmental perspective. Children
should:

1. be in a relationship that conveys a sense of warmth and acceptance while at
   the same time offers boundaries that must be respected;
2. have their difficulties as well as joys and satisfactions emphasized;

3. be helped to fully describe problems, strengths, the subtleties in their relationships, and the full range of their feelings;
4. have their abilities to elaborate intentions, wishes, feelings, and fears expanded;
5. be assisted in recognizing patterns in relationships, feelings, and difficulties;
6. be assisted in increasing their self-awareness of feelings, intentions, and interactive patterns that are not obvious to them;
7. be assisted in identifying opposite tendencies or conflicts;
8. be assisted in using imagery to understand inner life and when appropriate explore or construct new images to guide behavior;
9. be assisted in breaking down complex behavioral patterns into smaller, learnable steps;
10. have conditions for behavioral change created for them;
11. be assisted in increasing their tolerance for anxiety through systematic exposure to images or situations that are difficult;
12. be offered support and guidance to help them regulate and organize attention and mood. (adapted from Greenspan, 1997)

Children may have life situations in which a sense of coherence is difficult to maintain. They may need help in actively controlling the conditions of these situations. A sense of coherence consists of three important parts. The first is the need for a comprehensible life situation. Next, sufficient personal competence to manage the life situation must be sensed. Finally, life areas with worthwhile goals to which commitment can emotionally and actively be made must exist (Staemmleer, 2000).

To support the process of self-organization and to understand children with learning/behavior disorders, teachers must use open questions regarding what they perceive, experience, and think. They must be willing to learn something new from the children without trying to manipulate responses. The open-ended questions leave subject matter and its possibilities pending with a multitude of possible meanings.

> Teaching better strategies for solving social dilemmas to children who see no dilemma is as difficult as teaching arithmetic to children who see no reason for learning addition. (O'Leary, 1980, p. 91).

Chapter 9

CYCLE OF LEARNING

The wisdom of self-regulation is that
"I know as I am able to know."
(Clark, 1982, p. 53)

Piaget's concept of equilibration underlies all effective self-regulated learning models. In whatever manner they divert on the surface most intervention models retain the ideas of (1) awareness of contradiction and (2) contradiction promoting disequilibrium, which in turn leads to reequilibration at a higher, more adaptive level of cognitive reconstruction. It is an epistemological model detailing how children get to know about, organize, and respond to all the changes that effect them. This model serves both as a point of view about how children go about perceiving and gathering information as well as a structure that acts as a guide for organizing and knowing. It investigates the origins, structures, and validity of knowledge. It seeks an explanation of how internal awareness gets to know about awareness of others (Skolnik, 1987; Rosen, 1991).

Intrinsically children are motivated to engage in cognitive activity. The need for such engagement is a primary human function. The growth of intellectual functioning is determined to a large degree by interactions of the environment with inherited factors. The inherited factors may either restrict or facilitate this growth. During the interactions the processes of self-regulation permit continual cognitive organization and adaption. They are essential to cognitive growth, even if that growth pattern is disordered in any way (Wadsworth, 1978).

In biological, cognitive, and affective self-regulation there exists a system in which all parts are interdependent. The links among the parts as well as between the parts and the system are not passive but are the very source of action. The system forms a totality in order to assimilate the outside elements. As a totality the system is closed on itself and is completely coherent. All aspects are logically decidable within the totality. The totality derives its own cohesion by simultaneously integrating and differentiating it parts. However, its subsystems are not as closed and every aspect of the subsystems is not entirely decidable (Piaget, 1968).

Progressing from one closed state to another follows a developmental sequence that is valid for all behavioral areas and at all stages of development. A child always begins from an already closed state. This state is expanded when new information from the environment causes that child to experience a disturbance. Efforts to compensate for this disturbance are made and a new state of equilibrium is reconstructed. Closure is again arrived at but at a higher level of developmental proficiency (Furth, 1987).

Three principle stages of processing are described by developmental psychology: sensing, transforming, and acting. Sensing refers to the way in which the information being given by the senses is processed. Transforming involves the way personal meaning is made from the information. Acting includes the way children understand how the information can be put to use (Simpson & Gray, 1976).

Meaning-making deals with what children experience and the understanding that they attribute to the experiences. Meanings are arrived at through an evolutionary process of consciousness, which draws attention to the conditions of action. Intentional attention always involves an object of awareness and leads to thoughtful and freely chosen action.

Meaning-making progresses from the ability to interpret actual facts related to personal observations. Continued experience leads to the ability to interpret changes made on encountered situations. Ability to coordinate the inferences made from actions follows and leads to defining regulations and relationships between self and environment. At the final stage, inferences made from the relationships themselves can be grasped. Behavior, whether it is subjective awareness and meaning of one's own behavior, or the understanding of the logical cause and effect of an interaction, can be recognized (Piaget, 1985; Matzko, 1997).

It is under the jurisdiction of self-regulatory processes that learning operates as a variety of interacting motor, cognitive, and affective skills or procedures. Self-regulation is an executive system that coordinates, interprets, and evaluates the results of these procedures. To begin with, any learner must be capable of integrating new information with what is already known. To comprehend, a learner must have the ability to integrate new information with prior knowledge as well as coordinate new ideas with each other at different points in a situation. Other self-regulatory skills are the abilities to control activation of relevant structures and to detect inconsistent and contradictory information in a situation (Masson, 1982; London, 1990; Sabornie & deBettencourt, 1997; Wood & Swan, 1978).

Any immediate situation always contains a child as well as his or her environment and ongoing needs. The actual situation always provides examples of the realities a child encounters. Self-regulated learning takes into consideration the result of an immediate interpretation of the situational facts and inferences, whether subjective or logical. The immediate interpretation provides a measure of the elements, an indication of how children make note of the elements, and what results from manipulations of the elements. The inferences children make indicate how they elaborate new relationships and how they generalize to new situations (Schmid-Kitsikis, 1973; Cowan, 1978; Wigg, 1993).

Self-regulated learning details the steps in a contact experience and maintains that reflection on the experience and the many possible permutations and interruptions along the way results in more coordinated adaptation. It is a growth process based on an energy-awareness, contact-dialogue, closure-withdrawal cycle that brings children to:

> . . . clearly identify and experience needs and wants at any given moment and emphasizes the ability and flexibility necessary to satisfy these in a 'good enough' and contactful manner. (Matzko, 1997, p. 36)

The cycle of self-regulated learning consists of cumulative steps with the successful development of each step dependent for its success on the sufficient development of the previous ones. Should any step be prevented from completing its purpose, the proceeding steps will be less well-formed and self-regulation will be diminished or missed completely (Smith, E., 1986).

Essentially cognitive structures arise from children making their own meanings of their intrapersonal and interpersonal worlds. These meaning-making activities, in turn, help children discover their own assimilatory and accommodatory patterns of behavior. Coordination of these functions across domains promotes changes in their thinking and feelings. Optimal immediate adaptation and future motor, cognitive, and emotional maturity are enhanced when alternatives are envisioned and evaluated, when there is an engagement in perspective taking, and when reason flows according to the current developmental level (Gordon, 1988).

In normal development, as children attend to sensory, symbolic, transformational, or abstract processes, they come to realize that decisions are made from everything reported by these processes. Attention to the processes brings an awareness that some elements are in the foreground and others in the background. Children become aware that, from all possible interpretations of this data, a particular interpretation is made. This sole interpretation is treated as a concept of reality. What is next realized is that a whole system of interrelated concepts of reality is possible. Optimally, the final level of awareness would contain all interrelated concepts from past and present in addition to anticipations of the future (Titus, 1980).

Since the interaction of nature and experience results in the surfacing of qualitatively different characteristics throughout the life span, there are certain universal developmental tasks that all children progress through. The processes of action, cognition, and affect interact as children move through this order and as they experience the interactions with their environments. The stages with which these tasks are associated occur in relatively predictable order (Masson, 1982; London, 1990; Sabornie & deBettencourt, 1997; Wood & Swan, 1978).

Effective results come from the successful resolution of the task's most salient issue for a given developmental period. Some salient developmental issues to be considered would be (1) a secure attachment in infancy, (2) independent exploration and linguistic development during toddlerhood, (3) establishing effective peer relations during the preschool period, and eventually (9) a sense of autonomy (Cicchetti et al., 1991).

> Salience often becomes the basis for introducing activities. For example, the salient action or movement of the sensorimotor individual; the salient symbolic formation of the preoperational individual; the salient transformation of the concrete operational individual; and the salient ideation of the formal operational individual. (Gordon, 1988, p. 65)

Should the meaning of a salient feature prove to be unclear, faulty, or deficient, self-regulation will be weakened. Children will not make adequate judgments and consequently will be unable to adjust approaches to problem solutions. In addition, the feedback they receive during any dialogue can be jeopardized (Butler, 1998).

> In sum, strategic learning involves a complex and recursive cycle of cognitive activities, including analyzing tasks; selecting; adapting, or even inventing strategies; monitoring performance, and shifting approaches as required. (Butler, 1998, p. 376)

When the existing conceptualizations about the world are contradicted by new observations and information, children will puzzle over them, manipulate the information, and construct a new understanding. Whatever cognitive organization is available is actively used to select the information to be processed. The selection is made based on how relevant and meaningful the information is. This is how movement through the developmental stages of cognition and adaptation occurs (Jacobs, 1984).

Any newly acquired awareness results in curiosity, attention, emotional energy, and excitement. Awareness increases interest and motivates learners to try alternate, more appropriate behaviors. Self-regulated learners, when confronted with a problem, begin by drawing on personal knowledge and experiences to interpret what is required to solve it. Their interpretations of a task are crucial steps in self-regulation because they specify the goal sets that influence the strategies used for the execution of solutions. Cognitive awareness can be developed by turning any learning task regardless of the intellectual mode, sensorimotor, symbolic, part-whole transformational, or abstract into a stimulating elaboration of personal interpretations accompanied by recognition of the task's themes. Figure/ground development comes forth by turning the problems presented by children into stimulating meaning-making configurations. Elaboration of a configuration and the recognition of its themes foster awareness of ground. Fleshing out the specifics in the configurations enhances awareness of figure. The structures of the ground, the characteristics of the figures, and the coping mechanisms eventually are uncovered. If faulty, they can be reconstructed (Matzko, 1997).

An adaptive self-regulated learning cycle depends on establishing a balance between reliance on others for support and use of personal resources. Experiencing different modes of contact guides children to an awareness that they have broader ranges of choices at their disposal. Therefore, it is important to examine relationship styles. Past relationship styles are analyzed with the purposes of fostering the continuation of positive ones and avoiding the continuation of any negative ones. Children gain much by assessing their self-perceptions in regard to the flexibility and strength of their capacity for autonomy. Success occurs when children achieve that amount of integration that allows further development (Frew, 1986; Lobb, 1992).

The cycle initially begins with the accidental contacts children make between themselves and their environments. At each level of development, regardless of the vehicle used, contact emerges from private interpretations of self and other to coordinated meanings of self and other. Contact on the sensorimotor level is initially biological. The sensory, perceptual, and motoric behaviors eventually develop into object permanence. Initial contact at the preoperational level consists of linguistic and nonlinguistic symbols, that is, play, imitation, imagery, and language. However, the symbols have, at first, very privately defined meanings. Ultimately the symbols attain meanings that are mutually shared with others. The mutually shared meanings make social language possible. Concrete operational level contacts begin with transformations that are initially constricted by simple part-whole pathways. The transformations come about through a child's ability to classify, seriate, decenter, reverse, and conserve data. Eventually an awareness that transformations can be performed by various routes results in a search for alternates in problem solving. Formal operation contacts, although originally portraying private logical ideational systems, ultimately lead to rational objectivity that incorporates the ideational systems and agency of others. Hypothetical, propositional thinking comes about through the functions of identity, negation, inversion, and correlation (Piaget, 1962; 1971; Inhelder & Piaget, 1964).

Piaget distinguished two different modes of contact that result in behavior changes, namely, physical learning and operational thinking. Contact through physical learning concerns itself with how children interpret the properties of the environmental elements they relate to. It is a learning that is directly obtained from the environment. It consists of gaining information from environmental elements themselves through a simple process of abstracting their properties. Its repetitive and practical aspects enable children to better differentiate among various features in their environments and its activity serves to consolidate information. It changes what children experience (Elkind, 1970; Gallagher & Reid, 1981)

At the most elementary level, the structures children have already achieved enable them to observe facts. Observations occur when children become aware of the result of their own action on environmental elements. However, at first, the activity performed on elements in the environment does not demand any change in behavior or generate new knowledge. No inferences are made about how or why phenomena occur. Children focus instead on their own interpretations in a particular situation. At this level children are able to comprehend all features of what they already know, but are unable to coordinate the features or put them to use in novel situations.

Following this, children deliberately cause the elements to react. There is no resistance from the elements. Eventually contact through physical learning reaches the point where the activity children perform on elements leads to new knowledge, specifically to the discovery of the specific attributes of the elements. As a result, children come to trust the learning environment and the self in the search for knowledge. This encourages them to increase their capacity to contain more and more information and to explore their capacity to extend ego boundaries without breaking contact with others. They reach a greater ability to contain, as well as a greater flexibility with, new experiences. As children arrive at increased capacities to contain several elements in a pattern, they develop knowledge of the essential features that underlie personal or environmental patterns. Careful attention to the salience of a situation can bring them to the identification of features that may be significant to problem solving. They can pragmatically apply the knowledge of the relevant features in uncomplicated problem-solving situations. Elements are reordered, grouped, or put into correspondence. The exclusive properties of the elements can now be compared and manipulated into new coordinations. There is a conformity between the activities and the elements. Once again, no inferences are made. Children are limited to practical application of particular features (Cowan, 1978; Lobb, 1992; Palinscar et al., 1993; Wigg, 1993).

Particular abilities and knowledge bases interact with environmental/situational demands and continually change throughout the developmental process. Learning is also enhanced by the effective organization and refinement of strategy use as well as the abandonment of ineffective, or partially effective, strategies for more efficient ones (Reid, 1988; Meltzer, 1993).

Contact through operational learning focuses on how children act on these elements. Its exploratory nature provokes new externally derived information and consolidates the very mental activities of children. As they discover new relations among their actions, children gain knowledge indirectly by reflecting on their own activities. Contact through operational learning occurs whenever children are confronted with problems that demand new deductive instruments. Knowledge is acquired by applying logical rules. This contact results in the construction of nonproperties of situational elements or events. When children construct not only the properties but also the nonproperties in any element or event, their thought processes go beyond simple correspondences. The coordinating quality of contact through operational learning helps children organize events into larger wholes. It changes how children experience (Gallagher & Reid, 1981).

At the next point, inferences are necessary. Children learn about their actions by observing their effects on environmental elements. Not only do they observe the results of their own actions but children can now make inferences about how and why these actions cause the effects they do. Deductions can be made about the interrelationships of elements, thereby uniting the elements. The realization of the interrelationships is generally quite gradual and consists of the reconstruction on a conceptual level of what was previously carried out on a practical level. Mental activity is limited to causal explanations.

Children are now ready to coordinate their very inferences. Operational rather than causal explanations are forthcoming. They become aware of the operative actions they apply to environmental elements. There is a realization that inferences are necessary to understand the logic of an interaction. The necessity of a strategy or overall plan for action becomes apparent. Continued application of the plan reveals its effectiveness. Each trial leads to modification and improvement of any plan. Recognition that an old plan is inadequate leads to the construction of a new strategy. Logical reflection takes a lower level act, projects it onto a higher plane, and frames inferences (Elkind, 1970; Gallagher & Reid, 1981).

What follows this accomplishment is the ability to generalize personal knowledge bases and knowledge usages to increasingly more complex situations with more controlling variables. Independent application of acquired learning strategies in more challenging situations provides children with occasions for planning, organizing, editing, and revising the use of strategies. Feedback from the environment directs and supports the complexity, length, and difficulty of a learning situation as children model and practice new problem-solving alternatives. Children become informed as to the name, purpose, and sequential steps of a strategy; how to apply the strategy; and when and where the strategy would be appropriately used (Cowan, 1978; Palinscar et al., 1993; Wigg, 1993).

After this, children can select goals, create plans, identify perspectives to guide action, and formulate hypotheses. They become proficient holistical and automatic processors of information. As they become more fluent and flexible, they make readjustments and reconstructions only when a situation is too complex.

Finally, children reach a level of expertise that allows them to process with a rapid, fluent, flexible, and coherent intuitiveness (Wigg, 1993).

THE CYCLE OF LEARNING

The self-regulated learning cycle proceeds through the sequence of arousal to task demands, scanning knowledge and beliefs, choice, action, and satisfaction. It is very important to keep in mind that this sequence is applicable in each realm of intellectual development. It pertains whether content is processed through motor, sensory, perceptual modalities; play, imitation, imaginary, linguistic symbols; classificatory, seriational, reversible, decentering, or conserving part-whole transformations; or hypothetical, propositional, probabilistic abstractions.

The construction of a sensorimotor inference involves four aspects:

1. knowledge resulting from the physical elements that are present;
2. knowledge resulting from the physical elements known by children but are not present;
3. knowledge resulting from combining information discerned from both physically present and nonphysically present elements;
4. knowledge resulting from a construction that builds to a level of understanding beyond information discerned from both physically present and nonphysically present elements.

The construction of a preoperational inference involves four aspects:

1. knowledge resulting from the symbolic element that are mentally present;
2. knowledge resulting from the symbolic elements known by children but are not mentally present;
3. knowledge resulting from combining information discerned from both mentally present and nonmentally present symbolic elements;
4. knowledge resulting from a construction that builds to a level of understanding beyond information discerned from both mentally present and nonmentally present symbolic elements.

The construction of a concrete operational inference involves four aspects:

1. knowledge resulting from the transformational elements that are mentally present;

2. knowledge resulting from the transformational elements known by children but are not mentally present;
3. knowledge resulting from combining information discerned from both mentally present and nonmentally present transformational elements;
4. knowledge resulting from a construction that builds to a level of understanding beyond information discerned from both mentally present and nonmentally present transformational elements.

The construction of a formal operational inference involves four aspects:

1. knowledge resulting from the abstract elements that are mentally present;
2. knowledge resulting from the abstract elements known by children but are not mentally present;
3. knowledge resulting from combining information discerned from both mentally present and nonmentally present abstract elements;
4. knowledge resulting from a construction that builds to a level of understanding beyond information discerned from both mentally present and nonmentally present abstract elements.

CYCLE OF LEARNING				
	Sensorimotor	**Pre-operational**	**Concrete operational**	**Formal operational**
Arousal to task demands	Motor Actions	Play	Classification	Hypothetical thought
Scanning	Sensory data	Imitation	Seriation	Propositional
Choice	Perceptual data	Imagery	Reversibility	Probability
Action		Linguistics	Decentering	
Satisfaction			Conservation	

Arousal to Task Demands

The best, most effective learning results from the personal curiosity and deep involvement of the learner. It is enhanced by social situations that demand the learner take and defend a position, make decisions, and formulate and enforce their own rules. It is learning that helps learners develop the ability to govern themselves, to think for themselves, to make moral decisions about what is right and wrong, and to make intelligent decisions about what is true and untrue. In self-regulated teaching/learning alliances, learners are helped to explore stimulating situations. This attunes them to their awareness and efficiency in understanding what they are experiencing and what is being asked of them (Kamii, Clark, & Dominick, 1994).

Arousal focuses on the rhythms that motivate children to either reach into the environment for the satisfaction of needs or pull back into the self for rest until impelled by other needs. The mode of incorporation varies beginning with movement and perception and continuing to those of the higher mental operations. The occurrence of a need causes a state of arousal or excitement. Needs mobilize children to a state of higher energy. A primitive undifferentiated form is simply excitement, that is, heightened activity. From initial reactions there is a movement of energy into the entire system. This, in turn, becomes meaningful activity involving an appropriate interaction with elements in the environment. The particular need in question is fulfilled. Finally, activity pursues an evaluation of the experiences. The process is a spiraling one in which the reading of observable facts precedes their coordinations. Learners at first interpret what is observable with whatever tools of assimilation they have available to them. After they have decoded what they have observed, they make inferences about how and why the facts occur. Equilibration never leads back to the original state. The construction of new coordinations enriches and changes the nature of knowledge (Smith, E., 1988).

The first phase in the learning cycle is figure/ground differentiation during which some aspect of a situation calls attention to itself. Differentiation centers around how some element, internal or external, attracts interest and sparks a need to respond in problem-solving ways to the emerging figure. The sequence begins with excitements to stimuli whether they are in the sensorimotor, symbolic, transformational, or abstract modality. Initially any particular intellectual modality serves as the ground while the stimuli from the environment are figures. Excitement is generated, provokes active and deliberate interests, and elicits an active deliberate approach to need satisfaction. This newly acquired awareness results in emotional energy and excitement and increases interest and can motivate children to try alternate, healthier behaviors (Perls, Hefferline, & Goodman, 1951; Matzko, 1997; Burley, 1998).

Arousal begins at the point where discrepancies become of interest. It refers to those skills that lead to the cognizance and identification of the requirements of a problem solution. It makes children aware of both personal abilities and situational limitations as well as expectations that impact on the problem solution. The quality of awareness relates to learning and change. Learning takes place best when what actually occurs is different from what is expected. Learning and change will occur only if there is a difference between expectancy and what is observed. Elements of surprise help children to learn a different way of perceiving, acting, or thinking (Flavell & Wellman, 1977; Larson & Gerber, 1987; Burley, 1998).

The first step toward the integration of knowledge, the reawakening of the sense of reality, occurs when children experience self and environment in immediate time-space situations. Initially children learn to observe self-patterns of behavior in particular situations. After they have learned to command their immediate surroundings, they then are able to deal with the processes. They come to realize that personal experiences, behaviors, symptoms, and thoughts are processes. By understanding personal needs and managing their environment, children gain the awareness and conscious control required for semantic and social adjustment. Attending to the awareness processes brings to the foreground the continuous connection among psychomotor, cognitive, and affective behaviors. Children discover how they select from all the observable facts reported by their observations. Reporting on the observations leads to the discovery that selected data bring out how particular interpretations are made (Belasco, 1980; Titus, 1980).

Basic needs resulting from the contacts on whatever level provoke systematic searchings. Originally children do not experience a separation from their motoric, symbolic, or operational needs. The needs are sensed as mere extensions of the body. As needs become stronger and searches increase, adjustments are stimulated. Adaptive responses are made to these stimuli. As elaborations are made to these responses, knowledge evolves. The focus of the motoric, symbolic, or operational search becomes the center of interest. As searches continue they are marked by broader and broader exposures to the outside world (Sigel, 1981; Swanson, 1988).

Awareness evolves in a sequential fashion through the elaboration of the assimilatory function in whatever intellectual modality a child is processing. The process begins with an initial need that results in systematic searching. At the initial point, there is no independence of what action, symbol, transformation, or abstraction is searched for. The need is merely an extension of the self. As the need becomes stronger and the search in the particular modality increases, a dim awareness causes an adjustment to the immediate situation. Even though there is an active search, the need and the search are not yet separated. The search may be successful but a child may fail to transfer to other situations. A child initially may act as if an object, a symbol, a transformation, or abstraction owes its existence to his or her own behaviors. At the final stage, however, the search is marked by an opening up to the "outside" world. The search for a solution becomes the center of interest of its own (Swanson, 1988).

Awareness to the environment can be initiated and stimulated by having a child go through measured repetitions and pleasurable experiences in any processing modality. Repetition of behavior aids in a separation of assimilation and accommodation. As he or she repeats familiar intellectual patterns, subjective experience becomes stabilized. After sufficient repetition of whatever intellectual modal patterns being used, that child launches gradual variations of stimulations. When an adult joins in these behaviors, the child is urged to go beyond stereotyped repetitious intellectual patterns. Imitation of the stereotyped repetitions fosters the experience of familiarity and contact.

Next, partial mastery occurs. Rather than repeating the internal, autocentric experiences, a child repeats certain behaviors in order to recreate familiar intellectual modal patterns. He or she attempts new behaviors and expands the range of familiarity. Differentiation between self and others begins and facilitates circular interactions. Familiar parallel interactions expand to reciprocal ones. New intellectual modal patterns within the context of imitation and contact with adults occur (Bauer & Modarressi, 1977).

Following this, the ability to maintain mental images of an intellectual modal pattern in both its familiar, static state and in its expanded, dynamic state exists. This is the first time that a cognitive link between these often opposing states can be established. Recognition of the connection between two understandings of the same modal pattern can be grasped. However, the understanding of a modal pattern in two understandings is not apparent. That is, a child sees the two states existing in an either-or and not as a both-and relationship. Although aware of the concurrent existence of the static and dynamic states, they can only be in focus alternately and not simultaneously (Bauer & Modarressi, 1977).

By modifying and extending the static-dynamic balance, new observable cues are discovered and new coordinations are reached. Contrast between these two factors mutually influencing each other allows a child to distinguish between (1) the elements themselves, (2) the elements he or she personally notes and compares to previous coordinations, and (3) the result of his or her manipulations on the elements. At some point in time, these simple patterns reorganize themselves into more complex ones. The stability and flexibility of the patterns determine the capacity to integrate and generate new knowledge. As the patterns become more integrated, they lead to a more objective reality (Grobecker, 1998).

Awareness techniques serve as a powerful methodology to teach children how to correct their interrupted contacting. The goal of these experiments is to train the self, considered to be the constructor of experiences, in deliberate awareness. They strive for the achievement of a revived sense of the thinking, perceiving, feeling, and doing self. Awareness in the "here and now" moment with conscious experiencing immediately makes available symptoms to begin intervention. Casting light on the elements allows for the generation and practice of a new solution on the spot. It leads to revision of the whole pattern of existence from the perspective of the present moment. The experience and any expression of cognitive understanding and emotion allow for the formation of new constructions (Piaget, 1970b; Breshgold, 1989; Miller, 1989).

Cognitive structures develop only when childen make their own discoveries about the objective and interpersonal worlds. The observable aspects refer to the immediate "reading" of the facts themselves. Contact leads to awareness of the elements themselves, of how children manipulate the elements, and of the result of the manipulations on the elements (Piaget, 1970b).

Discrepancies arising from a lack of a clear figure/ground pattern call for meaning. A child needs to be guided in exploring the stimulating encounters and demands of the immediate task and in analyzing a particular situation. Becoming more attuned to the aspects that affect his or her cognitive and affective behaviors results in more active involvement in monitoring and controlling them. Awareness techniques serve as the vehicles to bring a child to a closer approximation of reality as well as make possible the discovery of limitations and distortions in his or her awareness. As mastery for awareness expands, the child is able to broaden personal responses. As a child relates to personal interpretations, or attends to a small portion of them, the actuality of many dimensions become apparent. More efficient and effective ways to use the powers of experimentation to serve personel development emerge (Mulgrew & Mulgrew, 1987; Davidove, 1988; Phillipson, 1990).

Developmentally delayed children seem to have dim awareness of the relevance of either active searching or of situations that require their personal active involvement. From this viewpoint they would be described as being more taken with the overt, easily observable, external aspects of task performance. They are less aware of the importance of the personal internal factors of motivation, interest, and concentration. Deficiencies or delays in children lie either in the lack of awareness of academic learning strategies or of social learning strategies (Loper, 1980).

Children with learning/behavior disorders are often characterized by a constricted or distorted view of their environment and/or a diminished awareness of their patterns of contact with others. Consequently, they may lack an adequate awareness of both internal and external occurrences. This insufficient awareness of personal internal bodily, emotional needs calls for their establishing a systemic way to observe emerging patterns of awareness (Davidove, 1988; Mulgrew & Mulgrew, 1987).

In the sensorimotor realm, children should be given activities that lead them to:

1. explore the stimulating sensory, perceptual, and motoric encounters and demands of the immediate task;
2. detect salient sensory, perceptual, and motoric features;
3. ignore irrelevant sensory, perceptual, and motoric details;
4. come to meaningful understanding of the sensory, perceptual, and motoric cues;

5. correctly decode (i.e., attend to appropriate sensory, perceptual, and motoric cues and store information);
6. become more actively involved in monitoring and controlling their sensory, perceptual, and motoric meaning-making;
7. recognize recurrent sensory, perceptual, and motoric themes and uncover coping mechanisms.

In the preoperational realm, children should be given activities that lead them to:

1. explore the stimulating symbolic encounters and demands of the immediate task;
2. detect salient symbolic features;
3. ignore irrelevant symbolic details;
4. come to meaningful understanding of the symbolic cues;
5. correctly decode (i.e., attend to appropriate symbolic cues and store information);
6. become more actively involved in monitoring and controlling their symbolic meaning-making;
7. recognize recurrent symbolic themes and uncover coping mechanisms.

In the concrete operational realm children should be given activities that lead them to:

1. explore the stimulating transformational encounters and demands of the immediate task;
2. detect salient transformational features;
3. ignore irrelevant transformational details;
4. come to meaningful understanding of the transformational cues;
5. correctly decode (i.e., attend to appropriate transformational cues and store information);
6. become more actively involved in monitoring and controlling their transformational meaning-making;
7. recognize recurrent transformational themes and uncover coping mechanisms.

In the formal operational realm, children should be given activities that lead them to:

1. explore the stimulating higher level thought encounters and demands of the immediate task;
2. detect salient higher level thought features;
3. ignore irrelevant higher level thought details;
4. come to meaningful understanding of the higher level thought cues;
5. correctly decode (i.e., attend to appropriate higher level thought cues and store information);
6. become more actively involved in monitoring and controlling their higher level thought meaning-making;
7. recognize recurrent higher level thought themes and uncover coping mechanisms.

Scanning Knowledge and Beliefs

The next stage of the learning cycle involves the mobilization of energy and scanning of the environment for solutions. The foundation of learning rests in the ability to interpret static states. Learning begins with and is the result of particular transformations. Knowledge develops with the understanding that events, forms, states, and apparently discrete materials are actually momentary points in time. Intervention must focus on process, movements, procedures, and the conversion of momentary states. Cognitive activities correspond to analysis or exploration. They identify field figures in space and time, compare field figures, actively transform and generalize field figures, and anticipate more and more distant reference figures. Any cognitive perception or operation is characterized by a step toward self-regulation (Piaget, 1973; Forman & Hill, 1981).

Scanning involves the ability to organize information into a variety of wholes. It is the vehicle by which children make some kind of meaning out of their experiences. It helps children form personal worldviews. At first, experiences are organized into personal histories with each experience referred to the self. Scanning grants access to a complex pattern of past experiences through memory, and to the ability to anticipate the future imaginatively on the basis of past experience (Crocker, 1988).

The basic elements of a situation contain the actions, thoughts, feelings, goals, alliances and conflicts, and interactions of a particular learner. There is no adequate comprehension of a situation unless there is an understanding of these aspects. There are verbal as well as nonverbal communicative resources available in the intervention encounter. They can be used to analyze various situations such as ideas, feelings states, motor activities, memory, and important life episodes. They permit shifts in self-awareness. The goal is the intentional rearrangement of the experiential elements into new patterns (Belasco, 1980).

Aspects of academic and affective behaviors, if they are to interact, need to be sufficiently differentiated from each other. To understand the growth process it is crucial to know how information is received and organized, and how that organization influences and determines further knowledge acquisition (Yontef in Perls et al., 1981).

Proficiency in scanning is evolutionary. Initially, processing information involves the application of a limited number of rules to context-free features. The approach is trial-and-error, disjointed, and unpredictable. As children advance to the next level of cognitive processing, recognition of similarities and comparison of differences are possible. New information is associated with already existing knowledge base. Even though able to classify and contrast aspects of new information, when faced with a complex situation, children detail no overall plan (Wigg, 1993; Butler, 1998).

Scanning is founded on a process with increasing sequential probabilities. At first only one dimension of an element or situation is considered. Should the repetition of this become tedious, the probability of another dimension being noticed becomes greater, causing fluctuation between the two. Reasoning takes on a new property at this point in that its concern is now with transformations and not merely configurations. This oscillation, in turn, increases the probability of awareness of some correlation between the two variations. When a sense of solidarity exists between variables, reasoning begins to be concerned with altering any aspect. Realization that any change can be reversed or that two simultaneous aspects can compensate each other increases. The more highly developed reasoning skills can correct less sophisticated ones (Schmid-Kitsikis, 1973).

As children indicate in some way what they are doing as they are doing it, they advance effective powers of self-observation. Even if inaccurate, these self-observations bring attention to automatic behavior. A realization of what is happening internally and externally may have the effect of opening up a crack, leading to exploration of a cognitive gap, and a heightened level of awareness (Piaget & Inhelder, 1969).

As a figure brightens, learners use their observations, memory, and reasoning to construct a set of possible solutions to a problem of interest. They separate the field into possibilities and probabilities.

The components of scanning are (1) defining the task, (2) selecting the lower order processed to do the task, (3) selecting the strategies to combine the lower order processes, (4) selecting a mental representation on which the lower order processes act, (5) allocating of mental resources on task performance, and (6) evaluating the task. Task performance must be brought into awareness before a particular problem can be solved (Kolligian & Sternberg, 1987).

Scanning the options of behavior mobilizes the initial energy into problem-solving action. As children actively participate in this cycle by responding to task variables and obstacles, they construct their own knowledge and understandings. The result is that they build domain-specific understandings as well as understandings about tasks, strategies, and themselves (Butler, 1998; Palinscar, 1998; Reid, 1998; Stone, 1998).

At a still higher cognitive level children become competent in selecting goals, creating plans, and identifying perspectives to guide action and to formulate hypotheses (Belasco, 1980).

Two basic ongoing processes are necessary for development: (1) the principle of contradiction or conflict holding that children must experience a situation as a dilemma not readily solved with their present structures; and (2) the principle of near-match, holding that growth to the next stage of development is advanced by the children being challenged by solutions slightly more advanced than their existing ones.

Contradiction, a major part of the dialectical principles proported by Piaget, is necessary for change. It maintains that change comes about through the acceptance of some information that once was unknown or resisted. This acceptance releases the internal energy that makes self-growth possible. Learning and adjustment processes come about from the integration of two contradictory opposites, namely, meaning and experience. Contradiction is necessary for change (Denes, 1980; Meltzer, 1984).

Any contradiction brings forth a void or sense of puzzlement. Incomplete compensation, that is, an incomplete balance between what is known and thought to be obvious and what has to be constructed, is created. Voids and puzzlements must be dealt with. Their resolutions necessitate constructive activity. The construction is between what the child knows and what he or she gains from the material (Gallagher & Quandt, 1981).

Contradiction, as distinguished from surprise, occurs when what actually happens is perceived as a transformation or variation on what was expected to happen. This motivates search. Making a contradictory statement or slipping in a contrasting objective stance at opportune times gives children opportunities to incorporate the conflicting data into their learning. This generates a state of disequilibrium that motivates search. The resolution of a contradiction occurs only when children can construct a new explanation or understanding of both the old concept and the new event (Piaget, 1977).

The conceptualization that behavior be viewed from contradictions or polarities is crucial to self-regulated learning. A major focus of intervention, then, would be on children's becoming aware of these opposite polarities in their behaviors. Separating the unconscious, automatic processes of learning from the conscious, intentional process involves the logic of opposition. The logic of opposition is required for bringing the unconscious, automatic processes of learning into awareness. That is, to learn about unconscious processes, it is necessary to put them in opposition with the aims of conscious intention (Breshgold, 1989; Jacoby, Lindsay, & Toth, 1992).

What is important for comprehension is the awareness that when two situational goals exist, it is impossible for both to be realized in their original form. Since the idea of contradiction is complex, no one should expect children with learning/behavior disorders to learn it in one step. The most basic prerequisite for recognizing a contradiction is the ability to distinguish between polarities. Initially, thoughts are dominated by opposites. An effective strategy to get children to become aware of opposites is to offer a countersuggestion and ask for a justification of both positions.

At first children will be unable to provide any logical justification for either goal. Even if able to provide a partial understanding of the contradiction, when asked if both goals can be reached, children will provide justifications that have both their conclusions and the countersuggestions ending in the same way. The justifications are based on the particular conclusions children happen to generate. Children display no knowledge of why both polarities can never be satisfied. However, because children now can generate several conclusions, they stand a better chance of finding those that really fit the situation logically. At this point children tend to relate their own private scripts and to be unaware of those of others. At the next level children are aware of the contradiction but provide conclusions without necessity. They usually give implausible conclusions in which the goals of both polarities are impossibly fulfilled. Children reinterpret the contradictions so as to avoid making the real-world inferences that adults would make. Finally, a mature understanding of contradiction is reached. Justifications are based on mutual exclusion (Breshgold, 1989; Jacoby, Lindsay, & Toth, 1992).

The ability of a child to distinguish among various sources of information, whether internal or external to the self, is in reference to task demands. This is not a unitary phenomena but develops as an awareness of various means and ends and the interrelationships between means and ends (Gavelek & Raphael, 1982).

It is important to determine ability and flexibility in (1) detecting salient features, (2) ignoring irrelevant details, and (3) shifting to more efficient approaches. Effective intervention challenges children to become aware of their own strategies, to pose questions to themselves, to practice strategies, and to check and self-monitor. It infuses in children a sense that they personally own the information they process (Reid, 1988; Meltzer, 1993).

Strategies are needed that call attention to children's natural processes and strive toward an increase of awareness so that maladaptive patterns of behavior are altered and adaptive personality patterns are coordinated. They must foster integration of sensory-motor actions, cognition, and affect (Rogers & Ridkin, 1981).

In the sensorimotor realm, children should be given activities that lead them to:

1. focus on their awareness and efficiency in understanding what sensory, perceptual, and motoric experiences they are having and what these experiences ask of them;
2. identify and scan options of their sensory, perceptual, and motoric behavior;
3. actively respond to task variables and obstacles to construct their own sensory, perceptual, and motoric knowledge bases and understandings;
4. establish systematic ways to observe their emerging patterns of sensory, perceptual, and motoric awareness;
5. elaborate and flesh out the specifics of their sensory, perceptual, and motoric meanings;
6. look for alternative possible sensory, perceptual, and motoric solutions to problems of interest;

7. form new sensory, perceptual, and motoric strategies;
8. shift to more efficient sensory, perceptual, and motoric problem-solving approaches.

In the preoperational realm, children should be given activities that lead them to:

1. focus on their awareness and efficiency in understanding what symbolic experiences they are having and what these experiences ask of them;
2. identify and scan options of symbolic behavior;
3. actively respond to task variables and obstacles to construct their own symbolic knowledge bases and understandings;
4. establish systematic ways to observe their emerging patterns of symbolic awareness;
5. elaborate and flesh out the specifics of their symbolic meanings;
6. look for alternative possible symbolic solutions to problems of interest;
7. form new symbolic strategies;
8. shift to more efficient symbolic problem-solving approaches.

In the concrete operational realm, children should be given activities that lead them to:

1. focus on their awareness and efficiency in understanding what transformational experiences they are having and what these experiences ask of them;
2. identify and scan options of transformational behavior;
3. actively respond to task variables and obstacles to construct their own transformational knowledge bases and understandings;
4. establish systematic ways to observe their emerging patterns of transformational awareness;
5. elaborate and flesh out the specifics of their transformational meanings;
6. look for alternative possible transformational solutions to problems of interest;
7. form new transformational strategies;
8. shift to more efficient transformational problem-solving approaches.

In the formal operational realm, children should be given activities that lead them to:

1. focus on their awareness and efficiency in understanding what higher level thought experiences they are having and what these experiences ask of them;
2. identify and scan options of their higher level thought behavior;
3. actively respond to task variables and obstacles to construct their own higher level thought knowledge bases and understandings;
4. establish systematic ways to observe their emerging patterns of their higher level thought awareness;
5. elaborate and flesh out the specifics of the meanings of their higher level thought processes;
6. look for alternative possible higher level thought processes solutions to problems of interest;

7. form new higher level thought strategies;
8. shift to more efficient higher level thought problem-solving approaches.

Children with learning/behavior disorders often are unable to understand the interrelationships between means and ends. Awareness is the intentional behavior of self-checking or monitoring one's understanding. It is influenced by the developmental and ability levels of the individual (Gavelek & Raphael, 1982).

These children are often confused by seeing only the static states. They must mentally and physically transform their own materials and personal worlds, generate questions about the nature of these changes, and find solutions that are extensions of their own personal conceptions (Forman & Hill, 1981).

Typical imbalances include avoidance of contradiction, refusal to disequilibrate, and/or unwillingness to use probabilistic cognitive terms. These children may evidence (1) considerable fluctuation between advanced and less mature levels of thought, (2) dominance of static over fluid imagery, (3) difficulties in applying anticipatory imagery in sequential tasks, and/or (4) egocentrism. All may lead them to a state where experimenting with alternative problem-solving behaviors is avoided. Therefore, it is important to determine their ability and flexibility in (1) detecting salient features, (2) ignoring irrelevant details, and (3) shifting to more efficient approaches (Gordon & Cowan, 1983).

Choice

When faced with an awareness that there is no immediate solution to a problem, children establish decision-making processes in which they hypothesize possible solutions. Options are considered in terms of their capacity to eliminate or reduce inappropriate or unrealistic solutions. They are then ranked in order according to some criteria such as feasibility, time-cost effectiveness, energy-cost effectiveness, desirability, possibility, and probability. When identifying with one of the solutions, while letting others fall into the background, children are freer to act appropriately (Matzko, 1997; Butler, 1998; Palincsar, 1998; Reid, 1998; Stone, 1998).

Making choices is based on and leads to further development of taking perspective, coordinating judgments from different domains of reasoning, envisioning and evaluating alternatives, as well as reasoning on chance and probability. Awareness mediated by cognition is the vehicle for discovering alternate problem solutions, evaluating them against several types of criteria, and then deciding in favor of an alternative. In enabling children to learn to learn—whether the context is academic, motoric, or affective—it is fundamental that the meanings that children make of the tasks at hand are understood. As the meanings of the tasks are incorporated into entire activities, self-direction is facilitated. Children can become engaged in attempting to use different routes, different rates, and a vast array of artifacts to augment their meaning-making abilities (Gordon, 1988; Palincsar, 1998).

Concepts that are interrelated with each other need to be strategically identified and integrated. Part/whole transformations demand compensation and self-regulation. If something is changed, something else must change to compensate for it. Self-regulation is the search for a better and extended field in the awareness of more possible logical alternatives and in awareness of a growth in coherence (Piaget, 1968).

The most important characteristic of this process is closure. Initially, relationships are not closed in a coherent structure. The closure of a structure designates a completeness or stability that is at least provisional but may be toppled at some later time as the system moves toward a broader and more stable equilibrium. Once it is closed in a set of implications and/or associations, more accurate deductions about the likelihood of certain events are possible. Consequences never actually experienced can be predicted. Closure does not mean completeness. One choice can always be replaced by another or it can always be integrated into a more general system constructed later (Piaget, 1974).

Children need to be led to an attitude of acting consciously and planfully by being allowed gradually to take over all mediating questions. Intervention can be recontexualized by showing children with learning/ behavior disorders the extent of the control they have over their own learning. Intervention methods that are deliberate, planful activities that render an information-gathering activity include such teachable strategies as: (1) clarifying the purpose of the action, (2) identifying the important aspects of the action, (3) attending and concentrating on the major content of the action, (4) monitoring the action to see if comprehension is occurring, (5) reviewing and self-questioning to see if understanding is occurring, (6) correcting actions when failure to understand occurs, (7) recovering from confusion and conflict (Inhelder & Piaget, 1964; Wiens, 1983).

If children become more aware of their maladaptive learning characteristics and attempt to compensate for them, they can learn to identify factors affecting their thinking. If reasons for using particular learning strategies are identified, they can be used to generalize and transfer specific strategies to other situations. As methods of self-direction are identified and utilized, they allow children to become more actively involved in controlling and monitoring their behaviors. Awareness of personal cognitive strategies leads to the use of those strategies for the correct thinking. Self-interpretation and awareness of personal patterns of academic and social behaviors, as well as the relationships of these patterns to earlier experiences, results (Gaskins & Baron, 1987).

Repudiation of earlier held ideas can be triggered by contradictions. Separating old ideas from new ones or coordinating previous ideas with new ones can result in new structures.

> Before sufficiently precise models are achieved, therefore, one witnesses a succession of states indicating progressive equilibration. The initial states of this progression achieve unstable forms of equilibrium only because of lacunae, because of perturbations, and above all, because of real or potential contradictions. (Reid, 1988 p. 47)

Children who suffer from weak, inadequate, or faulty self-regulatory functioning are apt to experience an overpowering disequilibrium. They may be unaware of a contradiction or uncertain if the new information really belongs in their structural makeup. Their knowledge base could end up as a compilation of unconnected information. However, if children are able to integrate the new information by changing their structures, they extend the possibilities for responding. They need to develop their power of imagination so that they are better able to conceive of possibilities and thereby increase their range of choice. Until past confusion has been met with cognitive and emotional satisfaction, assimilation of life's experiences cannot occur. Repairing cognitive and emotional confusion demands an intentional choice to bear but not necessarily condone one's own failings and those of others. Before children are internally empowered to change their lifestyles and belief systems, they must "challenge old habits, attitudes, values, and behaviors" (Matzko, 1997, p. 51). They must redefine and alter their relationships. Undoing cognitive and emotional confusion calls for being open to new ways of thinking and feeling. In order to acquire critical developmental skills when caught up in a void or impasse, children must learn to face the unknown and bear what is unchangeable with courage (Gordon, 1988).

Intervention must be flexible enough to adopt either an assimilative or accommodative stress. As a counterbalance to an imbalance, tipped in either direction, children should be encouraged to engage in activities that focus on the nondominant functional mechanism (Gordon, 1988).

In the sensorimotor realm, children should be given activities that lead them to:

1. make decisions about their responses (that is, evaluate the consequences of various sensory, perceptual, and motoric responses and estimate the probability of favorable outcomes);
2. indicate in some way how they rank sensory, perceptual, and motoric options in order according to their feasibility, cost effectiveness, desirability, possibility, and probability;
3. identify with one of the sensory, perceptual, and motoric solutions so they are freer to act appropriately;

   4. indicate in some way how they consider cognitive mind-sets and feeling states that lead to their sensory, perceptual, and motoric choices;
   5. make appropriate sensory, perceptual, and motoric choices and execute their decisions by experiencing sufficient internal and external support;
   6. uncover sensory, perceptual, and motoric problem-solving and coping mechanisms and, if faulty, reframe them.

In the preoperational realm, children should be given activities that lead them to:

   1. make decisions about their responses (that is, evaluate the consequences of various symbolic responses and estimate the probability of favorable outcomes);
   2. indicate in some way how they rank symbolic options in order according to their feasibility, cost effectiveness, desirability, possibility and probability;
   3. identify with one of the symbolic solutions so they are freer to act appropriately;
   4. indicate in some way how they consider cognitive mind-sets and feeling states that lead to their symbolic choices;
   5. make appropriate symbolic choices and execute their decisions by experiencing sufficient internal and external support;
   6. uncover symbolic problem-solving and coping mechanisms and, if faulty, reframe them.

In the concrete operational realm, children should be given activities that lead them to:

   1. make decisions about their responses (that is, evaluate the consequences of various transformational responses and estimate the probability of favorable outcomes);
   2. rank transformational options in order according to their feasibility, cost effectiveness, desirability, possibility and probability;
   3. identify with one of the transformational solutions so they are freer to act appropriately;
   4. consider cognitive mind-sets and feeling states that lead to their transformational choices;
   5. make appropriate transformational choices and execute their decisions by experiencing sufficient internal and external support;
   6. uncover transformational problem-solving and coping mechanisms and, if faulty, reframe them.

In the formal realm, children should be given activities that lead them to:

   1. make decisions about their responses (that is, evaluate the consequences of various higher level thought responses and estimate the probability of favorable outcomes);
   2. rank higher level thought options in order according to their feasibility, cost effectiveness, desirability, possibility, and probability;
   3. identify with one of the higher level thought solutions so they are freer to act appropriately;

4. consider cognitive mind-sets and feeling states that lead to their higher level thought choices;
5. make appropriate higher level thought choices and execute their decisions by experiencing sufficient internal and external support;
6. uncover higher level thought problem-solving and coping mechanisms and, if faulty, reframe them.

Children are disempowered when any action violates or interrupts the normal functioning of their self-regulating systems. On the other hand, they are empowered when able or allowed to choose between alternative behaviors and accept the consequences of their choices. As the ability to make choices grows, their sense of empowerment grows. If children were not allowed to make guesses, the presentation of facts by others might well go unassimilated to the existing knowledge base. More important, the new facts would not create the conflict needed to rework the existing knowledge base (Forman & Hill, 1981; Melnick & Nevis, 1986).

Children with learning/behavior disorders may have trouble making decisions. Should internal conflicts and/or confusion about priorities interrupt the normal self-regulating cycle, choice becomes dysfunctional. Inexperience, fear of failure, fear of possible consequences, or lack of courage can impair the ability to make choices. Children must experience sufficient internal and external support in order to make appropriate choices and to execute their decisions. They must learn to define ambivalent thoughts and feelings and to explore confusions. Behaviors that obstruct self-regulation can be eliminated or reduced (Crocker, 1988).

Action

Learning embraces all of development and results from the interaction of maturation, physical experience, social-cultural experience, and self-regulation. It is first the application of an assimilative structure that is in some way inadequate or inappropriate to the task at hand. Should a child have the developmental competence to recognize the inadequacy of the structure, he or she becomes aware of a sense of discomfort, disturbance, or contradiction. This will motivate attempts to negate or compensate for the conflict. As a result the original assimilative structure is modified. The attempts bring this child to richer levels of equilibration. An ever-growing number of possibilities for responding is developed. All behavior is adaptation and all adaptation is an establishment of a balance between self and environment. Momentary imbalance results in action. Such imbalances are felt as awareness of the unique sense of need (Piaget, 1977, 1981).

After the identification of a solution, if change is to occur, action must be taken. With action, children go beyond mere thought. Implementation of a solution is made according to (1) the cognitive model children hold of their environments and their places in these environments, (2) their past assimilations of experience, and (3) their past learnings and habits. Action, a system of behaviors, stems from these worldviews. As a system of adapting creatively to life's circumstances, action permits children to learn from experience, to analyze their past learning styles with the purpose of avoiding the continuation of negative learning behaviors and developing adaptive ones. Action helps children define ambivalent thoughts and feelings and explore the polarities of both. It calls for an openness to new ways of thinking and behaving. It causes children to reflect on how their actions monitor and systematize their knowledge. Misconceptions and errors need to be met and repaired with emotional satisfaction. This demands intentional awareness, but not acceptance, of mistakes. Past problem solutions and past relationships are altered. Old thinking habits, attitudes, values, and behaviors are challenged (Butler, 1998; Palincsar, 1998; Reid, 1998; Stone, 1998).

Action takes the form of defining ambivalent thought and feelings and exploring the polarities of both. Internal and external supports are extremely necessary.

> This process must necessarily consider feeling states and cognitive mind-sets because decisions are generally based on cognition and are readily made. Choiceful behaviors to execute these decisions, however, require emotional support of action. (Matzko, 1997, p. 48)

Exploration of the strategies the children have, those they need to develop, and those they need to learn to transfer is paramount. Questions directed at the ability to recognize, categorize, associate, analyze, synthesize, and create knowledge are to be raised. Being open to new ways of thinking and behaving is called for. Anaysis is demanded of the ways in which the self is monitored and knowledge, through representative or reflective thought, is systematized. Past learning styles are analyzed with the purposes of avoiding the continuation of negative ones and the developing of adaptive learning behaviors. Self-perceptions in regard to personal cognitive flexibility and strength are assessed (Lobb, 1992).

Effective, coherent, self-regulated learning calls for children to be problem solvers. To problem solve they need to generate options by:

> (a) isolating salient dimensions of communicative tasks and contexts; (b) recognizing patterns formed by the isolated dimensions; and (c) formulating hypotheses about the significance of the patterns relative to the communicative task, context, and/or objective. He or she must make decisions by selecting and organizing a plan of action for communication from among the options generated. Last, but not least, the speaker must monitor, self-evaluate, and

revise based on efficacy and outcome, among other considerations. (Wigg, 1993, p. 170)

The cycle of self-regulated learning can be interrupted at any stage of its process resulting in faulty academic and/or affective performance. For example, cognitive interpretation might be used to replace real sensation. Energy may be inactivated, dulled, undirected, or misdirected. Action may be random or rigid. If needs are incorrectly identified or unsuccessfully met, satisfaction will not be experienced in any contact attempts. These interruptions in the cycle impede closure and satisfaction (Matzko, 1997).

To enable children to take action they should be encouraged to increase their capacity to contain excitement rather than blocking it. If blocking is occurring, children must be helped to look at what resistant or defensive behavior is being used. Knowledge of the kinds of behaviors being used to block further learning indicates what phase of the contact-withdrawal cycle the child might be blocking (Lobb, 1992).

In the sensorimotor realm, children should be given activities that lead them to:

1. mobilize their initial sensory, perceptual, and motoric energy into problem-solving action;
2. act out a chosen sensory, perceptual, and motoric response;
3. first try to enact a solution to a problem by attempting to use whatever sensory, perceptual, and motoric knowledge or strategies they have available;
4. anticipate possible changes and easily accommodate their sensory, perceptual, and motoric structures to a variety of new meanings;
5. comprehend the environment in both its affirmative and negative sensory, perceptual, and motoric qualities, that is, polarities;
6. move on to more advanced sensory, perceptual, and motoric contacting activities that signify an awareness of causality;
7. monitor the sensory, perceptual, and motoric effects on the environment and regulate behavior accordingly.

In the preoperational realm, children should be given activities that lead them to:

1. mobilize their initial symbolic energy into problem-solving action;
2. act out a chosen symbolic response;
3. first try to enact a solution to a problem by attempting to use whatever symbolic knowledge or strategies they have available;
4. anticipate possible changes and easily accommodate their symbolic structures to a variety of new meanings;
5. comprehend the environment in both its affirmative and negative symbolic qualities, that is, polarities,
6. move on to more advanced symbolic contacting activities that signify an awareness of causality;

7. monitor the symbolic effects on the environment and regulate behavior accordingly.

In the concrete operational realm, children should be given activities that lead them to:

1. mobilize their initial energy into transformational problem-solving action;
2. act out a chosen transformational response;
3. first try to enact a solution to a problem by attempting to use whatever transformational knowledge or strategies they have available;
4. anticipate possible changes and easily accommodate their transformational structures to a variety of new meanings;
5. comprehend the environment in both its affirmative and negative transformational qualities, that is, polarities;
6. move on to more advanced transformational contacting activities that signify an awareness of causality;
7. monitor the transformational effects on the environment and regulate behavior accordingly.

In the formal realm, children should be given activities that lead them to:

1. mobilize their initial energy into higher level thought problem-solving action;
2. act out a chosen higher level thought response;
3. first try to enact a solution to a problem by attempting to use whatever higher level thought knowledge or strategies they have available;
4. anticipate possible changes and easily accommodate their higher level thought structures to a variety of new meanings;
5. comprehend the environment in both its affirmative and negative higher level thought qualities, that is, polarities;
6. move on to more advanced higher level thought contacting activities that signify an awareness of causality;
7. monitor the higher level thought effects on the environment and regulate behavior accordingly.

Satisfaction and Withdrawal

It is not the assimilation of observations that were already understood that stretches the mind in new directions. It is the accommodation of the mind to new information, to information that often seems contradictory to previous understanding, that causes the mind to try and test new hypotheses (Gallagher & Quandt, 1981).

Evaluation of the entire process follows. Attention is to be given to the ways in which children explain, describe, and justify their approaches. This last phase occurs when children appreciate their knowledge, their actions, and their lives as processes. This derives from a sense of doing a job well while struggling with self-limitations and doubts. If the contact is successful, the problems to which the children were responding are resolved and they can withdraw from the experience and assimilate it to a higher level of cognitive and affective functioning. Soon a new cycle begins (Butler, 1998; Palincsar, 1998; Reid, 1998; Stone, 1998).

Behavior stops when a need is satisfied. When children are able to bring closure to the learning situation, withdrawal without fixation is possible. A level of awareness of self is reached that enables children to foresee and improve learning behavior. Overcoming an obstruction brings a return to balance and is indicated by a feeling of satisfaction (Piaget, 1981).

An awareness of self that enables children to foresee and improve behavior brings them to experience need satisfaction. When this satisfaction is internally absorbed, children are able to end a learning experience and find closure. It is now possible for them to withdraw from the learning situation without difficulty (Frew, 1986; Lobb, 1992).

Achievement brings a healthy withdrawal and a rewarding self-environment interaction. However, the withdrawal phase of the cycle often creates a void at which point children are simultaneously intrigued by and repulsed by past events. Fear of letting go is commonly felt. To support any feelings of loss, internal and external supported systems, emotionally satisfying behavior alternatives, and healthy symptom management must be encouraged (Matzko, 1997).

In the sensorimotor realm, children should be given activities that lead them to:

1. actively focus on and construct understandings about their sensory, perceptual, and motoric activities (how they learn);
2. evaluate their entire sensory, perceptual, and motoric processes;
3. attend to the ways in which they indicate a justification of their sensory, perceptual, and motoric approaches;
4. adapt sensory, perceptual, and motoric strategies across different contexts;
5. take responsibility for implementing their sensory, perceptual, and motoric strategies and changing their structures.

In the preoperational realm, children should be given activities that lead them to:

1. actively focus on and construct understandings about their symbolic activities (how they learn);
2. evaluate their entire symbolic processes;
3. attend to the ways in which they indicate a justification of their symbolic approaches;
4. adapt symbolic strategies across different contexts;
5. take responsibility for implementing their symbolic strategies and changing their structures.

In the concrete operational realm, children should be given activities that lead them to:

1. actively focus on and construct understandings about their transformational activities (how they learn);
2. evaluate their entire transformational processes;
3. attend to the ways in which they explain, describe, and justify their transformational approaches;
4. adapt transformational strategies across different contexts;
5. take responsibility for implementing their transformational strategies and changing their structures.

In the formal realm, children should be given activities that lead them to:

1. actively focus on and construct understandings about their higher level thought activities (how they learn);
2. evaluate their entire higher level thought processes;
3. attend to the ways in which they explain, describe, and justify their higher level thought approaches;
4. adapt higher level thought strategies across different contexts;
5. take responsibility for implementing their higher level thought strategies and changing their structures.

Intervention approaches that are developmentally based sustain the dynamic focus crucial to a functional understanding of children. They lay the ground for developing strategies that can extend psychoeducational curricula meaningfully. While meeting children at their respective developmental levels, the strategies also govern core processes, renegotiate bypassed levels, and promote self-sufficiency. In order to connect a number of core developmental processes, it is necessary to build on natural inclinations and interests (Gordon, 1988).

The learning cycle directs evaluation of a child's cognitive developmental lags and personal needs as well as academic and psychological intervention (Matzko, 1997).

Children face a major task when they are not adequately problem solving. They must work through a continuum from the initial destruction and assimilation of any obstacles to the final satisfaction of their needs to create more viable learning habits (Cowan, 1978; Wigg, 1993).

Chapter 10

GUIDELINES:ESTABLISHING
SELF-REGULATED LEARNING ACTIVITIES

*. . . learning is provoked by situations–provoked by a
psychological experimenter; or by a teacher, with respect to
some didactic point; or by an external situation . . .*
(Piaget in Ripple & Rockcastle, 1964, p. 8)

The study of cognition concerns itself with structure; the study of affect focuses on energetics. These two aspects of behavior are inseparable and complementary and cannot be reduced to a single aspect. Cognitive structures are needed to construct an objective and decentered world, while affective structures are needed to construct an energized, motivated world (Piaget & Inhelder, 1969).

Since knowledge is the result of a process of bringing personal meaning to experience, any teaching/learning interaction must be embedded in a social perspective. Educators must be sensitive to (1) the way in which children organize learning activities, (2) what resources are brought to the activities, as well as (3) the relationships between the activities and children's understanding of them. These are to be viewed as meaningful attempts to communicate and inform (Palincsar, 1998).

The basic pedagogical problem is that of allowing learners to become aware of, and have access to, what is not consciously internalized within their cognitive systems (Piaget, 1970a).

Little progress will be made unless and until the child is aware that a problem exists. Self-awareness training must address the following questions:

1. Is the final target behavior in the child's response repertoire?
2. What is the complexity of the task?
3. Does the target behavior occur specifically or generally?
4. What is the cognitive skill level of the child?
5. What characteristics of the child might interact with the effectiveness of the intervention?
6. What are the available resources for teaching the cognitive skill?

The following activities are necessary for effective learning:

1. understanding the purpose of learning;
2. modifying learning strategies for different purposes;
3. identifying the important information in a learning situation;
4. recognizing the logical structure inherent in a learning situation;
5. considering how new information relates to what is already known;
6. attending to perceptual, symbolic, and semantic constraints;
7. evaluating the learning situation for clarity, completeness, and consistency;
8. dealing with failures to understand what was learned;
9. deciding how well the information has been understood.

Important aspects include:

1. timelines – children construct personal timelines based on their own critical life events;
2. conflicts – children use personal conflicts in the classroom as learning material, allowing others to voice their interpretations;
3. personal projection – children show they contribute to their own personal world through projective techniques;
4. descriptors – children learn how to uncover their range of personal, unique vocabularies by using personal descriptors;
5. metacognition – children learn the logical reasons for particular behaviors through questions such as: why are we doing this? Why are we learning this? (adapted from Rhodes, 1988)

Mental growth is fostered by:

1. designing and implementing treatment strategies that are matched to the level of a child's emerging stage of cognitive ability, assimilation-accommodation balance, meaning-making abilities, and sociocultural context;
2. joining a child in the context of how personal experiences are organized;
3. holding a child at the contact point where he or she has the capacity to maintain both thinking and self-awareness in the face of increasingly more difficult concepts and deepening feelings;
4. offering possibilities for reworking the quality of a child's self-other relationships in light of the context;
5. working at the experiential point where a child's dissociation is interrupted;
6. directing awareness of negative experiences and their consequences without having a child reach an intensity of emotion that would trigger the further use of maladaptive behaviors;
7. giving children safe ways of expressing their feelings in integrated, meaning-making ways;
8. helping children improve their perception of themselves and others resulting in appropriate social skills;
9. developing childrens' power of imagination so they are better able to imagine possibilities and thereby increase their range of choice;
10. providing a vehicle for self-interpretation and awareness of personal patterns of behavior as well as the relationships of these patterns to earlier experiences;

11. providing opportunities for children to expand their experience and to exercise disfavored capacities of emotions;
12. allowing children opportunities to take on roles and try out behaviors in order to get in touch with personal strengths and to broaden theory problem-solving abilities;
13. using group work in which children can receive and give support through sharing with others;
14. providing children with the organizing concepts operative in the figure-ground relationship;
15. extending learning over more trials than are needed merely to produce initial changes in the child's behavior;
16. identifying the similar elements in the structured learning setting and the application setting;
17. using a variety of relevant figures in multiple backgrounds by rotating role-playing parts;
18. including a program of self-reinforcement.

A developmental perspective looks at certain cognitive structural abilities of the self in addition to unaware affect. Children with learning/behavior disorders may not have the internal structures necessary to understand their own thoughts, actions, and emotions and those of others. They often fail to see how they operate and form patterns of behavior. They must learn to make better use of more advanced ego mechanisms. This, along with self-awareness, leads to ultimate flexibility.

Important principles underlie a developmentally focused intervention. Natural aptitudes and interests are build on in order to connect the developmental processes concerned with self-regulation, formation of intimate relationships, engagement in simple boundary-defining behaviors, and self-defining communication. Connections are to be made with the cognitive and affective levels that have been mastered. From that point children can become engaged in experiences that will facilitate growth into new levels.

After a general determination of any child's developmental level, the next step is to determine which modalities patterns—be they sensory, motor, symbolic, transformational, or ideational—will enable that child to be more easily attentive and which ones need extra practice. Most significant is to appropriately open and bring closure to exchanges of communication on whatever level.

Educators can determine the mastered development levels by observing personal inclinations, affects, and behaviors of any individual child. Other significant indicators of level mastery are spontaneous vocabulary and communication, as well as the degree to which themes can be organized. Essential themes such as dependency, intimacy, pleasure, excitement, assertiveness, curiosity, competition, anger, and empathy bear scrutiny.

To determine an effective intervention approach, it is crucial to construct a full developmental profile allowing for an understanding of both the content and structure of mental activity.

A full developmental profile must be constructed that:

1. Describes a child's regulatory capacities, i.e., his or her ability to stay calm and attentive, to process and respond rationally to the various sensations and communications surrounding him or her.
2. Describes a child's style and capacity for engaging and entering into reciprocal affective gesturing and discussion within a full range of emotions and themes.
3. Describes a child's ability to organize his or her behavior and feelings into purposeful patterns that include his or her understanding of environmental expectations.
4. Describes a child's ability to represent wants and ideas as well as his or her ability to create associations among different represented experiences. For each basic ability, there is a range of possible behavior patterns from very adaptive to disordered. (adapted from Greenspan, 1997)

Questions to be considered:

1. How does a child regulate activity and sensations, symbols and referents, part-whole transformations, or abstractions?
2. How does a child relate to others on the motoric, symbolic, transformation, and abstract levels?
3. How does a child read nonverbal, symbolic, transformational, and abstract cues?
4. How does a child represent motoric, symbolic, transformation, and abstract experiences?
5. How does a child build bridges between motoric, symbolic, transformation, and abstract cues?
6. How does a child integrate motoric, symbolic, transformation, and abstract polarities?
7. How does a child discern feelings on the motoric, symbolic, transformation, and abstract levels?
8. How does a child reflect on internal wishes and feelings from motoric, symbolic, transformation, and abstract levels?
9. How does a child's picture of the world take shape, i.e., personal narratives with the events and people in them? (adapted from Greenspan, 1997)

Two components of faulty academic and affective behavior must be separated out in the intervention process. First, determination has to be established as to how the difficulty with stage-related communication is correlated with the inability to get certain needs met, that is, how it relates to self-regulation. Next, determination has to be established as to how the stage-related patterns are connected to the original state of mind. The separation of these two components leads children to identify and experience the states associated with the needs for self-regulation and to read more correctly the communication of other people (Greenspan, 1997).

Three aspects to academic and affective deficits require attention. The first, constitutional and maturational aspects, are determined by observing a child's sensorimotor processing, time-space processing, and underactivity-overactivity. The second, interactive aspects, are determined by observing a child's relationships with peers and adults. The third, dynamic fantasy aspects, are determined by observing how a child shapes pictures of his or her world, that is, personal narratives with the events and people in them. Knowledge gained from these observations helps to create an ability for self-observation in a child (Greenspan, 1997).

EVALUATION OF SENSORIMOTOR PROCESSING

Important questions:

1. Does the child have any sense of separation of his or her action from his or herself?
2. Does the child have any recognition of others and their actions? Does the child have any sense of separation from these actions?
3. Does the child see objects as sharing a common physical space?
4. How does a child select actions from his or her repertoire?
5. How does he or she incorporate actions received from others?
6. How does he or she use available objects as means to achieve a goal?
7. How does he or she understand spatial arrangements between objects located in his or her immediate environment?
8. How does he or she understand spatial arrangements between objects moving through a familiar space?
9. Does he or she cause a reoccurrence of various events and thus reveal his or her concept of the cause of these events?
10. Does he or she have evocative memory, i.e., permanent object?

The construction of a sensorimotor inference involves four aspects:

1. knowledge resulting from the physical elements that are present;
2. knowledge resulting from the physical elements known by a child but are not present in his or her physical world;
3. knowledge resulting from combining information discerned from both physically present and nonphysically present elements;
4. knowledge resulting from a construction that builds to a level of understanding beyond information discerned from both physically present and non-physically present elements.

CYCLE OF LEARNING AND SENSORIMOTOR PROCESSING

Arousal

Children processing information with sensorimotor structures should be given activities that lead them to:

1. explore the stimulating sensory, perceptual, and motoric encounters and demands of the immediate task;
2. detect salient sensory, perceptual, and motoric features;
3. ignore irrelevant sensory, perceptual, and motoric details;
4. come to meaningful understanding of the sensory, perceptual, and motoric cues;
5. correctly decode (i.e., attend to appropriate sensory, perceptual, and motoric cues and store information);
6. become more actively involved in monitoring and controlling their sensory, perceptual, and motoric meaning-making;
7. recognize recurrent sensory, perceptual, and motoric themes and uncover coping mechanisms.

Scanning

Children processing information with sensorimotor structures should be given activities that lead them to:

1. focus on their awareness and efficiency in understanding what sensory, perceptual, and motoric experiences they are having and what these experiences are asking of them;
2. identify and scan options of their sensory, perceptual, and motoric behavior;
3. actively respond to task variables and obstacles to construct their own sensory, perceptual, and motoric knowledge bases and understandings;
4. establish systematic ways to observe their emerging patterns of sensory, perceptual, and motoric awareness;
5. elaborate and flesh out the specifics of their sensory, perceptual, and motoric meanings;
6. look for alternative possible sensory, perceptual, and motoric solutions to problems of interest;
7. form new sensory, perceptual, and motoric strategies;
8. shift to more efficient sensory, perceptual, and motoric problem-solving approaches.

Choice

Children processing information with sensorimotor structures should be given activities that lead them to

1. make decisions about their responses (that is, evaluate the consequences of various sensory, perceptual, and motoric responses and estimate the probability of favorable outcomes);
2. indicate in some way how they rank sensory, perceptual, and motoric options in order according to their feasibility, cost effectiveness, desirability, possibility, and probability;
3. identify with one of the sensory, perceptual, and motoric solutions so they are freer to act appropriately;
4. indicate in some way how they consider cognitive mind-sets and feeling states that lead to their sensory, perceptual, and motoric choices;
5. make appropriate sensory, perceptual, and motoric choices and execute their decisions by experiencing sufficient internal and external support;
6. uncover sensory, perceptual, and motoric problem-solving and coping mechanisms and, if faulty, reframe them.

Action

Children processing information with sensorimotor structures should be given activities that lead them to:

1. mobilize their initial sensory, perceptual, and motoric energy into problem-solving action;
2. act out a chosen sensory, perceptual, and motoric response;
3. first try to enact a solution to a problem by attempting to use whatever sensory, perceptual, and motoric knowledge or strategies they have available;
4. anticipate possible changes and easily accommodate their sensory, perceptual, and motoric structures to a variety of new meanings;
5. comprehend the environment in both its affirmative and negative sensory, perceptual, and motoric qualities, that is, polarities;
6. move on to more advanced sensory, perceptual, and motoric contacting activities that signify an awareness of causality;
7. monitor the sensory, perceptual, and motoric effects on the environment and regulate behavior accordingly.

Satisfaction

Children processing information with sensorimotor structures should be given activities that lead them to:

1. actively focus on and construct understandings about their sensory, perceptual, and motoric activities (how they learn);
2. evaluate their entire sensory, perceptual, and motoric processes;
3. attend to the ways in which they indicate a justification of their sensory, perceptual, and motoric approaches;
4. adapt sensory, perceptual, and motoric strategies across different contexts;
5. take responsibility for implementing their sensory, perceptual, and motoric strategies and changing their structures.

EVALUATION OF PREOPERATIONAL PROCESSING

Important questions:

1. Does the child have any sense of separation of his or her symbols from his or herself?
2. Does the child have any recognition of others and their symbols? Does the child have any sense of separation from these symbols?
3. Does he or she see symbols as sharing a common psychological space?
4. How does the child select symbols from his or her repertoire?
5. How does he or she incorporate symbols received from others?
6. How does he or she use available symbols as means to achieve a goal?
7. How does he or she understand sequential mental arrangements between symbols located in his or her immediate psychological environment?
8. How does he or she understand sequential mental arrangements between symbols moving through familiar psychological space? How does he or she reveal his or her concept of the cause of these events?
9. Does he or she cause a reoccurrence of various symbolic events and thus reveal his or her concept of the cause and sequence of these symbols and what they represent?
10. Can he or she differentiate between symbols and their referents?
11. Can he or she differentiate between self-created symbols and reality?

The construction of a preoperational inference involves four aspects:

1. knowledge resulting from the symbolic elements that are mentally present;
2. knowledge resulting from the symbolic elements known by children but are not mentally present;
3. knowledge resulting from combining information discerned from both mentally present and nonmentally present symbolic elements;
4. knowledge resulting from a construction that builds to a level of understanding beyond information discerned from both mentally present and nonmentally present symbolic elements.

CYCLE OF LEARNING AND PREOPERATIONAL PROCESSING

Arousal

Children processing information with preoperational structures should be given activities that lead them to:

1. explore the stimulating symbolic encounters and demands of the immediate task;
2. detect salient symbolic features;
3. ignore irrelevant symbolic details;
4. come to meaningful understanding of the symbolic cues;
5. correctly decode (i.e., attend to appropriate symbolic cues and store information);
6. become more actively involved in monitoring and controlling their symbolic meaning-making;
7. recognize recurrent symbolic themes and uncover coping mechanisms.

Scanning

Children processing information with preoperational structures should be given activities that lead them to:

1. focus on their awareness and efficiency in understanding what symbolic experiences they are having and what these experiences are asking of them;
2. identify and scan options of symbolic behavior;
3. actively respond to task variables and obstacles to construct their own symbolic knowledge bases and understandings;
4. establish systematic ways to observe their emerging patterns of symbolic awareness;
5. elaborate and flesh out the specifics of their symbolic meanings;
6. look for alternative possible symbolic solutions to problems of interest;
7. form new symbolic strategies;
8. shift to more efficient symbolic problem-solving approaches.

Choice

Children processing information with preoperational structures should be given activities that lead them to:

1. make decisions about their responses (that is, evaluate the consequences of various symbolic responses and estimate the probability of favorable outcomes);
2. indicate in some way how they rank symbolic options in order according to their feasibility, cost effectiveness, desirability, possibility, and probability;
3. identify with one of the symbolic solutions so they are freer to act appropriately;
4. indicate in some way how they consider cognitive mind-sets and feeling states that lead to their symbolic choices;
5. make appropriate symbolic choices and execute their decisions by experiencing sufficient internal and external support;
6. uncover symbolic problem-solving and coping mechanisms and, if faulty, reframe them.

Action

Children processing information with preoperational structures should be given activities that lead them to:

1. mobilize their initial symbolic energy into problem-solving action;
2. act out a chosen symbolic response;
3. first try to enact a solution to a problem by attempting to use whatever symbolic knowledge or strategies they have available;
4. anticipate possible changes and easily accommodate their symbolic structures to a variety of new meanings;
5. comprehend the environment in both its affirmative and negative symbolic qualities, that is, polarities;
6. move on to more advanced symbolic contacting activities that signify an awareness of causality;
7. monitor the symbolic effects on the environment and regulate behavior accordingly.

Satisfaction

Children processing information with preoperational structures should be given activities that lead them to:

1. actively focus on and construct understandings about their symbolic activities (how they learn);
2. evaluate their entire symbolic processes;
3. attend to the ways in which they indicate a justification of their symbolic approaches;
4. adapt symbolic strategies across different contexts;

5. take responsibility for implementing their symbolic strategies and changing their structures.

EVALUATION OF
CONCRETE-OPERATIONAL PROCESSING

Important questions:

1. Does the child have any sense of separation of his or her transformations of part/whole relationship from him or herself?
2. Does the child have any recognition of others and their transformations of part/whole relationships? Does the child have any sense of separation from these transformations?
3. Does the child have any sense of the transformations sharing a common psychological space?
4. How does the child select transformations from his or her repertoire?
5. How does he or she incorporate transformations received from others?
6. How does he or she use available transformations as means to achieve a goal?
7. How does he or she understand simultaneous arrangements between transformations located in his or her immediate psychological environment?
8. How does he or she understand simultaneous arrangements between transformations moving through a familiar psychological space?
9. Does he or she cause a reoccurrence of various simultaneous transformations and thus reveal his or her concept of the cause and interaction of these transformations?
10. Can he or she combine and recombine parts without distorting the parts or the whole?
11. Does he or she have a value hierarchy by which he or she can evaluate how his or her own activities play a role in situations?
12. Can he or she stay on topic, remain in a defined set, and clearly distinguish between what is "inside" and what is "outside" the system?
13. Can he or she take mental detours or alternative routes to the same goal?
14. In a two-person situation can he or she think from the other's point of view?

The construction of a concrete operational inference involves four aspects:

1. knowledge resulting from the transformational elements that are mentally present;
2. knowledge resulting from the transformational elements known by children but are not mentally present;
3. knowledge resulting from combining information discerned from both mentally present and nonmentally present transformational elements;

4. knowledge resulting from a construction that builds to a level of understanding beyond information discerned from both mentally present and nonmentally present transformational elements.

CYCLE OF LEARNING AND CONCRETE OPERATIONAL PROCESSING

Arousal

Children processing information with concrete operational structures should be given activities that lead them to:

1. explore the stimulating transformational encounters and demands of the immediate task;
2. detect salient transformational features;
3. ignore irrelevant transformational details;
4. come to meaningful understanding of the transformational cues;
5. correctly decode (i.e., attend to appropriate transformational cues and store information);
6. become more actively involved in monitoring and controlling their transformational meaning-making;
7. recognize recurrent transformational themes and uncover coping mechanisms.

Scanning

Children processing information with concrete operational structures should be given activities that lead them to:

1. focus on their awareness and efficiency in understanding what transformational experiences they are having and what these experiences are asking of them;
2. identify and scan options of transformational behavior;
3. actively respond to task variables and obstacles to construct their own transformational knowledge bases and understandings;
4. establish systematic ways to observe their emerging patterns of transformational awareness;
5. elaborate and flesh out the specifics of their transformational meanings;
6. look for alternative possible transformational solutions to problems of interest;
7. form new transformational strategies;
8. shift to more efficient transformational problem-solving approaches.

Choice

Children processing information with concrete operational structures should be given activities that lead them to:

1. make decisions about their responses (that is, evaluate the consequences of various transformational responses and estimate the probability of favorable outcomes);
2. rank transformational options in order according to their feasibility, cost effectiveness, desirability, possibility, and probability;
3. identify with one of the transformational solutions so they are freer to act appropriately;
4. consider cognitive mind-sets and feeling states that lead to their transformational choices;
5. make appropriate transformational choices and execute their decisions by experiencing sufficient internal and external support;
6. uncover transformational problem-solving and coping mechanisms and, if faulty, reframe them.

Action

Children processing information with concrete operational structures should be given activities that lead them to:

1. mobilize their initial energy into transformational problem-solving action;
2. act out a chosen transformational response;
3. first try to enact a solution to a problem by attempting to use whatever transformational knowledge or strategies they have available;
4. anticipate possible changes and easily accommodate their transformational structures to a variety of new meanings;
5. comprehend the environment in both its affirmative and negative transformational qualities, that is, polarities;
6. move on to more advanced transformational contacting activities that signify an awareness of causality;
7. monitor the transformational effects on the environment and regulate behavior accordingly.

Satisfaction

Children processing information with concrete operational structures should be given activities that lead them to:

1. actively focus on and construct understandings about their transformational activities (how they learn);
2. evaluate their entire transformational processes;

3. attend to the ways in which they explain, describe, and justify their transformational approaches;
4. adapt transformational strategies across different contexts;
5. take responsibility for implementing their transformational strategies and changing their structures.

EVALUATION OF FORMAL OPERATIONAL PROCESSING

Important questions:

1. Does the adolescent have any sense of separation of his or her abstrct thoughts from him or herself?
2. Does the adolescent have any recognition of others and their abstract thoughts? Does he or she have any sense of separation from these thoughts?
3. Does the adolescent see his or her abstract thoughts as sharing a common psychological space?
4. How does the adolescent select these thoughts from his or her repertoire?
5. How does he or she incorporate abstract thoughts received from others?
6. How does he or she use available abstract thoughts as means to achieve a goal?
7. How does he or she understand mental arrangements between abstract thoughts located in his or her immediate psychology environment (thought system)?
8. How does he or she understand mental arrangements among abstract thoughts moving through a familiar psychological space (comparison of abstract thought systems)?
9. Does he or she cause a reoccurrence of various abstract thought systems and thus reveal his or her concept of the cause and relationship of these thought systems?
10. Can he or she arrange abstract elements in such a way as to systematically test all possible combinations?
11. Can he or she coordinate two abstract thought systems rather than two variables?
12. In a two-person situation can he or she distinguish each party's point of view from that of a third person, i.e., be an impartial spectator?
13. Can he or she think about his or her own abstract thoughts?
14. Can he or she see him or herself in an infinite variety of possibilities?
15. Can he or she see him or herself as a balanced thought system?

The construction of a formal operational inference involves four aspects:

1. knowledge resulting from the abstract elements that are mentally present;
2. knowledge resulting from the abstract elements known by children but are not mentally present;

3. knowledge resulting from combining information discerned from both mentally present and nonmentally present abstract elements;
4. knowledge resulting from a construction that builds to a level of understanding beyond information discerned from both mentally present and nonmentally present abstract elements.

CYCLE OF LEARNING AND FORMAL OPERATIONAL PROCESSING

Arousal

Children processing information with formal operational structures should be given activities that lead them to:

1. explore the stimulating higher level thought encounters and demands of the immediate task;
2. detect salient higher level thought features;
3. ignore irrelevant higher level thought details;
4. come to meaningful understanding of the higher level thought cues;
5. correctly decode (i.e., attend to appropriate higher level thought cues and store information);
6. become more actively involved in monitoring and controlling their higher level thought meaning-making;
7. recognize recurrent higher level thought themes and uncover coping mechanisms.

Scanning

Children processing information with formal operational structures should be given activities that lead them to:

1. focus on their awareness and efficiency in understanding what higher level thought experiences they are having and what these experiences are asking of them;
2. identify and scan options of their higher level thought behavior;
3. actively respond to task variables and obstacles to construct their own higher level thought knowledge bases and understandings;
4. establish systematic ways to observe the emerging patterns of their higher level thought awareness;
5. elaborate and flesh out the specifics of the meanings of their higher level thought processes;
6. look for alternative possible transformational solutions to problems of interest;
7. form new higher level thought strategies;

8. shift to more efficient higher level thought problem-solving approaches.

Choice

Children processing information with formal operational structures should be given activities that lead them to:

1. make decisions about their responses (that is, evaluate the consequences of various higher level thought responses and estimate the probability of favorable outcomes);
2. rank higher level thought options in order according to their feasibility, cost effectiveness, desirability, possibility, and probability;
3. identify with one of the higher level thought solutions so they are freer to act appropriately;
4. consider cognitive mind-sets and feeling states that lead to their higher level thought choices;
5. make appropriate higher level thought choices and execute their decisions by experiencing sufficient internal and external support;
6. uncover higher level thought problem-solving and coping mechanisms and, if faulty, reframe them.

Action

Children processing information with formal operational structures should be given activities that lead them to:

1. mobilize their initial energy into higher level thought problem-solving action;
2. act out a chosen higher level thought response;
3. first try to enact a solution to a problem by attempting to use whatever higher level thought knowledge or strategies they have available;
4. anticipate possible changes and easily accommodate their higher level thought structures to a variety of new meanings.
5. comprehend the environment in both its affirmative and negative higher level thought qualities, that is, polarities;
6. move on to more advanced higher level thought contacting activities that signify an awareness of causality;
7. monitor the higher level thought effects on the environment and regulate behavior accordingly.

Satisfaction

Children processing information with formal operational structures should be given activities that lead them to:

1. actively focus on and construct understandings about their higher level thought activities (how they learn);
2. evaluate their entire higher level thought processes;
3. attend to the ways in which they explain, describe, and justify their higher level thought approaches;
4. adapt higher level thought strategies across different contexts;
5. take responsibility for implementing their higher level thought strategies and changing their structures.

Methodology must assume that the self, the mind, or the human consciousness is the action of any child's reality. Any intervention procedures must aim toward helping children generate or construct their own reality with the self as the central referent and director of that reality.

The following general objectives must be incorporated into intervention:

1. encourage children to produce novel forms of knowledge,
2. ask children to demonstrate how they constructed their knowledge,
3. present open problematic situations that are new problems to the children,
4. have children contrast their rules of knowledge organization with each other,
5. allow children to identify and become progressively aware of their personal cognitive systems,
6. support the construction of problem-solutions in new environmental situations,
7. support the solution of more complex problems at the "growing edge" of a student's ability and at the contact point with the environment. (adapted from Pontecorvo & Zucchermaglio, 1990)

The following principles reflect a developmental perspective:

1. create warm and accepting relationships that offer boundaries that must be respected;
2. place emphasis on children's joys and satisfactions as well as their difficulties;
3. allow children to fully describe their problems, strengths, the full range of their feelings, and the nuances in their relationships;
4. help children to recognize patterns in their relationships, feelings, and difficulties;
5. bring into awareness children's feelings, intentions, and interactive patterns that are not obvious to them;
6. help children to identify opposite tendencies, polarities, or conflicts in their actions, thoughts, and feelings;
7. help children to use imagery to understand their inner lives and, when appropriate, explore or construct new images to guide their behaviors;
8. help children to break down complex behavioral patterns into smaller, learnable steps;
9. create conditions that foster behavioral changes;
10. help children to increase tolerance for anxiety through systematic exposure to images or situations that are difficult;
11. offer support and guidance to help children regulate and organize attention and moods. (adapted from Greenspan, 1997)

CONSTRUCTIVIST TREATMENT

1. learning depends on children's ability to control transformations

   present problems to children that involve puzzling transformations; children then make efforts to control and understand the problematic transformations

2. having goals to work toward while experiencing transformations helps children regulate structure

   allow children to set goals before they try to deal with the transformations (goal provides structure that aids reasoning so children can anticipate outcome)

3. experiencing transformations helps children control and understand them

   present concrete material that permits children to experience and impose kinds of change (children learn to devise solutions that fit their own immediate and internal needs)

4. creating problem-solving strategies facilitate the growth of knowledge

   present problems, not solutions, to children and accept their methods of problem solving even if unconventional or certain to lead to failure (the activity of creating facilitates resolution of problems)

5. effective learning occurs when children anticipate the results of their actions and compare the results of their actions with outcomes to verify success or failure

   require children to anticipate outcomes; encourage them to compare their hypothesized outcome with the results of their predictions; (contradictions stimulate developmentally significant efforts to resolve the contradiction)

6. the ability to control and understand transformations develops as the result of reflexive abstraction; this involves making inferences and reorganizing knowledge

   create situations that stimulate children to infer and reason spontaneously (learning to reason, to make inferences, to think about personal actions, and observe phenomena helps children cope with their own and environmental shortcomings, and consequently fosters self-regulation)

7. telling children that their actions are good or bad, right or wrong, rein-forces dependence on a controlling environment; responding to children by fashioning further interactions that stimulate creativity and reasoning strengthens internal regulation

   allow children to enjoy their problem-solving efforts; if these efforts are inadequate, pose new problems and allow children to experiment further (stimulating internal control of behav-ior and environment facilitates greater development then does imposing external control) (Moses, 1981)

Intervention with Children Manifesting Resistive Behaviors:

Resistive behaviors, which include cutting, tardiness, refusal to cooperate, walking out, excessive restlessness, inattention, inability to remember procedures, interrupting, monopolizing, digressing, jumping out of role, apathy, and minimal participation, can be managed by such strategies as:

A. using empathic encouragement:

   1. let students explain any difficulty in participating
   2. clearly express your understanding of the student's feelings
   3. if appropriate, respond with a viable alternative
   4. present your own view in greater detail with reasons
   5. express the appropriateness of delaying a resolution difference between teacher and student
   6. urge the student to tentatively participate

B. reinstructing and simplifying:

   1. have students follow one behavioral step rather than a series of steps
   2. have students play a passive role in a role-playing scene
   3. instruct students in what to say in the role-play
   4. reinforce students for improvements over their own prior performances rather than live up to standards set for other students

C. reducing threat:

   1. model a particular task before asking the students to try the task;
   2. reassure students with such comments as, "I know it's not easy"; "Take your time"; "Give it a try"; and "I'll help you through it"
   3. clarify any aspect of the task that is still not clear

D. eliciting responses:

   1. call on volunteers
   2. introduce topics for discussion
   3. ask a specific student to participate, preferably one who shows some sign of interest or attention

E. terminating responses: If attention is diverted from the task at hand, take a direct stand.

   1. interrupt ongoing inappropriate behavior
   2. extinguish inappropriate behavior
   3. cease interaction with a resistant student and ask others to participate
   4. urge students to get back on the correct topic (adapted from Goldberg et al., 1983)

Mental growth can be fostered by:

1. designing and implementing intervention strategies that are matched to the level of a child's emerging stage of cognitive ability, assimilation-accommodation balance, meaning-making abilities, and sociocultural context;
2. joining a child in the context of how personal experiences are organized;
3. holding a child at the contact point where he or she has the capacity to maintain both thinking and self-awareness in the face of increasingly more difficult concepts and deepening feelings;
4. offering possibilities for reworking the quality of a child's self-other relationships in light of the context;
5. working at the experiential point where a child's dissociation is interrupted;
6. directing awareness of negative experiences and their consequences without having a child reach an intensity of emotion that would trigger the further use of maladaptive behaviors.

CYCLE OF LEARNING

1. AROUSAL TO TASK DEMANDS:

Teachers should use activities that can lead learners to:

1. explore the stimulating encounters
2. detect salient features
3. ignore irrelevant and demands of the immediate task
4. come to meaningful understanding of the cues
5. correctly decode (i.e., attend to appropriate cues and store information)
6. become more actively involved in monitoring and controlling their meaning-making
7. recognize recurrent themes and uncover coping mechanisms

In the following areas:

Movement	Symbolic functioning	Transforming part/Whole relationships	Ideas
Sensations, Psychomotor skills	Play, Imitation, Imagery, Drawing/graphics, Language	Classification, Seriation, Reversibility, Conservation, Decentration	Hypothetical thought, Propositional thought, Proportionality

2. SCANNING KNOWLEDGE AND BELIEFS OF CHILDREN:

Teachers should use activities that can lead children to:

1. focus on their awareness and efficiency in understanding what they are experiencing and what is being asked of them
2. identify and scan options of behavior
3. actively respond to task variables and obstacles to construct their knowledge bases and understandings
4. establish systematic ways to observe their emerging patterns of awareness
5. elaborate and flesh out of the specifics of their meanings
6. look for alternative possible solutions to problems of interest
7. form new strategies
8. shift to more efficient approaches

In the following areas:

Movement	Symbolic functioning	Transforming part/Whole relationships	Ideas
Sensations, Psychomotor skills	Play, Imitation, Imagery, Drawing/graphics, Language	Classification, Seriation, Reversibility, Conservation, Decentration	Hypothetical thought, Propositional thought, Proportionality

3. CHOICE:

Teachers should use activities that can lead children to:

1. make decisions about responses, evaluate the consequences of various responses, estimate the probability of favorable outcomes

2. rank options in order according to their feasibility, cost-effectiveness, desirability, possibility and probability

3. identify with one of the solutions so they are free to act appropriately

4. consider cognitive mind-sets and feeling states that lead to their choices

5. make appropriate choices and execute their decisions by experiencing sufficient internal and external support

6. define ambivalent feelings and explore confusion

7. uncover problem solving and coping mechanisms and, if faulty, reframe them

In the following areas;

Movement	Symbolic functioning	Transforming part/Whole relationships	Ideas
Sensations, Psychomotor skills	Play, Imitation, Imagery, Drawing/graphics, Language	Classification, Seriation, Reversibility, Conservation, Decentration	Hypothetical thought, Propositional thought, Proportionality

4. ACTION:

Teachers should use activities that can lead children to:

1. mobilize their initial energy into problem-solving action
2. act out a chosen response
3. first try to enact a solution to a problem by attempting to use whatever knowledge or strategies they have available
4. anticipate possible transformations and easily accommodate their structures to a variety of new meanings
5. comprehend the environment in both its affirmative and negative qualities, that is, polarities
6. move on to more advanced contacting activities that signify an awareness of causality
7. monitor the effects on the environment and regulate behavior accordingly

In the following areas:

Movement	Symbolic functioning	Transforming part/Whole relationships	Ideas
Sensations, Psychomotor skills	Play, Imitation, Imagery, Drawing/graphics, Language	Classification, Seriation, Reversibility, Conservation, Decentration	Hypothetical thought, Propositional thought, Proportionality

5. SATISFACTION AND WITHDRAWAL:

Teachers should use activities that can lead children to:

1. actively focus on and construct understandings about their cognitive activities (how they learn)
2. evaluate their entire processes
3. attend to ways in which they explain, describe and justify their approaches
4. adapt strategies across different contexts
5. take responsibility for implementing their strategies and changing their structures

In the following areas:

Movement	Symbolic functioning	Transforming part/Whole relationships	Ideas
Sensations, Psychomotor skills	Play, Imitation, Imagery, Drawing/graphics, Language	Classification, Seriation, Reversibility, Conservation, Decentration	Hypothetical thought, Propositional thought, Proportionality

REFERENCES

Achenbach, T. M. (1974). *Developmental Psychology.* New York: Wiley.

Anderson, T. (1996). What in the world is constructivism? *Learning,* March/April, 49–52.

Anthony, E. J. (1956). The significance of Jean Piaget for child psychiatry. *British Journal of Medical Psychology, 29,* 20–34.

Baker, L. (1982). An evaluation of the role of metacognitive deficits in learning disabilities. *Topics in Learning Disabilities, 2,* 27–35.

Bauer, R., & Modarressi, T. (1977). Strategies of therapeutic contact: Working with children with severe object relationship disturbances. *American Journal of Psychotherapy, 31,* 605–617.

Beilin, H., & Pufall, P. B. (1992). In conclusion: Continuing implication. In H. Beilin & P. B. Pufall (Eds.), *Piaget's theory: Prospects and possibilities* (pp. 311–326). Hillsdale, NJ: Lawrence Erlbaum.

Belasco, B. (1980). Anthropological reflections on Gestalt therapy. *The Gestalt Journal, III,* 54–63.

Bereiter, C. (1985). Toward a solution of the learning paradox. *Review of Educational Research, 55,* 201–226.

Bhavnagri, N. P., & Samuels, B. G. (1996). Making and keeping friends: A thematic unit to promoting understanding of peer relationship in young children. *Childhood Education, 72,* 219–232.

Biemiller, A., & Meichenbaum, D. (1998). The consequences of negative scaffolding for students who learn slowly – A commentary on C. Addison Stone's "The metaphor of scaffolding: Its utility for the field of learning disabilities." *Journal of Learning Disabilities, 4,* 365–369.

Bondy, E. (1984). Thinking about thinking: Encouraging children's use of metacognitive processes. *Childhood Education,* (March/April), 234–238.

Borkowski, J. G., & Konarski, E. A. (1981). Educational implications of efforts to train intelligence. *Journal of Special Education, 1,* 289–305.

Bos, C. S., & Filip, D. (1982). Comprehension monitoring in disabled and average students. *Topics in Learning and Learning Disabilities, 2,* 79–85.

Bovet, M. C., (1981). Learning research with Piagetian lines. *Topics in Learning and Learning Disabilities, 1,* 1–9.

Bower, E. (1972). Psychology in the school: Conceptions, processes, and territories. *Psychology in the Schools, 42,* 3–11.

Breshgold, E. (1989). Resistance in Gestalt therapy: An historic-theoretical perspective. *The Gestalt Journal, XII,* 73–102.

Breslow, L. (1988). Possibilities and pitfalls in clinical application of cognitive-developmental theory. In E. D. Nannis & P. A. Cowan (Eds.), *New Directions for Child Development, 39,* 147–164. San Francisco: Jossey-Bass.

Bronfenbrenner, U., Kessel, F., Kessen, W., & White, S., (1986). Toward a critical social history of developmental psychology, *American Psychologist, 41,* 1218–1230.

Brown, G. I. (1971). *Human Teaching for Human Learning: An Introduction to Confluent Education.* New York: Viking Press.

Brown, G. I. (Ed.). (1975). *The Living Classroom: Innovation through Confluent Education and Gestalt.* New York: Viking Press.

Brown, A. L., & Palinscar, A. S. (1982). Inducing strategic learning from texts by means of informed, self-control training. *Topics in Learning and Learning Disabilities, 2,* 1–17.

Bryan, T., Sullivan-Burstein, K., & Mathur, S. (1998). The influence of affect on social-information processing. *Journal of Learning Disabilities, 31,* 418–426.

Burley, T. (1998). Mind and brains for Gestalt therapists. *Gestalt Review, 2,* 131–142.

Butler, D. L. (1998). In search of the architect of learning: A commentary on scaffolding as a metaphor for instructional interactions. *Journal of Learning Disabilities, 31*, 374–385.

Byrd, D. M., & Gholson, B. (1985). Reading, memory, and metacognition. *Journal of Educational Psychology, 77*, 428–436.

Cahalan, W. (1983). An elaboration of the Gestalt personality theory: The experience of self in social relations. *The Gestalt Journal, VI,* 39–53.

Chapman, M. (1992). Equilibrium and the dialectics of organization. In H. Beilin & P. B. Pufall (Eds.), *Piaget's theory: Prospects and possibilities* (pp. 39–59). Hillsdale, NJ: Lawrence Erlbaum.

Child, I. L. (1973). *Humanistic Psychology and the Research Tradition: Their Several Virtues.* New York: Wiley.

Chrzanowski, G. (1982). Interpersonal formulations of psychotherapy. In J. C. Anchin & D. J. Kiesler (Eds.), *Handbook of interpersonal psychology.* (pp. 25–45). New York: Pergamon Press.

Cicchetti, D. (1984). The emergence of developmental psychopathology. *Child Development, 55,* 1–7.

Cicchetti, D., Toth, S. L., Bush, M. A., & Gillespie, J. F. (1988). Stage-salient issues: A transactional model of intervention. In E. D. Nannis & P. A. Cowan (Eds.), *New directions for child development* (pp. 123–145). Hillsdale, NJ: Lawrence Erlbaum.

Cicchetti, D., & Beeghly, M. (Eds.) (1990). *The Self in Transition: Infancy to Childhood.* Chicago: University of Chicago Press.

Cicchetti, D., Beeghly, M., Carlson, V., Coster, W., Gersten, M., Rieder, C., & Toth, S. (1991). Development and psychopathology: Lessons from the study of maltreated children. In D. P. Keating & H. Rosen (Eds.), *Constructivistic perspectives on developmental psychopathology and atypical development* (pp. 69–102). Hillsdale, NJ: Lawrence Erlbaum.

Cicchetti, D., & Toth, S. L. (1998). The development of depression in children and adolescents. *American Psychologist, 53,* 221–241.

Clark, A. (1982). Grief and Gestalt therapy. *The Gestalt Journal, V,* 49–63.

Clarkson, P. (1997). Variations on I and thou. *Gestalt Review, 1,* 56–70.

Cocking, R. (1981). Continuities and discontinuities in structuralism and constructivism. In I. E. Sigel, D. M. Brodzinsky, & R. M. Golinkoff (Eds.), *New directions in Piagetian theory and practice.* (pp. 71–86). Hillsdale, NJ: Lawrence Erlbaum.

Combs, A. W. (1981). Human education: Too tender for a tough world? *Phi Delta Kappan, 62,* 446–449.

Cooney, E. W. (1977). Social-cognitive development: Applications to intervention and evaluation in the elementary grades. *The Counseling Psychologist, 8,* 6–9.

Cowan, P. A. (1978). *Piaget with Feeling: Cognitive, Social, and Emotional Dimensions.* New York: Holt, Rinehart & Winston.

Crocker, S. F. (1983). Truth and foolishness in the Gestalt prayer. *The Gestalt Journal, VI,* 4–16.

Crocker, S. F. (1988). Boundary processes, states, and the self. *The Gestalt Journal, XI,* 81–124.

Crocker, S. F. (1992). *A philosophical framework for understanding developmental issues.* Paper presented at the 14th Annual Meeting of The Theory and Practice of Gestalt Therapy, Boston, MA.

Davidove, D. M. (1988). Exhibition in disarray. *The Gestalt Journal, XI,* 61–80.

Denes, M. (1980). Paradoxes in the therapeutic relationship. *The Gestalt Journal, III,* 41–51.

Dougherty, D. (1988). Children's mental health problems and services. *American Psychologist, 43,* 808–812.

Eisenhart, M., & Borko, H. (1993). *Designing Classroom Research: Themes, Issues, and Struggles.* Boston: Allyn & Bacon.

Elias, M. J., & Maher, C. A. (1983). Social and affective development of children: A programmatic. *Exceptional Children, 49,* 339–346.

Elkind, D. (1970). *Children and Adolescents: Interpretative Essays on Jean Piaget.* New York: Oxford University Press.

Elkind, D. (1989). Developmentally appropriate practice: Philosophical and practical implications. *Phi Delta Kappan, 71,* 113–117.

Elkind, D. (1981). Stages in the development of reading. In I. E. Sigel, D. M. Brodzinsky & R. M. Golinkoff (Eds.), *New directions in Piagetian theory and practice.* (pp. 267–279). Hillsdale, NJ: Lawrence Erlbaum.

Ellis, E. S. (1998). Watering up the curriculum for adolescents with learning disabilities, part 2. *Remedial and Special Education, 19,* 91–105.

Emde, R. N., & Sorce, J. F. (1982). Emotional expression in infancy. *Journal of Child Psychology and Psychiatry and Applied Discipline, 23,* 145–158.

Flavell, J. E. (1979). Metacognition and cognitive monitoring: A new area of cognitive-developmental inquiry. *American Psychologist, 34,* 906–911.

Flavell, J. H., & Wellman, H. M. (1977). Metamemory. In R. V. Kail & J. W. Hagen (Eds.), *Perspectives on the development of memory and cognition.* (pp. 3-33). Hillsdale, NJ: Lawrence Erlbaum.

Forman, G. E., & Hill, F. (1981). The power of negative thinking: Equilibration in the preschool. In I. E. Sigel, D. M. Brodzinsky, & R. M. Golinkoff (Eds.), *New directions in Piagetian theory and practice.* (pp. 345–352). Hillsdale, NJ: Lawrence Erlbaum.

Frew, J. (1986). The functions and patterns of occurrence of contact styles during the developmental phases of the Gestalt group. *The Gestalt Journal, VIII,* 55–60.

Frew, J. (1992). From the perspective of the environment. *The Gestalt Journal, XV,* 39–60.

Frew, J. (1997). A Gestalt therapy application to the practice of group leadership. *Gestalt Review, 1,* 131–149.

Fuhr, R. (1998). Gestalt therapy as a transrational approach: An evolutionary perspective. *Gestalt Review, 2,* 6–27.

Fuhr, R., Sreckovic, M., & Grennler-Fuhr, M. (2000). Diagnosis in Gestalt therapy. *Gestalt Review, 4,* 237–252.

Furth, H. (1981). *Piaget and Knowledge: Theoretical Foundations.* Chicago: University of Chicago Press.

Furth, H. (1983). Symbolic formation: Where Freud and Piaget meet. *Human Development, 26,* 26–41.

Furth, H. (1987). *Knowledge as Desire: An Essay on Freud and Piaget.* New York: Columbia Press.

Furth, H. (1991). Thinking without language: A perspective and review of research with deaf people. In D. P. Keating & H. Rosen (Eds.), *Constructivistic perspectives on developmental psychopathology and atypical development* (pp. 203–227). Hillsdale, NJ: Lawrence Erlbaum.

Furth, H. (1992). The developmental origin of human societies. In H. Beilin & P. B. Pufall (Eds.), *Piaget's theory: Prospects and possibilities* (pp. 251–265). Hillsdale, NJ: Lawrence Erlbaum.

Gallagher, J., & Quandt, I. J. (1981). Piaget's theory of cognitive development and reading comprehension. *Topics in Learning and Learning Disabilities, 1,* 21–30.

Gallagher, J. M., & Reid, D. K. (1981). *The Learning Theory of Piaget and Inhelder.* Austin, TX: Pro-Ed.

Gaskins, I. W., & Baron, J. (1987). Teaching poor readers to cope with maladaptive cognitive styles: A training program. *Journal of Learning Disabilities, 18,* 390–394.

Gavelek, J. R., & Raphael, T. E. (1982). Instructing metacognitive awareness of question-answer relationships: Implications for the learning disabled. *Topics in Learning and Learning Disabilities, 2,* 69–77.

Gelfand, D. M., & Peterson, L. (1985). *Child Development and Psychopathology.* Beverly Hills, CA: Sage.

Gerber, M. (1983). Learning disabilities and cognitive strategies: Case for training or constraining problem solving? *Journal of Learning Disabilities, 16,* 255–260.

Giordano, G. (1981). The re-emergence of Gestalt psychology and implications for reading readiness. *Journal of Learning Disabilities, 14,* 121–123.

Glaser, R. (1990). The re-emergence of learning theory within instructional research. *American Psychologist, 45,* 29–39.

Glenn, D. S., Rueda, R., & Rutherford, R. B. (1984). Cognitive approaches to social competence with behaviorally disordered youth. In J. K. Grosenick, E. McGinnis, S. L. Huntz, & C. R. Smith (Eds.), *Social/Affective Interventions in Behavioral Disorders,* EC 170 044.

Goldberg, A., Sprafkin, R. P., Gershaw, J., & Klien, P. (1983). Structured learning: A psychoeducational approach for teaching social competencies. *Behavioral Disorders, 8,* 161–170.

Gordon, D. E. (1988). Formal operations and interpersonal and affective disturbances in adolescents. In E. D. Nannis & P. A. Cowan (Eds.), *New directions for child development* (pp. 51–73). Hillsdale, NJ: Lawrence Erlbaum.

Gordon, D. E., & Cowan, P. (1983). *A Piagetian approach to psychopathology: Scheme differences in children's play.* Paper presented at the 91st Annual Meeting of the American Psychological Association Anaheim, CA. August 26–30, 1983.

Graham, S., & Harris, K. R. (1993). Teaching writing strategies to students with learning disabilities: Issues and recommendations. In L. J. Meltzer (Ed.), *Strategy assessment and instruction for students with learning disabilities: From theory to practice.* (pp. 271–292). Austin, TX: Pro-Ed.

Greenberg, L. S., & Safran, J. D. (1987). *Emotions in Psychotherapy.* New York: Guilford Press.

Greenspan, S. I. (1997). *Developmentally based psychotherapy.* Madison, CT: International University Press.

Grobecker, B. (1998). The new science of life and learning differences. *Learning Disability Quarterly, 21,* 207–227.

Gruber, H. E., & Voneche, J. (1977). *The Essential Piaget.* London: Routledge & Kegan Paul.

Harter, S. (1983). Cognitive-developmental considerations in the conduct of play therapy. In C. E. Scharfeer & K. J. O'Connor (Eds.), *Handbook of play therapy* (pp. 95–127). New York: Wiley.

Henker, B., Whalen, C. K., & Hinshaw, S. P. (1980). The attributional contexts of cognitive intervention strategies. *Exceptional Education Quarterly, 1,* 17–30.

Henley, M. (1980, April). *A developmental model for the education of children evaluated mentally retarded.* Paper presented at the Annual Presidential Lecture Series, Westfield, MA.

Heshusius, L. (1989). Holistic principles: Not enhancing the old but seeing a-new: A rejoinder. *Journal of Learning Disabilities, 22,* 595–602.

Hilgard, E. R. (1948). *Theories of Learning.* New York: Appleton-Century-Crofts.

Hoemann, H. (1991). Piagetian perspectives on research with deaf subjects. In D. P. Keating & H. Rosen (Eds.), *Constructivistic perspectives on developmental psychopathology and atypical development* (pp. 229–245). Hillsdale, NJ: Lawrence Erlbaum.

Hycner, R. H. (1985). Dialogical Gestalt therapy: An initial proposal. *The Gestalt Journal, VII,* 23–49.

Hycner, R. A. (1990). The I-Thou relationship and Gestalt therapy. *The Gestalt Journal, XIII,* 41–54.

Inhelder, B. (1968). *The Diagnosis of Reasoning in the Mentally Retarded* (W. B. Stephens, Trans.). New York: The John Day Company.

Inhelder, B. (1992). Foreword. In H. Beilin & P. B. Pufall (Eds.), *Piaget's theory: Prospects and possibilities* (pp. xi-xii). Hillsdale, NJ: Lawrence Erlbaum.

Inhelder, B., & Piaget, J. (1958). *The Growth of Logical Thinking from Childhood to Adolescence; An Essay on the Construction of Formal Operational Structures*. New York: Basic Books.

Inhelder, B., & Piaget, J. (1964). *The Early Growth of Logic in the Child*. London: Routledge & Kegan Paul.

Inhelder, B., Sinclair, H., & Bovet, M. (1974). *Learning and the Development of Cognition*. Cambridge, MA: Harvard University Press.

Jacobs, L. (1984, Spring). Cognition and learning disabilities. *Teaching Exceptional Children*, 213–217.

Jacobs, L. (1989). Dialogue in Gestalt therapy verbatim. *The Gestalt Journal, XII*, 25–68.

Jacobs, L. (1992). Insights from psychoanalytic self-psychology and intersubjectivity theory for Gestalt therapists. *The Gestalt Journal, XV*, 25–60.

Jacoby, L. L., Lindsay, D. S., & Toth, J. P. (1992). Unconscious influences revealed: Attention, awareness, and control. *American Psychologist, 47*, 802–809.

Jarman, R. F., Vavrik, J., & Walton, P. D. (1995). Metacognitive and frontal lobe processes: At the interface of cognitive psychology and neuropsychology. *Genetic, Social, and General Psychology Monographs, 121*(2), 153–210.

Johnson, S. M. (1985). *Characterological Transformation: The Hard Work Miracle*. New York: W. W. Norton.

Johnston, E. B., & Johnston, A. V. (1984). *The Piagetian Language Nursery*. Rockville, MD: Aspen Systems Publications.

Jones, V. F. (1992). Integrating behavioral and insight-oriented treatment in school-based programs for seriously emotionally disturbed students. *Behavioral Disorders, 17*, 225–236.

Kagan, J. (1978). On emotion and its development: A working paper. In M. Lewis & L. A. Rosenblum (Eds.), *The development of affect* (pp. 11–41). New York: Plenum Press.

Kamii, C. (1975). One intelligence indivisible. *Young Children, 30*, 228–238.

Kamii, C., Clark, F. B., & Dominick, A. (1994). The six national goals: A road to disappointment. *Phi Delta Kappan, 75*, 672–677.

Keating, D. P. (1991). Constructivism and diversity. In D. P. Keating & H. Rosen (Eds.), *Constructivistic perspectives on developmental psychopathology and atypical development.* (pp. 1–9). Hillsdale, NJ: Lawrence Erlbaum.

Keating, D. P., & Rosen, H. (Ed.). (1991). Constructivistic Perspectives on Developmental Psychopathology and Atypical Development. Hillsdale, NJ: Lawrence Erlbaum.

Kegan, R. (1980). Making meaning: The constructive-developmental approach to persons and practice. *Personnel and Guidance Journal, 58*, 373–380.

Kelly, C. R. (1972). *The New Education*. Santa Monica, CA: Interscience Research Institute.

Keogh, B. K., & Glover, A. T. (1980). The generality and durability of cognitive training effects. *Exceptional Education Quarterly, 1*, 75–82.

Kim, T. Y., Lombardino, L. J., Rothman, H., & Vinson, B. (1989). Effects of symbolic play intervention with children who have mental retardation. *Mental Retardation, 27*, 159–165.

Kimmel, E., & McGinitie, W. W. (1984). Identifying children who use perservative text-processing strategy. *Reading Research Quarterly, 19*, 162–172.

Kneedler, R. D. (1980). The use of cognitive training to change social behaviors. *Exceptional Education Quarterly, 1*, 64–73.

Kohlberg, L. (1987). *Child Psychology and Childhood Education*. New York: Longman.

Kolligian, J. J., & Sternberg, R. L. (1987). Intelligence, information processing, and specific learning disabilities: A triarchic synthesis. *Journal of Learning Disabilities, 20*, 8–17.

Kreger, R. D., & Kreger, L. R. (1981, April). *Looking at emotional disturbance from a developmental perspective: An assessment and treatment.* (ERIC Document Reproduction Service No. ED239426)

Kuhn, D. (1981). The role of self-directed activity in cognitive development. In I. E. Sigel, D. M. Brodzinsky, & R. M. Golinkoff (Eds.), *New directions in Piagetian theory and practice.* (pp. 353–358). Hillsdale, NJ: Lawrence Erlbaum.

Lago-DeLello, E. (1998). Classroom dynamics and the development of serious emotional disturbance. *Exceptional Children, 64,* 479–492.

Larson, K. A., & Gerber, M. M. (1987). Effects of social metacognition training for enhancing overt behavior in learning disabled and low achieving delinquents. *Exceptional Children, 54,* 201–211.

Latner, J. (1982). The thresher of time: On love and freedom on Gestalt therapy. *The Gestalt Journal, V,* 20–38.

Latner, J. (1984). The kingdoms of experience. *The Gestalt Journal, VII,* 84–109.

Liben, L. S., & Downs, R. M. (1993). Understanding person-space map relations: Cartolographic and developmental perspectives. *Developmental Psychology, 29,* 739–752.

Licht, B. G. (1983). Cognitive-motivational factors that contribute to the achievement of learning-disabled children. *Journal of Learning Disabilities, 16,* 483–489.

Licht, B. G. (1993). Achievement-related beliefs in children with learning disabilities: Impact on motivation and strategic learning. In L. J. Meltzer (Ed.), *Strategy assessment and instruction for students with learning disabilities: From theory to practice.* (pp. 195–220). Austin, TX: Pro-Ed.

Lobb, M. S. (1992). Childbirth and re-birth of the mother. *The Gestalt Journal, XV,* 7–38.

Loevinger, J. (1976). *Ego Development: Conceptions and Theories.* San Francisco: Jossey-Bass.

London, C. B. G., (1990). A Piagetian constructivist perspective on curriculum development. *Reading Improvement, 27*(2), 82–95.

Long, N. J., Fecser, F. A., & Brendtro, L. K. (1998). Life space crisis intervention: New skills for reclaiming students showing patterns of self-defeating behavior. *Healing Magazine, 3,* 2–22.

Loper, A. B. (1980). Metacognitive developmentally: Implications for cognitive training. *Exceptional Education Quarterly, 1,* 1–8.

Loper, A. B. (1982). Metacognitive training to correct academic deficiency. *Topics in Learning Disabilities, 2,* 61–68.

Malerstein, A. J., & Ahern, M. (1982). *A Piagetian Model of Character Structure.* New York: Human Science Press, Inc.

Martin, K. (1998). Learning together. *The Constructivist, 12,* 12–19.

Masson, M. E. J. (1982). A framework of cognitive and metacognitive determinants of reading skill. *Topics in Learning and Learning Disabilities, 2,* 37–43.

Mastropieri, M. A., Scruggs, T. E., & Whedon, C. (1997). Using mnemonic strategies to teach information about U.S. presidents: A classroom-based investigation. *Learning Disability Quarterly, 20,* 13–19.

Matzko, H. M. G. (1997). A Gestalt therapy treatment approach for addictions: Multiphasic transformation process. *Gestalt Review, 1,* 34–56.

McCormick, P. A., Campbell, J. W., Pasnak, R., & Perry, P. (1990). Instruction of Piagetian concepts for children with mental retardation. *Mental Retardation, 28,* 359–366.

McNutt, G., & Mandelbaum, L. H. (1980). General assessment competencies for special education teachers. *Exceptional Education Quarterly, 1,* 21–29.

Meichenbaum, D. (1980). Cognitive behavior modification with exceptional children: A promise yet unfulfilled. *Exceptional Education Quarterly, 1,* 83–88.

Melnick, J., & Nevis, S. N. (1986). Power, choice, and surprise. *The Gestalt Journal, IX,* 43–52.

Meltzer, L. J. (1984). Cognitive assessment and the diagnosis of learning problems. In M. D. LeVine & P. Satz (Eds.), Middle childhood: Development and dysfunction (pp. 131–152). Baltimore, MD: University Park Press.

Meltzer, L. J. (1993). (Ed.) *Strategy assessment and instruction for students with learning disabilities: From theory to practice.* Austin, TX: Pro-Ed.

Miller, L. (1989). The ideas of conflict: A study of the development of story understanding. *New Directions for Child Development, 6.* pages.

Montangero, J., & Maurice-Naville, D. (1997). *Piaget, or The Advance of Knowledge.* Mahwah, NJ: Lawrence Erlbaum.

Morgan, S. B. (1986). Autism and Piaget's theory: Are the two compatible? *Journal of Autism and Developmental Disorders, 6,* 441–457

Morozas, D. S. (1983). Curricula development for the severely handicapped through the use of art. *The Forum, 9,* 16–17.

Moses, N. (1981). Using Piagetian principles to guide instruction of the learning disabled. *Topics in Learning and Learning Disabilities, 1,* 11–19.

Moshman, D. (1998). *Identity as a theory of oneself.* Paper presented at the Meeting of the Jean Piaget Society, Chicago, IL.

Mulgrew, E., & Mulgrew, J. (1987). Awareness of self and others in Gestalt therapy. *The Gestalt Journal, XI,* 67–72.

Murray, F. B. (1992). Restructuring and constructivism: The development of American educational reform. In H. Beilin & P. B. Pufall (Eds.), *Piaget's theory; Prospects and possibilities* (pp. 287–308). Hillsdale, NJ: Lawrence Erlbaum.

Nannis, E. D. (1988). Cognitive-developmental differences in emotional understanding. In E. D. Nannis & P. A. Cowan (Eds.) *New directions for child development* (pp. 31–50). Hillsdale, NJ: Lawrence Erlbaum.

Neimark, E. D. (1980). Intellectual development in the exceptional adolescent as viewed within a Piagetian framework. *Exceptional Education Quarterly, 1,* 47–55.

Nevis, E. C. (1997). Gestalt therapy and organization development: A historical perspective, 1930–1996. *Gestalt Review, 1,* 110–130.

Nichols, P. (1986). Down the up staircase: The teacher as therapist. *Teaching Behaviorally Disordered Youth, 2,* 1–13.

Noam, G. G. (1988). A constructivist approach to developmental psychopathology. In E. D. Nannis & P. A. Cowan (Eds.), *New directions for child development,* 91–121.

Noam, G. G., Hauser, S. T., Santostefano, S., Garrison, W., Jacobson, A. M., Powers, S. I., & Mead, M. (1984). Ego development and psychopathology: A study of hospitalized adolescents. *Child Development, 5,* 84–194.

O'Hara, M. (1998). Gestalt therapy as an emancipatory psychology for a transmodern world. *Gestalt Review, 2,* 154–168.

Oldfather, P., & Dahl, K. (1994). Toward a social constructivist reconceptualization of intrinsic motivation for literacy learning. *Journal of Reading Behavior, 26,* 139–156.

O'Leary, S. G. (1980). A response to cognitive training. *Exceptional Education Quarterly, 1,* 89–94.

Oyama, S. (1999). Locating development: Locating developmental systems. In S. A. Gelman, P. H. Miller, K. Nelson, E. Kofski-Scholnick (Eds.), *Conceptual development: Piaget's legacy,* (pp. 185–208). Mahwah, NJ: Lawrence Erlbaum.

Palincsar, A. S. (1998). Keeping the metaphor of scaffolding fresh: A response to C. Addison Stone's "The metaphor of scaffolding: Its utility for the field of learning disabilities." *Journal of Learning Disabilities, 4,* 370–373.

Palincsar, A. S., Winn, J., David, Y., Snyder, B., & Stevens, D. (1993). Approaches to strategic reading instruction reflecting different assumptions regarding teaching and learning. In L. J. Meltzer (Ed.), *Strategy assessment and instruction for students with learning disabilities: From theory to practice* (pp. 247–270). Austin, TX: Pro-Ed.

Paris, S. G., Cross, D. R., & Lipson, M. Y. (1984). Informed strategies for learning: A program to improve children's reading awareness and comprehension. *Journal of Educational Psychology, 76,* 1239–1252.

Paris, S. G., & Jacobs, J. E. (1984). The benefits of informed instruction for children's reading awareness and comprehension skills. *Child Development, 55,* 2083–2093.

Paris, S. G., & Lindauer, B. K. (1982). The development of cognitive skills during childhood. In B. Wolman (Ed.), *The handbook of developmental psychology* (pp. 333–349). Englewood Cliffs, NJ: Prentice-Hall.

Paris, S. G., & Myers, M. (1981). Comprehension monitoring, memory, and study strategies of good and poor readers. *Journal of Reading Behavior, 13,* 5–22.

Paris, S. G., & Winograd, P. (1990). Promoting metacognition and motivation of exceptional children. *RASE, 11,* 7–15.

Perls, F. S. (1980). *The Gestalt Approach and Eyewitness to Therapy.* New York: Bantam.

Perls, F. S., Hefferline, R. F., & Goodman, P. (1951). Gestalt Therapy: Excitement and Growth in the Human Personality. New York: Dell.

Phillipson, P. (1990). Awareness, the contact boundary, and the field. *The Gestalt Journal, XIII,* 73–84.

Piaget, J. (1929). *The Child's Conception of the World.* London: Routledge & Kegan Paul.

Piaget, J. (1932). *The Moral Judgment of the Child.* London: Routledge & Kegan Paul.

Piaget, J. (1950). *The Psychology of Intelligence.* London: Routledge & Kegan Paul.

Piaget, J. (1952). *The Origins of Intelligence in Children.* New York: International Universities Press.

Piaget, J. (1954). *The Construction of Reality in the Child.* New York: Basis Books.

Piaget, J. (1962). *Plays, Dreams, and Imitation in Childhood.* New York: W. W. Norton.

Piaget, J. (1964). *Development and Learning.* In R. E. Ripple & V. N. Rockcastle (Eds.), Piaget rediscovered: A report on the conference on cognitive studies and curriculum development (pp. 7–20). Ithaca NY: Cornell University.

Piaget, J. (1968). *Six Psychological Studies.* New York: Vintage Books.

Piaget, J. (1970a). *Main Trends in Psychology.* London: George Allen & Unwin Ltd.

Piaget, J. (1970b). *Structuralism.* New York: Basic Books.

Piaget, J. (1971). Piaget's theory. In P. H. Mussen (Eds.), *Carmichael's manual of child psychology* (pp. 702–733). New York: Wiley.

Piaget, J. (1972). Intellectual evolution from adolescence to adulthood. *Human Development, 15,* 1–12.

Piaget, J. (1973). *The Child and Reality: Problems of Genetic Epistemology* (A. Rosin, Trans.). New York: Grossman.

Piaget, J. (1974). *To Understand is to Invent: The Future of Education.* New York: The Viking Press.

Piaget, J. (1975). *The Equilibration of Cognitive Structures: The Central Problem of Intellectual Development.* Chicago: University of Chicago Press.

Piaget, J. (1976). *The Grasp of Consciousness: Action and Concept in the Young Child.* Cambridge, MA: Harvard University Press.

Piaget, J. (1977). Problems of equilibration. In M. H. Appel & L. S. Goldberg (Eds.), *Topics in cognitive development: vol. I Equilibration: theory, research, and application* (pp. 3–13). New York: Plenum.

Piaget, J. (1981). *Intelligence and Affectivity.* Palo Alto, CA: University of California at Berkeley.

Piaget, J. (1985). *The Equilibration of Cognitive Structures* (T. Brown & J. Thampy, Trans.). Chicago: University of Chicago Press.

Piaget, J., & Garcia, R. (1991). *Toward a Logic of Meaning.* Hillsdale, NJ: Lawrence Erlbaum.

Piaget, J., & Inhelder, B. (1969) *The Psychology of the Child* (Henel Weaver, Trans.). New York: Basic Books.

Pontecorvo, C., & Zucchermaglio, C. (1990). In Y. M. Goodman (Ed.), *How children construct literacy* (pp. 59–98). Newark, DE: International Reading Association.

Poplin, M. S. (1988a). The reductionist fallacy in learning disabilities: Replicating the past by reducing the present. *Journal of Learning Disabilities, 21,* 389–400.

Poplin, M. S. (1988b). Holistic/constructivist principles of the teaching/learning process: Implications for the field of learning disabilities. *Journal of Learning Disabilities, 21,* 401–416.

Pritchard, I. (1998). *Good Education: The Virtues of Learning.* Norwalk, CT: Judd Publishing, Inc.

Pullis, M., & Smith, D. C. (1981). Social-cognitive development of learning disables children. *Topics in Learning and Learning Disabilities, 1,* 43–55.

Putnam, M. L., Deshler, D. D., & Schumaker, J. B. (1993). The investigation of setting demands: A missing link in learning strategy instruction. In L. J. Meltzer (Ed.), *Strategy assessment and instruction for students with learning disabilities: From theory to practice* (pp. 325–353). Austin, TX: Pro-Ed.

Reid, D. K. (1981). Learning and development for a Piagetian perspective: The exceptional child. In I. E. Sigel, D. M. Brodzinsky, & R. M. Golinkoff (Eds.), *New directions in Piagetian theory and practice.* (pp. 339–344). Hillsdale, NJ: Lawrence Erlbaum.

Reid, D. K. (1988). Reflections on the pragmatics of a paradigm shift. *Journal of Learning Disabilities, 21,* 417–419.

Reid, D. K. (1993). Learning disorders and the flavors of cognitive science. In L. J. Meltzer (Ed.), *Strategy assessment and instruction for students with learning disabilities: From theory to practice* (pp. 5–22). Austin, TX: Pro-Ed.

Reid, D. K. (1998). Scaffolding: A broader view. *Journal of Learning Disabilities, 4,* 386–396.

Resnick, R. W. (1997). The "recursive loop" of shame. *Gestalt Review, 1,* 256–270.

Rhodes, W. C. (1988). The controlling self and self-control. *The Pointer, 32,* 15–20.

Rhyne, J. (1980). Gestalt psychology/Gestalt therapy: Forms/contexts. *The Gestalt Journal, III,* 76–84.

Rogers, L., & Kegan, R. (1991). Mental growth and mental health as distinct concepts in the study of developmental psychopathology: Theory, research, and clinical implications. In D. P. Keating & H. Rosen (Eds.), *Constructivistic perspectives on developmental psychopathology and atypical development* (pp. 103–147). Hillsdale, NJ: Lawrence Erlbaum.

Rogers, R., & Ridkin, M. (1981). Dynamics of pathological aggression. *The Gestalt Journal, IV,* 65–74.

Rosen, H. (1985). *Piagetian Dimensions of Clinical Relevance.* New York: Columbia University Press.

Rosen, H. (1991). Constructivism, personality, psychopathology, and psychology. In D. P. Keating & H. Rosen (Eds.), *Constructivistic perspectives on developmental psychopathology and atypical development* (pp. 149–172). Hillsdale, NJ: Lawrence Erlbaum.

Saarni, C. I. (1993). Piagetian operations and field independence as factors in children's problem solving. *Child Development, 44,* 338–345.

Sabornie, E. J., & deBettencourt, L. U. (1997). *Teaching Students with Mild Disabilities at the Secondary Level.* Upper Saddle River, NJ: Merrill, Prentice-Hall.

Sadler, W. A., & Whimbey, W. A. (1985). A holistic approach to improving thinking skills. *Phi Delta Kappan, 67,* 199–203.

San Miguel, S. K., Forness, S. R., & Kavale, K. A. (1996). Social skills deficits in learning disabilities: The psychiatric comorbidity, hypothesis. *Learning Disability Quarterly, 19,* 252–261.

Santostefano, S. (1991). Coordinating outer space with inner self: Reflections on developmental psychopathology. In D. P. Keating & H. Rosen (Eds.), *Constructivistic perspectives on developmental psychopathology and atypical development* (pp. 11–40). Hillsdale, NJ: Lawrence Erlbaum.

Saxe, L., Cross, T., & Silverman, N. (1988). Children's mental health: The gap between what we know and what we do. *American Psychologist, 43,* 800–807.

Schmid-Kitsikis, E. (1973). Piagetian theory and its approach to psychology. *American Journal of Mental Deficiency, 77,* 694–705.

Schoen, S. (1989). A note on Gestalt responsibility and Buddhist nonattachment. *The Gestalt Journal, VII,* 70–75.

Scruggs, T. E., Mastropieri, M. A., & Sullivan, G. S. (1994). Promoting relational thinking: Elaborative interrogation for students with mild disabilities. *Learning Disabilities Quarterly, 60,* 450–463.

Selman, R. L. (1980). *The Growth of Intrapersonal Understanding: Developmental and Clinical Analysis.* New York: Penguin Press.

Sherrill, R. E. (1986). Gestalt therapy and Gestalt psychology. *The Gestalt Journal, IX,* 67–76.

Short, E. J., & Ryan, E. B. (1984). Metacognitive differences between skilled and less skilled readers: Remediating deficits through story grammar and attribution training. *Journal of Educational Psychology, 76,* 225–235.

Shub, N. (1981). Gestalt therapy with the schizophrenic patient. *The Gestalt Journal, IV,* 47–56.

Sigel, I. (1981). Social experience in the development of representational thought: Distancing theory. In I. E. Sigel, D. M. Brodzinsky, & R. M. Golinkoff (Eds.), *New directions in Piagetian theory and practice.* (pp. 203–217). Hillsdale, NJ: Lawrence Erlbaum.

Sigel, I. E., Brodzinsky, D. M., & Golinkoff, R. M. (1981). *New Directions in Piagetian Theory and Practice.* Hillsdale, NJ: Lawrence Erlbaum.

Silverman, H. J. (1980). *Piaget, Philosophy, and the Human Sciences.* New Jersey: Humanities Press.

Simpson, E. L., & Gray, M. A. (1976). *Humanistic Education: An Interpretation.* Cambridge, MA: Ballinger.

Skolnik, T. (1987). What do we call survival? Restructuring the Gestalt therapy position in your mind. *The Gestalt Journal, X,* 5–25.

Skolnik, T. (1990). Boundaries, boundaries, boundaries. *The Gestalt Journal, XIII,* 55–68.

Slife, B. D., Weiss, J., & Bell, T. (1985). Separability of metacognition and cognition: Problem solving in learning disabled and regular students. *Journal of Educational Psychology, 77,* 437–445.

Smith, C. D. (1985). Making educational sense of Piaget's psychology. *Oxford Review of Education, 11,* 181–191.

Smith, E. W. L. (1986). Retroflection: The forms of nonenactment. *The Gestalt Journal, VIX,* 36–54.

Smith, E. W. L. (1988). Self-interruptions in the rhythm of contact and withdrawal. *The Gestalt Journal, XI,* 37–58.

Smock, C. D. (1981). Constructivism and educational practices. In I. E. Sigel, D. M. Brodzinsky, & R. M. Golinkoff (Eds.), *New directions in Piagetian theory and practice* (pp. 51–69). Hillsdale, NJ: Lawrence Erlbaum.

Solomon, R. (1997). Children who learn differently. *The Journal of Developmental and Learning Disorders, 1,* 343–378.

Spivack, G., & Swift, M. (1976). Behavior management in the open classroom. *International Review of Applied Psychology, 25,* 41–52.

Sroufe, L. A., & Rutter, M. (1984). The domain of developmental psychopsychology. *Child Development, 83,* 173–189.

Staemmleer, F. M. (2000). Like a fish in water: Gestalt therapy in times of uncertainty. *Gestalt Review, 4*(3), 205–218.

Stolorow, R. D., & Lachmann, F. M. (1983). *Psychoanalysis of Developmental Arrests: Theory and Treatment.* New York: International Universities Press.

Stone, C. A. (1998). The metaphor of scaffolding: Its utility for the field of learning disabilities. *Journal of Learning Disabilities, 4*, 344–364.

Stone, C. A., & Conca, L. (1993). The origin of strategy deficits in children with learning disabilities: A social constructivist perspective. In L. J. Meltzer (Ed.), *Strategy assessment and instruction for students with learning disabilities: From theory to practice* (pp. 23–59). Austin, TX: Pro-Ed.

Stone, C. A., & Reid, D. K. (1994). Social and individual forces in learning: Implications for instruction of children with learning difficulties. *Learning Disabilities Quarterly, 17*, 72–86.

Swanson, H. L. (1987). Information-processing theory and learning disabilities: An overview. *Journal of Learning Disabilities, 20*, 3–7.

Swanson, H. L. (1993). Principles and procedures in strategy use. In L. J. Meltzer (Ed.), *Strategy assessment and instruction for students with learning disabilities: From theory to practice.* (pp. 61–92). Austin, TX: Pro-Ed.

Swanson, H. L., & Alexander, J. E. (1997). Cognitive processes as predictors of word recognition and reading comprehension in learning-disabled and skilled readers: Revisiting the specificity hypotheses. *Journal of Educational Psychology, 89*, 128–158.

Swanson, J. L. (1988). Boundary processes and boundary states. *The Gestalt Journal, XI*, 5–24.

Swap, S. (1974). Disturbing classroom behavior: A developmental and ecological view. *Exceptional Children, 40*, 163–172.

Swicegood, P. R., & Linehan, S. L. (1995). Literacy and academic learning for students with behavioral disorders: A constructivist view. *Education and Treatment of Children, 18*, 335–347.

Tenzer, A. (1983). Piaget and psychoanalysis: Some reflections on insight. *Contemporary Psychoanalysis, 19*, 126–136.

Thompson, R. A. (1991). Construction and reconstruction of early attachment: Taking perspective on attachment theory and research. In D. P. Keating & H. Rosen (Eds.), *Constructivistic perspectives on developmental psychopathology and atypical development* (pp. 41–67). Hillsdale, NJ: Lawrence Erlbaum.

Thorndyke, P. W. (1977). Cognitive structures in comprehension and memory of narrative discourse. *Cognitive Psychology, 9*, 77–110.

Urbain, E. S., & Kendall, P. C. (1980). Review of social-cognitive problem-solving interventions with children. *Psychologist Bulletin, 88*, 109–143.

Van der Kooij, R., & Vrijhof, H. J. (1981). Play and development. *Topics in Learning and Learning Disabilities, 1*, 57–67.

Voyat, G. (1983). Conscious and unconscious. *Contemporary Psychoanalysis, 19*, 348–357.

Wadsworth, B. (1978). *Piaget for the Classroom Teacher.* New York: Longman.

Wadsworth, B. (1996). *Piaget's Theory of Cognitive and Affective Development: Foundations of Constructivism (5th ed.).* White Plains, NY: Longman.

Wadsworth, B. (1997). Is there a logic to feelings? *The Constructivist, 12*, 6–13.

Welch, L. (1940). A preliminary investigation of some aspects of the hierarchical development of concepts. *Journal of General Psychology, 22*, 359–378.

Wenar, C. (1982). Developmental psychology: Its nature and models. *Journal of Clinical Child Psychology, 11*, 192–201.

Werner, H. D. (1982). *Cognitive Therapy: A Humanistic Approach.* New York: Free Press.

Westman, J. (1990). *Handbook of Learning Disabilities: A Multisystem Approach.* Boston: Allyn & Bacon.

Wiens, J. W. (1983). Metacognition and the adolescent passive learner. *Journal of Learning Disabilities, 16*, 144–149.

Wigg, E. H. (1993). Strategy training for people with language-learning disabilities. In L. J. Meltzer (Ed.), *Strategy assessment and instruction for students with learning disabilities: From theory to practice* (pp. 167–194). Austin, TX: Pro-Ed.

Wong, B. Y. L. (1998). Analysis of intrinsic and extrinsic problems in the use of the scaffolding metaphor in learning disabilities intervention research: An introduction. *Journal of Learning Disabilities, 4,* 340–343.

Wood, M. M., & Swan, W. W. (1978). A developmental approach to educating the disturbed young child. *Behavior Disorders, 3,* 197–209.

Wright, G. (1984). Reflections at the speed of thought. *The Gestalt Journal, VII,* 75–83.

Yontef, G. In Perls, L., Polster, E., Yontef, G., Zinker, J., & Miller, M. (1981). The future of Gestalt therapy: A symposium. *The Gestalt Journal, IV,* 3–18.

Youniss, J., & Damon, K. (1992). Social construction in Piaget's theory. In H. Beilin & P. B. Pufall (Eds.), *Piaget's theory: Prospects and possibilities* (pp. 267–286). Hillsdale, NJ: Lawrence Erlbaum.

Zinker, J. (1991). Creative process in Gestalt therapy: The therapist as artist. *The Gestalt Journal, XVI,* 71–88.

AUTHOR INDEX

SUBJECT INDEX

A

Accommodation (*see* Cognitive structures)
Adaptation, 61-65, 86, 126, 132, 176
    organization, 63-65
American Orthopsychiatric Association, 11
Assimilation (*see* Cognitive structures)
Attention Deficit Hyperactive Disorder
        (ADHD) (*see* Learning/behavior
        disorders)
Auditory-vocal-verbal processing, 116-117,
        119
Awareness, 33, 37, 80-86, 109, 132, 169,
        176-178, 185
    and emotion, 82-86
    insight, 81

B

Behavior, 18, 22, 32, 68, 120-121, 193
    imitation, 38-39, 86, 177
    intentional gestures, 32-33, 35
    motorskills, 85, 95
    nature of, 12
    symbolic play, 39, 114

C

Classification (*see* Concrete operational
        processing)
Cognitive structures, vi, 27-28, 66-77, 111,
        133, 135, 153
    abstraction, 18, 48
    Accommodation, 47, 59-61, 69-70, 87-88,
            90, 111, 132-133, 138, 192
    assimilation, 47, 59-61, 69-70, 87-89, 111,
            132-133, 138, 187, 192
    development of, 14-15
    ego, 30-31, 35, 51
    emotions, 51, 84-85, 116, 197
    empathy, 21, 197
    figural/operational, 67-69
    identification, 21-22

    imagery, 39
    intelligence, 18
    language, 37, 40, 62, 170, 197
    logic and reason, 18, 42, 49-50, 89, 95,
            131, 163
    stages, 25-27
        definition, 17, 63
        milestones, 63
    subsystems, 17
    symbols, 37-41, 62, 77, 84
    values and morality, 66, 174
Concrete operational processing, 29, 42-48
    classification, 43-44
    conservation, 44, 47-48
    decentration, 44-47, 62, 84, 114, 157
    evaluation, 205-208
    reversibility, 14, 27, 44-45
    seriation, 43-44
    (*see also* meaning making)
Conservation (*see* Concrete operational
        processing)
Constructivism, v-vi, 11-25
    and environment, 12-13
    developmental markers, 23
    equilibration, 55-57
        definition, 15
    evaluation, 212-214
Contact, 86-91, 170
    categories, 89-90
    process, 90-91

D

Decentration (*see* Concrete operational
        processing)
Developmental models,
    adolescents, 49, 123, 125-126
    adult interactions, 91, 101
    children, 4, 169
    classroom education, 158-159
    constructivism (*see* Constructivism)
    cultural factors, 77, 89
    education personnel, 147, 154, 195

238

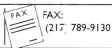